CW01091432

Map of Penllyn Parish

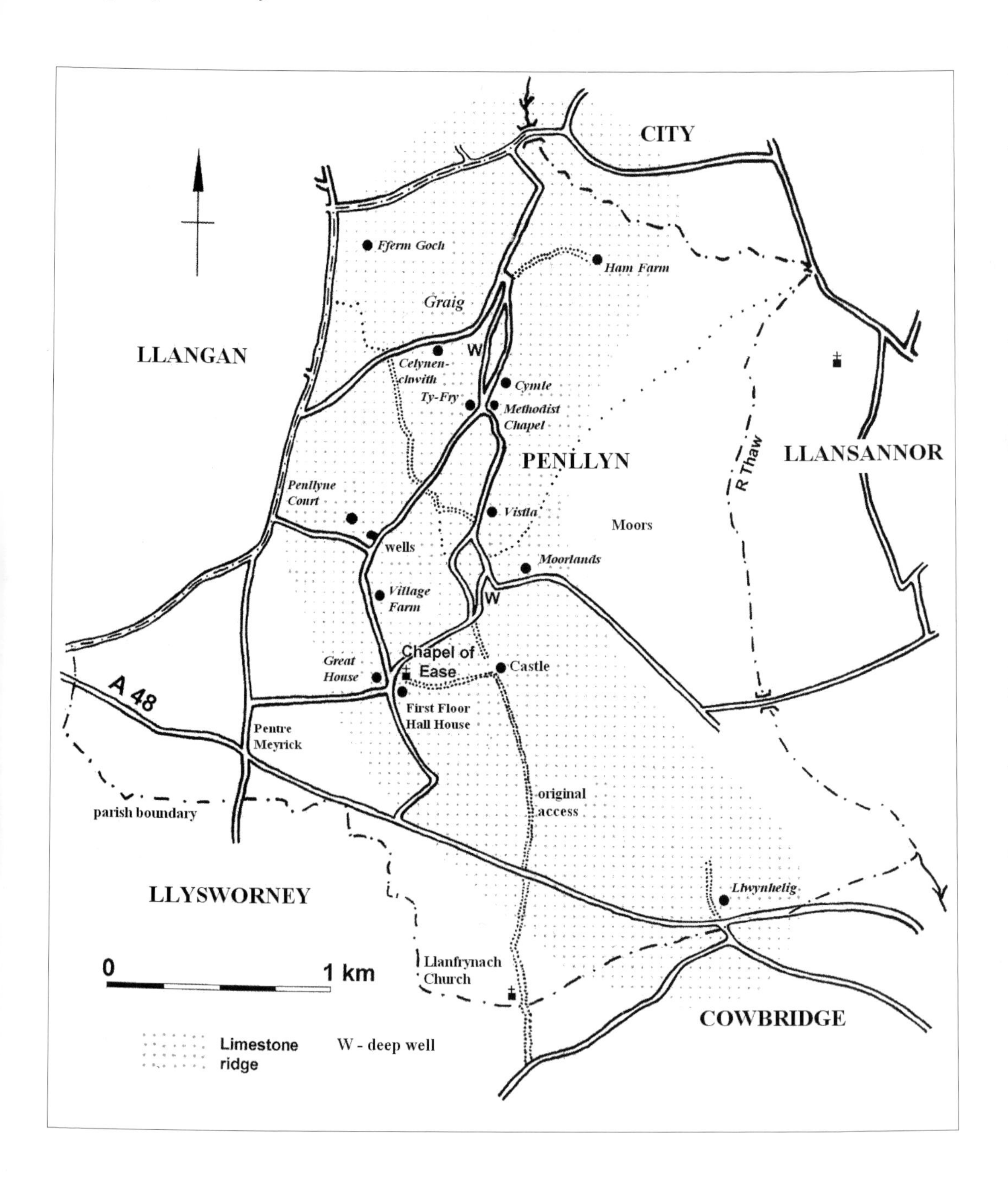

PENLLYN

A celebration of the history of a Vale of Glamorgan Community

Edited by Stephen White and Susan Clarke

Published by

Graig & Penllyn Residents Association
&
Penllyn History Society

ISBN-978-0-9555443-0-9

© 2007 by Graig & Penllyn Residents Association
All rights reserved. No part of this publication may be reproduced, stored in a retrieval system, or transmitted in any form or by any means, electronic, mechanical, photocopying, recording or otherwise, without the prior permission of the copyright owner.

Printed and bound in the UK. Designed by Angelo Bellandi of RG Printing.

Contents

Foreword

Penllyn

Penllyn is a small rural parish in the Vale of Glamorgan in South Wales. As can be seen from the parish map, the parish boundary stretches from Llwynhelig, just outside Cowbridge, down to Llanfrynach Church to the west of Cowbridge. It then extends northwest up to and including Pentre Meyrick, north along the road to Ruthin, then east at Fferm Goch along a minor road until it meets the River Thaw at Rhyd Forge. Finally, it follows the river south before cutting west to rejoin the start point at Llwynhelig.

The spelling of Penllyn

Villagers maintain that there is only one village, Penllyn, of which Craig Penllyn is the bottom part and Penllyn the top part. However, there is no common acceptance of the spelling of Penllyn.

Alternative historical spellings include Pennelane, Penlin, Penllin, Penlline, Penllyne, Pentlyne and many others. Current road signs include Penlline and Penllyn, Penllyne is still commonly used, while the community's website can be found at www.penlline.org.uk. Craig Penllyn is often known as the Graig (the rock or the crag) and also shares variations of Penllyn's spelling.

In July 1949, the Ordnance Survey asked the Parish Council for the correct form. They decided on Penllyn, which we have adopted in this book. The commonly accepted meaning of Penllyn is "Head of the Lake" from the Welsh pen (head or end) and llyn (lake), though a reference to flax (llin) has also been postulated given the alternative spellings.

Except for direct quotations, we have used the names Penllyn, Craig Penllyn and the Graig throughout, except for J. B. Davies' chapter; "The Descent of the Manor of Penllin" which we felt should be reproduced as written.

The book's gestation

The parish was largely untouched by the 19th century boom in coal mining and it relied for centuries on its agricultural output. Now, in the 21st century much has changed. Affluence and demographic trends have altered the composition of the community. Agriculture remains but is now concentrated in a small number of farms. Settlements have grown, particularly the Graig, although the increase in house numbers has not been matched by a proportionate increase in population.

The decline in agriculture and farm numbers led to far fewer people working on the land. An influx of new residents followed, to whom the history of the community was largely unknown. Yet tantalising reminders of the history of the community were to be seen from house remains and lumps and bumps in the ground. The decision to conserve and restore the ancient village wells sparked further interest and, in 1998, the local residents determined to research, write down and publish an account of the community and its history. Over the intervening years enthusiasms waxed and waned and at times it seemed that the book would not proceed. Sadly, the journey of discovery proved too long in some cases, with ill health and mortality impacting. More fortunately, we were able to gain access to much historic photographic material, never previously published, as well as recording the recollections of elder members of the community.

So, albeit by fits and starts, we persevered and some nine years after the whole process began, the results of this collaborative effort have now come to fruition. We hope that this book will help to give both residents and visitors a sense of place and community.

Recollections

Interspersed throughout the text are residents' recollections, highlighted by blue shading. Participants are either identified in the text or by their initials as follows: Anthony John Powell **(A.P.)** Pauline Elizabeth **(Betty)** Powell née Thomas **(B.P.)** Albert James Newton **(A.N.)** Ena Robinson née Hughes **(E.R.)** and her sister, Edith **(Nancy)** Jenkins née Hughes **(N.J.)** Herbert **(Herbie)** John Gane **(H.G.)** Elizabeth Gane **(E.G.)** John Bagg **(J.B.)** Elizabeth **(Betty)** Thomas née Thomas **(B.T.)** Graham Phillips **(H.G.P.)** and Gwyneth May Salmon née David **(G.D.)** who was born in Winchfield House in 1907 and died in 1993. Interviewers were Eiryn Petty **(E.P.)** Kay Hopkins née Davey **(K.H.)** Margaret Todd, Gwyneth Salmon's daughter, **(M.T.)** and Stephen White **(S.W.)**

Foreword

Acknowledgements:

Over this period, there have been many contributions by members and friends of the community and a full list of thanks would indeed be long. We are deeply appreciative of all these efforts, and to those kind enough to also make financial contributions, but we would like to pay particular thanks to:

• Mary Clay and John Homfray, for allowing us to reproduce photos from the Homfray albums dating from 1894 -1939

• J. B. Davies for contributing the chapter on the descent of the manor of Penllin

• Paul Jones (for the Penllyn Castle drawing) and Nick Hawksworth (for the Mari Lwyd drawing)

• Linda Harmer, Elizabeth Madge, Mary Barasi, Stephen Barasi, Bryan Gillard, Ellen Davies, John Homfray, Ray Caple, Stephen White, Anthony Powell, Nancy Jenkins, Robert Evans, David Francis, Pam Harris, Dave Harris, Rose Morgan, Gill Morgan, Pat Smith and Jeff Alden for donations, advice, research, photos and written contributions

• Elizabeth Madge and Catherine Kelly for proof reading

• Stephen White, Stephen Barasi, Renate Askew and Ray Caple of Penllyn History Society and the officials and committee of Graig & Penllyn Residents Association

• Anthony Powell, Betty Powell, Albert Newton, John Bagg, Herbie Gane, Elizabeth Gane, Ena Robinson, Nancy Jenkins, Betty Thomas and Graham Phillips for their recollections of Penllyn past and to Eiryn Petty, Kay Davey and Stephen White for taping and transcribing

• Margaret Todd for her photographs, and her taped recollections of Gwyneth Salmon

• The Vale Centre for Voluntary Services for providing a Kick Start II grant towards publication costs

• Creative Rural Communities for providing a grant towards editorial and printing costs

• Barbara Whitehouse and Sue Clarke for helping with the "final push" towards publication

We hope that we have fully acknowledged all external references, sources and contributors either above or in the individual chapters. If there are omissions, we apologise unreservedly.

March 2007

Penllyn History Society and Graig & Penllyn Residents Association

List of Illustrations

Illustrations

Chapter 5. The Turbervilles and Their Faith

Chapter 6. Dr. William Salmon

Chapter 7. The Arrival of the Homfrays

Chapter 8. Church and Chapel

Chapter 9. The Village Wells

Illustrations

Chapter 10. Farming and Daily Life

Chapter 11. Education

Chapter 13. Law and Order

Chapter 14. Mining and Quarrying

Chapter 15. The Hunt and the Races

Illustrations

Chapter 16. Pubs

Chapter 17. Folklore and Legends

Chapter 18. Leisure and Celebration

Chapter 19. Parish Field and Coed y Graig

Chapter 20. Images

Chapter 1

The Shaping of the Land

The Vale of Glamorgan comprises the southern half of the terrain map of Glamorgan. However, as Mary Gillham[1] points out, "the 'Vale' of Glamorgan is no vale, but a plateau, 200 or 400 feet or more above sea level, the high points bevelled off to give pleasantly undulating farmland, with the few steeper slopes picked out by dark patches of woodland".

Figure 1. Terrain Map of Glamorgan (location of Penllyn Castle superimposed). Reproduced by permission of Dr. Peter Brabham, School of Earth, Ocean & Planetary Sciences, Cardiff

The two most noticeable features of Penllyn Parish are easily identified on the terrain map. These are the crescent shaped carboniferous limestone ridge, and the Thaw Valley to the immediate east. There is a stark contrast between the dry limestone ridge, with its overlay of thin brown earths, and the flat moorlands of the Thaw Valley, with its deep layers of wet, acidic soils.

To understand how our landscape and scenery evolved, we need to understand how the deposition of rocks laid down millions of years ago, and the impacts of weathering and erosion that have occurred since, have given rise to the shape and surface features of the land today.

Geological Time Scale (commencing with Devonian)		
Era	Period	Millions of year ago
Cenozoic	Quaternary	2 - present
	Tertiary	65 - 2
Mesozoic	Cretaceous	144 - 65
	Jurassic	213 - 144
	Triassic	248 - 213
	Permian	286 - 248
Paleozoic	Carboniferous	360 - 286
	Devonian	408 - 360

The Shaping of the Land

Devonian

The oldest rock in the Vale of Glamorgan is Devonian Old Red Sandstone. This formed from the eroding surrounding landmass of the Old Red Sandstone continent over 390 million years ago.

Sediment accumulating on semi-arid land, in rivers, overbanks and flood plain environments, including deltas, gave rise to deposits of red marl and sandstone. Hematite staining gave these deposits their red appearance. Locally, Stalling Down is the only area where such sandstone can be seen. Later deposits included coarse quartzite and pebbly grit.

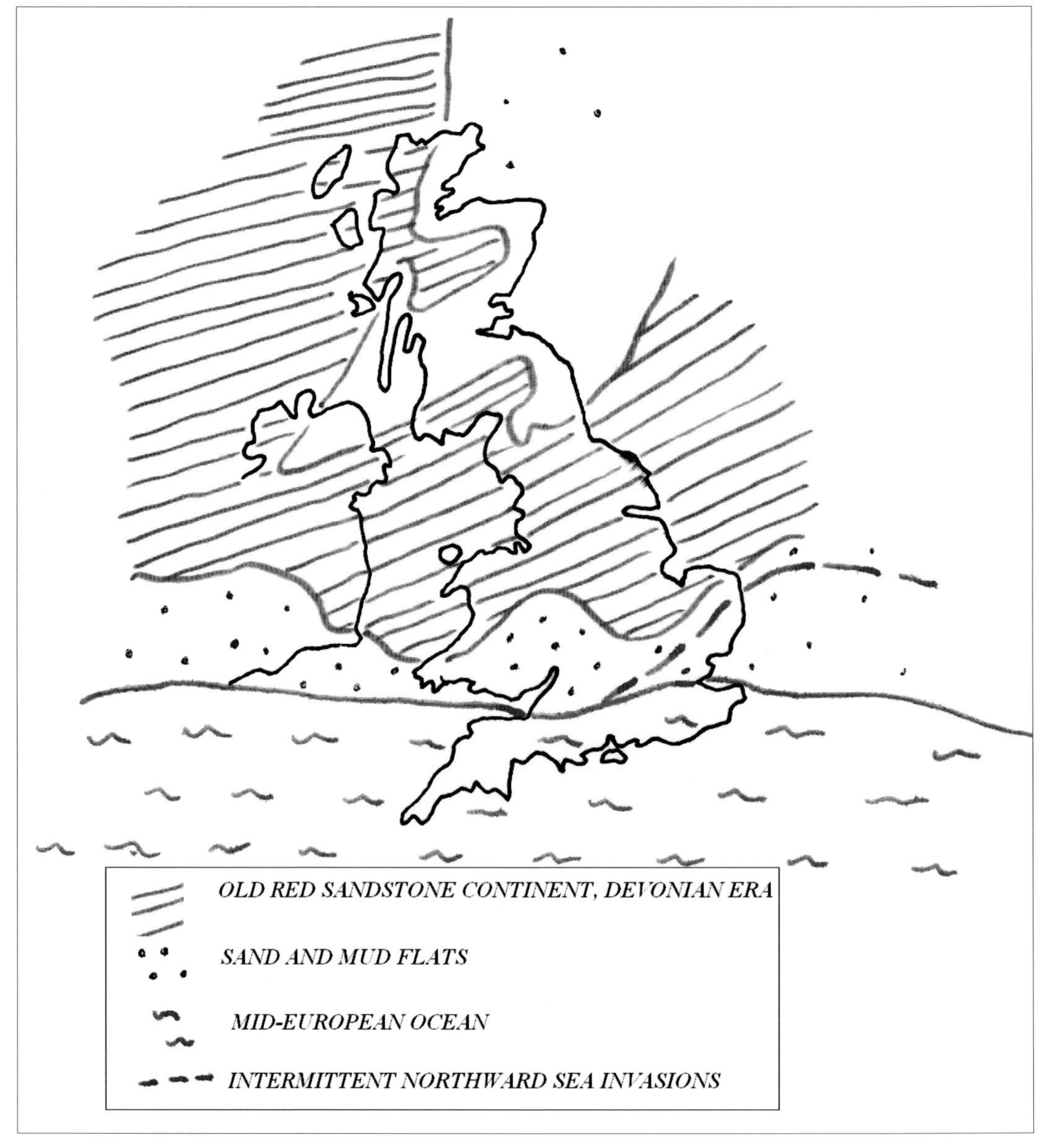

Figure 2. Map of Old Red Sandstone.

Figure 3. Crinoid at Craig Penllyn. These can be seen wherever the underlying limestone is exposed.

Carboniferous

At the end of The Devonian period, earth movements and subsidence allowed tropical marine waters to flood the South Wales lowlands, resulting in new shallow seas, estuaries and lagoons of clear warm water. Limestone deposits resulted, incorporating the skeletons of marine organisms, shellfish and corals. Some Lower Carboniferous deposits (e.g. Friar's Point limestone) contain numerous fossils of crinoids (sea lilies), brachiopods, bryozoans and corals.

The formation of limestone

Most fresh water and sea water contains dissolved calcium carbonate. Limestone forms when calcium carbonate crystalises out of solution as the water evaporates. The high temperatures of tropical shallow seas and lagoons causes the surface water to evaporate, leaving a white lime mud to fall to the bottom of the seabed. This slowly hardens to form a fine-grained limestone. Limestone is also formed by marine aquatic organisms (e.g. shellfish, corals and sea urchins). They absorb the calcium carbonate from the seawater to form their shells and skeletons. When they die their skeletons fall to the ocean floor, accumulate and become cemented together. Chemically limestone contains calcium carbonate (CaCO3), magnesium carbonate (MgCO3) iron (CaFe (CO3)2) and silica (SO4) plus other minerals.

Locally named beds include the Cornelly Oolite formation, with the Stormy Limestone Formation, Pant Mawr Sandstone and Oxwich Head Limestone Formation deposited above. These last three beds have many fissures and fractures in the rock, which allow rainwater and groundwater to permeate through, and collect above the Cornelly Oolite band of rock. This water then seeps out in a series of springs and streams. Other features relating to the abrasion and dissolving powers of water result in swallow holes, sinking streams and caves. As this area stores a massive volume of water the whole area is classed as a major aquifer, añd Dwr Cymru (Welsh Water) use this as a supply of drinking water.

The Shaping of the Land

Currently, spring water comes from Pwllwy springs (situated about one and a half km from Trebettyn Farm, Moorlands), and Schwyll (on the road from Ewenny to Ogmore-by-Sea).

Further earth movement, possibly increasing the gradient of the land, resulted in a more coarse land-derived input from the rivers into the shallow seas. Sandstone and shale predominated and the resulting rock formations are called the Millstone Grit. Vegetation incorporated in these deposits gave rise to significant coal measures – the South Wales coalfields.

At the close of the Carboniferous era large scale earth movements (the Variscian mountain building epoch) resulted in folding of the strata to produce an anticline (a long fold of the rock strata) running in an east-west direction. This formed the Cowbridge - Cardiff anticline and the ridge at Stalling Down.

Figure 4. Diagram of strata/folds in the Vale of Glamorgan

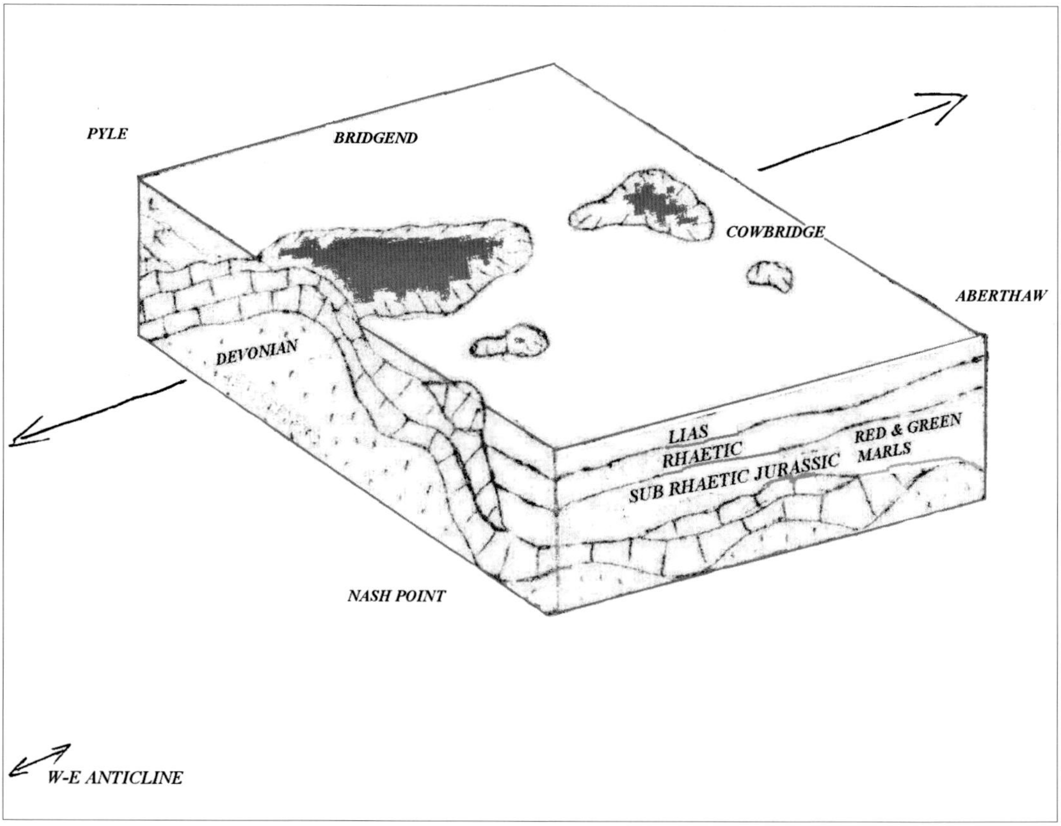

Permian

No Permian deposits are to be found in South Wales. However considerable lateral pressure resulted in faults and cracks appearing (e.g. Slade, Dunraven and Penllyn) coupled with upward movements of the land.

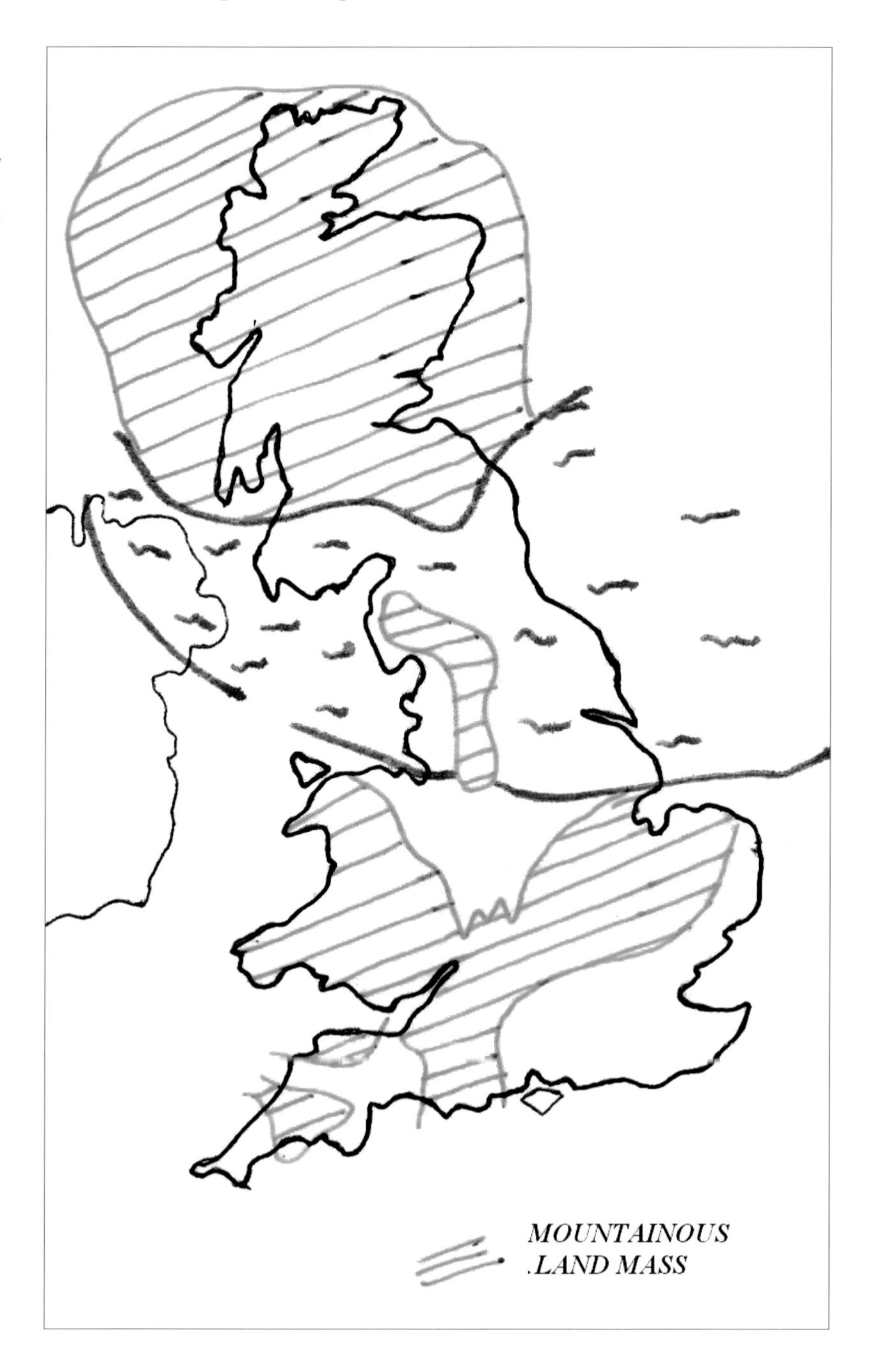

Figure 5. Paleogeographic Map of Permian Britain. The Zechstein Sea extended to Northern Europe and Western Russia. As it rapidly dried, extensive evaporates formed. At this time what is now Wales was known at St George's Land.

The Shaping of the Land

Triassic

During the Triassic era our landmass was situated near the equator. Sub-arid climatic conditions with intermittent torrential rainfall resulted in massive erosion of surface sediments during flash floods. Large quantities of eroded mud, coarse debris and boulders were deposited on the lower levels. Evaporation and oxidation of the sediment occurred, leaving behind salts of gypsum (visible at Penarth) and haematite iron oxides (e.g. Llanharry).
These deposits are called the Tea Green Marls (sub-rhaetic sediments).

Further rises in the sea level at the end of the Triassic period covered the area that is now the Vale. Only the highest areas of land remained above water. Marine deposits of warm water limestone were laid down, and more sandy deposits nearer the land. This sandstone is the 'Quarella Sandstone', and has been used on many houses in the village as a window stone.

Jurassic

The rising sea level during Jurassic times deposited carbonate rich sediments in warm temperature seas. Coarser limestone, like the Sutton Stone (a creamy white stone often with particles of galena [lead]) was laid down close to land. This is a tough hard stone that increases in hardness with exposure to the elements. It was often used for buildings and ornamental work such as church fonts. This was followed by the Southerndown Beds that are made of thin, crystalline limestone, the Lias (Porthkerry Formation), a more offshore, thin limestone, and grey calcareous shale containing numerous fossils. The Lias forms much of the visible cliffs along the Heritage Coast at Southerndown.

Quaternary - Ice Ages

Movement of the landmass to more northerly regions, together with a dramatic reduction of the average temperature, introduced several ice ages.

In South Wales, glaciers radiated out from the higher ground of the Brecon Beacons. Glamorgan lay at the southernmost tip of the furthest extent of these. The movement of these ice sheets resulted in grinding and abrasion of the surface rock. This formed stony clay. As the climate warmed and the ice melted this was swept away and deposited as boulder clay in the lower lying areas, such as the River Thaw Valley at Moorlands. The base layer of these deposits is sand and gravel, covered by mud and sediment - in some places up to 40 meters thick. Rounded pebbles and boulders from the Pennant sandstone, which lies to the north of Penllyn, can be found along the flanks of the Thaw Valley.

As climatic conditions finally warmed and the ice sheets receded, a diverse range of flora and fauna began to evolve. The Thaw Valley north of Cowbridge would comprise marshland and lakes with meandering river channels. Scrub and then forest would dominate the higher ground. Without man, the landscape was very different from that we can see today, but that was about to change.

Figure 6. Thaw Valley at end of Ice Age (location of Penllyn Castle superimposed). Reproduced by permission of Dr. Peter Brabham, School of Earth, Ocean & Planetary Sciences, Cardiff

Acknowledgements:
Dr. Lesley Cherns, School of Earth, Ocean & Planetary Sciences, Cardiff
Mr. Gareth Farr, Groundwater & Contaminated Land Team, Environment Agency Wales
Dr. Peter Brabham, School of Earth, Ocean & Planetary Sciences, Cardiff
Mr. Tony Dauncey, Ruthin Quarry
David & Charles, Publishers -'Geology Explained in South Wales' by T. R. Owen (Fig. 4)
Dr. Mike Brooks and others generous with their help.

1 'Limestone Downs', Mary E Gillham, Glamorgan Wildlife Trust, 1991

Chapter 2

First Settlers

At some point after the end of the Ice Age, people established a presence in what would become Penllyn Parish, but the evidence of their activity tends to diminish the further one goes back in time. Our distant ancestors' wooden structures and organic materials have rotted away and evidence that had been preserved underground for centuries ploughed out.

Archaeological periods		
Neolithic	4,000 BC	2,300 BC
Bronze Age	2,300 BC	700 BC
Iron Age	700 BC	43 AD
Romano - British	43 AD	410 AD
Early Medieval	410 AD	1066 AD

In addition to this there are the attentions of treasure seekers. Mr. R.C. Nicholl-Carne, of Nash Manor, wrote to Archaeologica Cambrensis in 1865, concerned with workmen repairing the turnpike about 100 yards south of Pentre Meyrick, and digging into a barrow for stone:

"one of them struck his pickaxe against a flat stone, which, on removing the earth they found to be covering the mouth of what they called a "butter stean" but which was doubtless an ancient sepulchral urn. In their anxiety to obtain, what they thought would prove to be gold, they knocked it all to pieces; so that when I visited the spot, I was not able to obtain a fragment more then three inches long by two wide."

Against the odds, some things do remain to provide insights into the past. Archaeological research and excavations throw light on our ancestors. Artifacts are still being found, especially if they register on a metal detector, while the trained eye can still observe evidence of ancient ploughing, field systems, track-ways and roads. All such archaeological records for Glamorgan are entered on the Sites and Monuments Record, maintained by Glamorgan-Gwent Archaeological Trust. It is one such record, the discovery of a stone adze, that indicates our local history timeline began over 5000 years ago, in the Neolithic Era.

Neolithic, 4000BC - 2300BC

In 1862, George Montgomery Traherne found this stone adze on Penllyn Moor in the Thaw Valley. Twenty years later he donated it to the National Museum and Galleries of Wales (N.M.G.W.). In 2002 curators dated the adze at 3,500 BC - 3,000 BC. At over 5,000 years old, this is the earliest dated artifact found in the Parish. It would have been used for cutting and working timber. Unfortunately, tracing its origins has proved problematic. A shaving of the adze was taken and analysed but the composition[1] of the rock corresponds to no local deposit or Welsh/English axe factory. A possible Scottish link has been postulated but it may simply have been worked from a glacial erratic.

The unusual shape of the adze, and the fact that it is only partly polished, may indicate that it has been reshaped by later flaking, perhaps to fit the butt into a new haft.

If one considers the adze's unusual shape and petrology an intriguing puzzle emerges, with three possible solutions. It may simply be a British axe of unknown origin and unusual shape, or it could be a Neolithic axe from a non-British source, or it could be an imported ethnographic axe, though in the latter two cases one has to wonder how it reached Penllyn[2]. Certainly there is no suggestion that Traherne was anything other than a respectable member of the gentry and we are not aware of any "exotic" finds at the moors that would suggest deposition by a collector of artifacts.

Figure 1. Stone adze, 3,500-3,000 BC. (Reproduced courtesy of Amgueddfa ac Orielau Cenedlaethol Cymru, National Museum & Galleries of Wales)

Bronze Age, 2300BC - 700BC

Use of stone tools continued well into the Bronze Age. Flint scatters have been found on Vistla Bank and near Pentre Meyrick. This would suggest that there was a settlement or settlements nearby, either Neolithic or perhaps Early Bronze Age. Flint, which is not a local rock, was used to produce a number of tools.

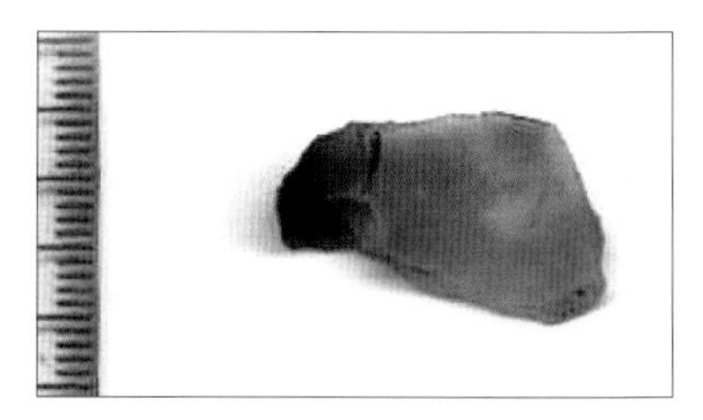

Figure 2. Flint Blade

This flint blade was found in unstratified deposits during the Village Wells excavation and conservation in 2000. Examination of the blade confirmed that it had been used for cutting[3]. Though there is no evidence to support the dating of the blade to prehistory, it is tempting to imagine a scene, several thousand years in the past, where a hunter cleaned his catch by these natural springs, using this very blade. As evidence of the effectiveness of the stone tools, a local man continues to this day to use, as a work-knife, a flint blade he found near Vistla Farm.

Some 4,000 years ago the need for pasture and crops would have resulted in the partial clearance of higher ground. However, the low lying Thaw Valley in the north and east of the Parish would have been mostly marsh, fed by the River Thaw and local springs. Even today, after 200 years of drainage activity, the water table is very close to the surface, and maps refer to this area as Penllyn Moor and Newton Moor. It is this area that has produced a notable concentration of finds, mainly by keen metal detectorists. The bronze finds range from spearheads to axes, and date from early to late Bronze Age.

The close proximity of many Bronze Age objects suggests that their deposition was not accidental but deliberate, while the presence of water further suggests that the objects were votive offerings, gifts to a deity or spirit.

Figure 3. Examples of Bronze Age Axes/Palstaves found in Penllyn and Newton Moors (Reproduced courtesy of Amgueddfa ac Orielau Cenedlaethol Cymru, National Museum & Galleries of Wales)

Votive Offerings

Votive offerings, a gift to a deity or spirit, are often linked with water. Frequently the object deposited would have significant value, such as an axe, spear or piece of jewellery, which was often deliberately damaged before deposition. Ritual deposition of valuable objects has a long history, both in Wales and in much of Europe. Numerous British examples can be found, from the Flag Fen site in East Anglia, to Llyn Cerrig Bach on Anglesey and Llyn Fawr in Glamorgan. The shrine to the water goddess Coventina at Carrawburgh on Hadrian's Wall had a well in its centre, which was found to contain thousands of Roman coins among a variety of other offerings.

The concentration of finds in a small area at Penllyn and Newton Moor, which would have had significant standing water pre drainage, suggests that this was a votive offering area, probably commencing in the Bronze Age and continuing into Roman times.

Offerings appear to have continued for thousands of years and we still have modern, local examples where offerings have taken place, albeit in a debased form. The village wells used to be cleaned out regularly pre mains water supply in 1934, but the 2000 excavation discovered numerous low value coins dating from the Second World War. More recently, people throw coins into the fountain at the new Cowbridge Physic Garden in exchange for "wishes".

Figure 4. Thaw Valley, 1990 excavation (Reproduced courtesy of Amgueddfa ac Orielau Cenedlaethol Cymru, National Museum & Galleries of Wales)

In 1990, Dr. Mark Redknapp of the N.M.G.W. undertook a geophysical examination and small excavation in the Penllyn Moor and Newton Moor area. He uncovered worked timber (that has since been radiocarbon dated to 1500BC) suggesting that there was a structure of some form.

The timber was laid flat to the ground without any vertical posts, a crude method of creating a trackway. It is possible that it may have had several sections, linking the areas of drier land rising above the marsh surface.

If the timber in the excavation is part of an ancient trackway, it may have been constructed in a manner similar to Abbot's Way, an ancient cordwood trackway in Somerset. A reconstruction indicates how it might have looked when originally laid down.

Bronze Age people left further evidence of their lifestyle in their burial places. Cremation was practiced and Mr. Nicholl-Carne also recounted how the funerary urn destroyed at Pentre Meyrick had contained

"burnt matter and half-charred human bones; among which, a skull, two thigh bones, a lower jaw, and several good teeth, were plainly distinguishable".

Apart from the barrow south of Pentre Meyrick, other possible barrows have been noted north of Pentre Meyrick and at Vistla Bank.

Figure 5. Modern reconstruction of Abbot's Way, an ancient trackway

Iron Age, 700BC - 43AD

Aerial Photos and Settlement

Aerial photography in other areas has shown that Iron Age valley settlements were more numerous than first thought and both these and upland settlements could be lightly defended or even undefended. Aerial photos of Penllyn, dating back to WW2, appear to show a possible prehistoric feature on Vistla bank, while another seems to show a circular feature north of the Graig on the Thaw Valley river terrace.

Whether these features are indicative of prehistoric settlement, or have some more mundane explanation, remains to be settled in the future.

From the late Bronze Age and for the duration of the Iron Age, the development and continuing presence of hill forts, such as Caer Dynnaf, located near Cross Inn, indicate a time of social change from the peaceful era of the Neolithic and Early Bronze Age. Climate change and population pressures may have been the reasons that led to the need to group together in these defensive encampments.

Figure 6. Caer Dynnaf Iron Age Hillfort, Llanfrynach Church in background. © Crown copyright: Royal Commission on the Ancient and Historical Monuments of Wales/© Hawlfraint y Goron: Comisiwn Brenhinol Henebion Cymru

'This humble iron object is one of the earliest iron artifacts from Wales. It is an axe, whose form copied the socketed bronze axes of the late Bronze Age, but in the newly discovered metal of the Iron Age. It provides support to the idea that Iron Age communities in Wales were quick to exploit the many Welsh iron ore sources and experiment with new smelting and smithing technologies'. Source: **www.gtj.org.uk**.

Figure 7. Iron Axe, found at Penllyn Moor (Reproduced courtesy of Amgueddfa ac Orielau Cenedlaethol Cymru, National Museum & Galleries of Wales)

Caer Dynnaf would have dominated the landscape and the surrounding fields and what was to become the Parish of Penllyn may already have been divided into a network of estates, with farms dotted around.[4] Despite this, no known Iron Age settlements exist in the Parish. The nearest such settlement is at Mynydd Bychan *(known locally as the Humpty Dumpty Mounds),* an Iron Age defended farm, which borders the Parish south of Pentre Meyrick. Excavations commenced in 1949 and were led by H. N. Savory. His reports were published in Archaeologica Cambrensis in 1954 and 1955. He concluded that the site was in occupation from 50BC to 100AD (with a later period of medieval settlement).

Interestingly, one of the objects discovered at Mynydd Bychan was a beehive quern, very similar to the quern featured, which was found at Ham Farm in the 1960's by Jim Jarvis, a farmer from Llansannor. It should be noted that a similar quern was also found in Cowbridge and this was dated AD200 - 300. Grain would have been poured through the hole on to a base quern and ground into flour by moving the upper stone from side to side, using a wooden handle inserted in the side. The Ham Farm quern has a broad dating of 400BC - 400AD and, while it demonstrates human activity on the terraces of the River Thaw, there is no associated evidence of Iron Age buildings.

Figure 8. Top section of beehive quern, found at Ham Farm, dated 400BC - 400AD (Reproduced courtesy of Amgueddfa ac Orielau Cenedlaethol Cymru, National Museum & Galleries of Wales)

One other local find relating to the Iron Age is the La Tène[5] brooch, found at Newton Moor, and dating to approximately 4th century BC. The brooch is cast in copper alloy with a repaired "mock-spring" mechanism i.e. the brooch's pin is connected to only one of the coils, so acting as a hinge rather than a spring. The "Wessex" form, as seen here, is more normally found in southern England, so this deposit is a geographical outlier[6].

Figure 9. Circa 4th century BC, La Tène brooch, found at Newton Moor (Reproduced courtesy of Amgueddfa ac Orielau Cenedlaethol Cymru, National Museum & Galleries of Wales)

Romano - British, 43AD - 410AD

The Battle for South Wales

The Romans did not walk unopposed into Wales in AD43. Tacitus Annals XII details the battle between the forces of Ostorius Scapula, the second governor of Britain, and those of Caractacus. Their final battle was in AD51:

"The army then marched against the Silures, a naturally fierce people and now full of confidence in the might of Caractacus, who by many an indecisive and many a successful battle had raised himself far above all other generals of the Britons. Inferior in military strength, but deriving an advantage from the deceptiveness of the country, he at once shifted the war by a stratagem into the territory of the Ordovices, where, joined by all who dreaded peace with us, he resolved on a final struggle. He selected a position for the engagement in which advance and retreat alike would be difficult for our men and comparatively easy for his own, and then, on some lofty hills, wherever their sides could be approached by a gentle slope, he piled up stones to serve as a rampart. A river too of varying depth was in his front, and his armed bands were drawn up before his defences". Despite these defences and a fierce battle, Caractacus was defeated, subsequently captured and taken before the Emperor's Tribunal in Rome, where he said *"I had men and horses, arms and wealth. What wonder if I parted with them reluctantly? If you Romans choose to lord it over the world, does it follow that the world has to accept slavery?"*

Penllyn was in the territory of the Silures at the time of the Roman invasion and despite the Silures' initial resistance, the Vale was to become a Romanised agricultural landscape with Cowbridge at its centre. Cowbridge had vicus[7] status and is also a candidate for the elusive town of Bomium (Bovium) identified in the Antonine Itinerary. Its central position on the main road between Caerwent and Carmarthen meant it probably had an agricultural marketing role and it also undertook some industrial production.

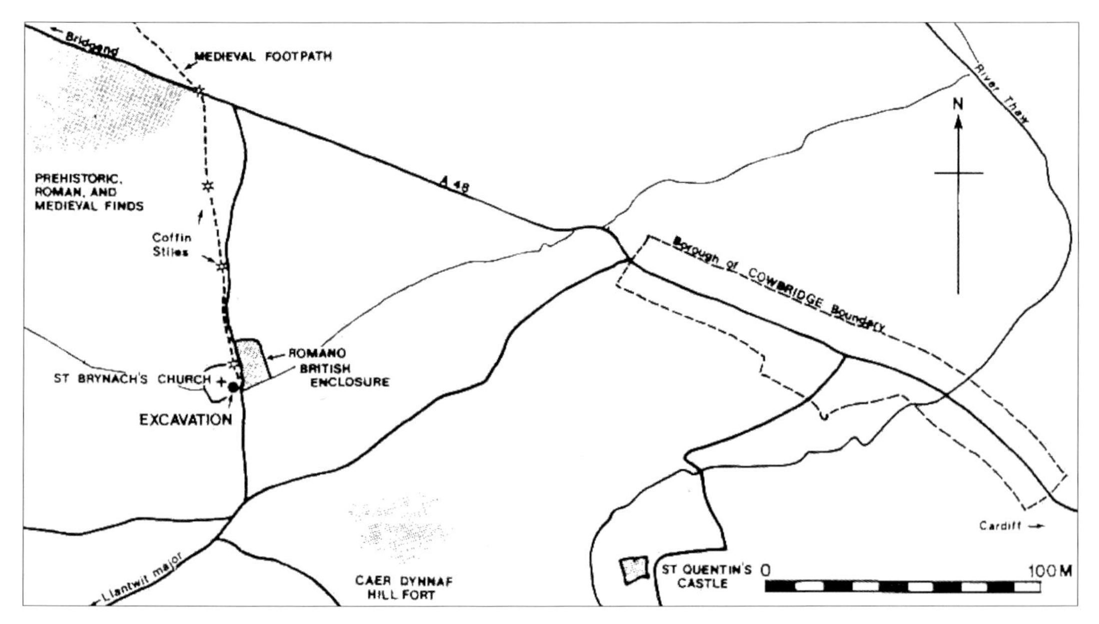

Figure 10. Location of Romano - British enclosure[8]

The Roman road rising out of Cowbridge, now known as the A48, cuts through the Parish, while Roman field systems and lynchets[9] have been noted south of the road. This activity level is suggestive of settlement and evidence exists of a settlement opposite Llanfrynach Church in the south of the Parish.

In the 1880's, David Jones of Wallington[10] noted an enclosure on the east side of Llanfrynach Church and wrote: *"of the village which once stood here, some few traces still remain in the irregularities of the ground in the field across the lane from the churchyard. Which shows where buildings once stood and the lines of small enclosures around them".*

Samian ware (a kind of bright red Roman pottery also known as terra sigillata) was found on this site, as well as numerous shards of 2nd to 4th century coarseware. It is interesting to note that a small stream runs by the side of the current church, which may indicate why the site was chosen for settlement. It is also a possibility that there was settlement here prior to the Roman period, as the site is extremely close to Caer Dynnaf and would have been suitable as a farmstead.

Early Medieval, 410AD - 1066AD

With the fragmentation of authority after Roman occupation, Wales split into minor kingdoms. The kingdom of Glywysing, which later merged with Gwent to become Morgannwg, covered the area between the Usk and Tawe rivers. The first king of Glywysing was Glywys, born c.415 AD. He was to become a holy man and his name is inscribed on a stone found in Ogmore Castle in 1929 *"Be it [known to all men] that Arthmail gave (this) field to God and Glywys (PN) and Nertat (PN) and his daughter".*[11] Penllyn was located in Gwrinydd cantref, one of seven to form Morgannwg.

The Early Medieval period is sometimes known as the Dark Ages. There is a paucity of evidence available, most notably an almost complete absence of pottery. We know from the pottery found at Llanfrynach[12] that there was a Romano-British settlement there in the 2nd - 4th centuries. What we do not know is whether the settlement at Llanfrynach remained in occupation for the period between the Romano-British settlement and the building of the Norman church. Additionally, without archaeological evidence, we can only speculate whether, during the Romano-British settlement period, the site had a shrine that was subsequently dedicated to St. Brynach. However, Llanfrynach's dedication to an early Christian saint is indicative of a pre-Norman religious site and it would have been a logical step, in the Norman era and as the community prospered, to replace any pre-existing wooden structure with the stone church that stands today. However, there is no firm evidence to support continuity of occupation.

St. Brynach

W. J. Rees[13] published a translation of a Latin manuscript (MS Vespasian A xiv, British Museum), chronicling the life of St. Brynach, who lived in the middle of the 5th century. St. Brynach was an evangelical missionary, and either he founded Llanfrynach or it was dedicated to him.

The manuscript emphasizes St. Brynach's pious and humble nature and relates his many achievements:

- How he killed a pestilential beast near Rome by the power of prayer alone: *"At that time, a pestilential beast raged in the country about Rome, which either tore with its bloody jaws all such persons as it saw, or inflicted death on them by its poisonous breath. It likewise tore in pieces the bodies of a great many brute animals to satisfy its fury; and its inbred rage could not by any means be appeased. It caused such fear to the inhabitants, that he accounted himself very fortunate, who, by leaving his habitation and the neighbourhood, was able to escape from this dreadful evil. But the holy man, being desirous to relieve the distress of the district, which the multitude of inhabitants were not able to do, by the sole use of prayer, he prostrated to the earth, and killed the deadly beast. For which, and also other goodly acts, all persons admired the holy man, and continually extolled him with magnificent praises."*

• His determined resistance to the charms of the daughter of a nobleman: *"She therefore, as almost every woman who is invincibly prepared by the devil, and has his ancient armour, and is an ample vessel of malignity, and every crime, endeavoured by every means to inthral the servant of God with her snares of alluring pleasure; and from the performance of better things, she endeavoured to allure him to her luxurious habits, she mixed wolfsbane with lustful ingredients formally prepared, she ceased not to get it for him to drink; but she prepared the mixture in vain; the holy servant of God did not thirst for such a cup; but refused it, and, as the apostle advised, he avoided the assaults of fornication. For in this conflict, he better fights, who gives way than he who resists; he conquers bravely who bravely flees."*

• His discourse with angels on Carn Ingli: *"And Saint Brynach, being a faithful performer of divine service, studied to cut off the superfluities of corporeal affection, so much did he desire to live agreeably to the divine will; he wasted his body by continual fastings, he diminished the insolence of his flesh by frequent watchings, he restrained the luxury of clothing by cold treatment, dipping it daily in the coldest water; what he could withdraw from his mouth, from his hand, and from his whole body, he converted to the use of the poor, and what he could acquire he received to relieve their poverty; he was always engaged in prayers, except when he refreshed his body either with food or sleep. Thus he led a life so pleasing to God, that as he deserved, he enjoyed frequently the sight and discourse of angels; and the mountain on which they met, at the foot of which a church was built, was called the Mountain of Angels."*

Although the 'Dark Ages' are generally regarded as a time of cultural poverty and isolation, local craftsmen were capable of the most intricate and beautiful workmanship, as evidenced by this pennanular brooch (Fig.11) found at Penllyn/ Newton moor. The pin would be passed through the cloth, then through the two finials, finally the brooch would be turned through the ring until the pin rested on the exterior face of the brooch, so providing a safe and ingenious fastening. In 1994 Dr. Mark Redknapp of the N.M.G.W identified this as "the only silver brooch of early medieval date from Wales".[14] Pennanular brooches would have been used to fasten cloaks and Dr. Redknapp believed this may either have been "a casual loss in the wet boggy moor that once ran along the River Thaw" or that it may have a more complex explanation. Whether the brooch was lost, or deliberately deposited, it was a high status piece of jewellery that would not have been lightly discarded.

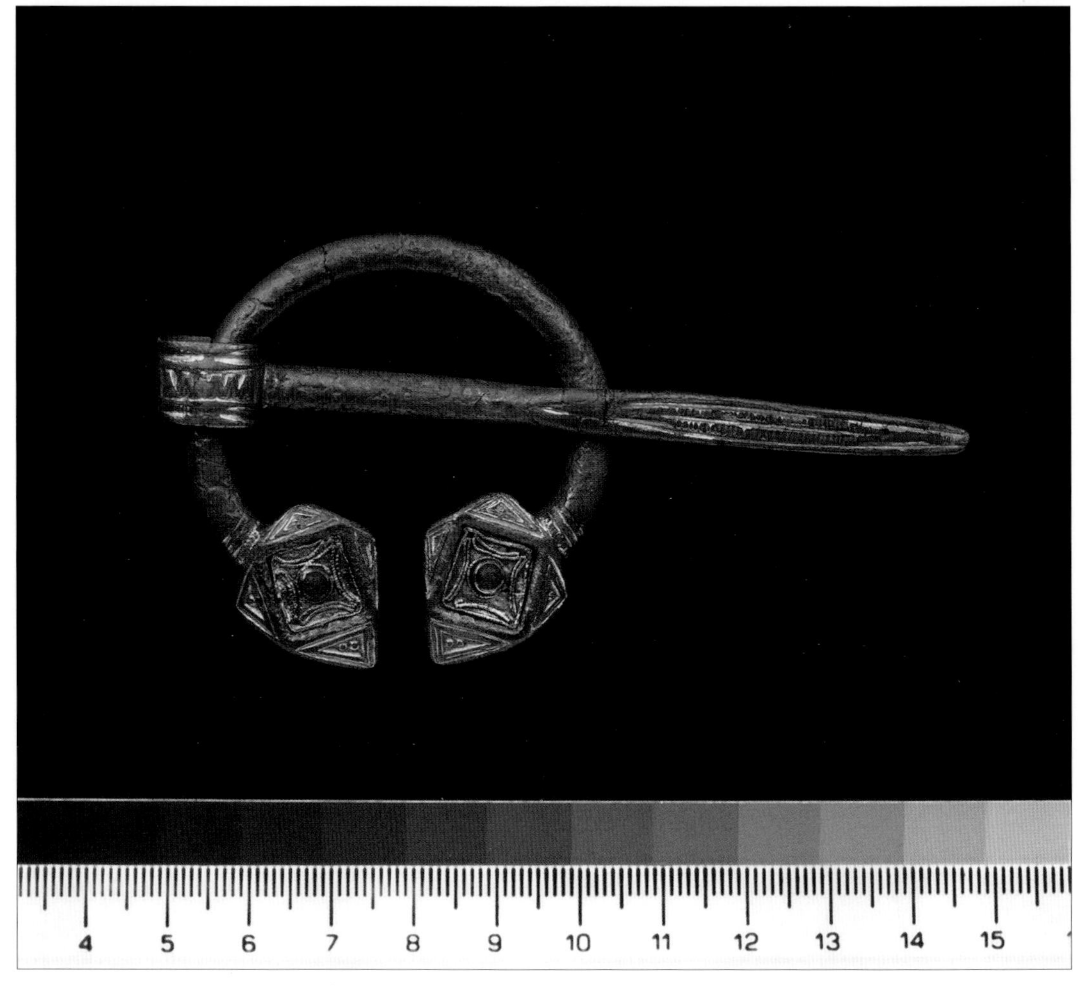

Figure 11. 8th Century Silver Brooch, found Penllyn/Newton Moor (Reproduced courtesy of Amgueddfa ac Orielau Cenedlaethol Cymru, National Museum & Galleries of Wales)

Towards the end of the Early Medieval period South Wales suffered Viking raids and incursions, though only a few settlement names are of Viking origin. There is little evidence of Viking linkage with Penllyn, though in 1893 a stirrup burial[15] was discovered at St. Mary Hill. Almost the only artifact that is suggestive of Viking influence is the bronze brooch (Fig.12) also found at Penllyn/Newton Moor. Dr. Redknapp considered that the repeated stamped patterns resemble those on Viking silver, even though the form of the brooch stems from local tradition

If the Vikings left little sign of their presence, the next set of invaders, the Normans, would have a far greater impact and result in the establishment of settlements in the north of the Parish.

Figure 12. 9th Century Bronze Pennanular Brooch, found Penllyn/Newton Moor
(Reproduced courtesy of Amgueddfa ac Orielau Cenedlaethol Cymru, National Museum & Galleries of Wales)

---

1 Magnetite rich Tertiary basalt containing clinopyroxene, biotite and orthopyroxene

2 Pers comm., Derek Roe, Pitt Rivers Museum, Oxford

3 Pers comm., Elizabeth Walker, N.M.G.W.

4 Parkhouse & Robinson, Glamorgan Gwent Archaeological Trust annual report 1981-2.

5 The name La Tène is from the place in Switzerland that the first definite artifacts of a Celtic culture were found. The term is associated with the development of a particular style of artwork, metalwork, goldsmithing, and pottery.

6 Archaeology in Wales 40, 2000, Philip McDonald, N.M.G.W.

7 A district, suburb or quarter of a town or village adjacent to a fort

8 Parkhouse & Robinson, Glamorgan Gwent Archaeological Trust annual report 1981-2

9 A bank formed at the end of a field by soil which, loosened by the plough, gradually moves down slope through a combination of gravity and erosion.

10 David Jones of Wallington was born the son of a successful Cowbridge tradesman and, after a good local education, accepted a clerical job in London from which, with an early inheritance and with some wise investment, he was able to retire early and settle in Wallington. In the 1880/1890 period he spent long holidays in Wales indulging in his hobby of going around churches recording information from tombstones, stories from older residents and examining old documents with the intention of writing history and guide books. He intended to write one of Penllyn parish, which he started but did not complete. His diaries and notebooks were rescued and are now in Cardiff Library, ref. 2.358.

11 RCAHMW 1976 translation (PN = personal name)

12 Llanfrynach: "Llan" originally referred to an enclosed area of land

13 'The Lives of the Cambro - British Saints', W J Rees, 1853

14 ' From the Isles of the North', proceedings of the Third International Conference on Insular Art, edited by Cormac Bourke, HMSO, 1994

15 Stirrups were an important military invention, allowing riders far greater flexibility in weapons use. Stirrup mounts have been frequently associated with Viking burials.

Chapter 3

Penllyn Castle

Although the battle of Hastings was in 1066 Penllyn would not feel the impact of the Norman invasion for many years. It was not until around 1090 that Robert Fitzhamon defeated Iestyn ap Gwrgan in battle to become lord of Glamorgan. On Robert Fitzhamon's death, his daughter Maud inherited his estate and she married Robert the Consul, Earl of Gloucester in 1121. The following year, Earl Robert appointed Robert Norreis[1] as Sheriff of Glamorgan, a post he was to hold for 27 years, continuing as Sheriff of Glamorgan under William, Earl Robert's son.

Sheriffs played a vital role. *"In Wales fewer records have survived, but sheriffs appear as powerful officials of the Marcher lord. They held his courts, enforced law and order, ensured the collection of his dues and are formally recorded as witnesses to important events and transactions within the lordship. They could, and did, use force when violent situations demanded it".*[2]

The Norreis name may derive from the Noyers area of Normandy and we know that William de Noers was steward to King William I (the Conqueror), and that he was granted 33 manors, mostly in Suffolk and Norfolk. The Domesday Book also mentions a Robert de Noyers in Buckinghamshire and a Howard de Noyers in Hertfordshire. We do not know whether our Robert Norreis was a descendant of any of these individuals.

Sometime prior to 1135 (possibly at the same time as he was made Sheriff), Robert Norreis was granted Penllyn and Llanmihangel as two knights fees[3] and it is likely that Norreis would have built Penllyn castle at this time, as one of the earliest stone castles in Glamorgan. From its bluff above the valley of the River Thaw it commanded the route from the Welsh-held lordship of Senghenydd into what would soon be the Borough of Cowbridge, whilst also acting as a bastion against the Welsh-held Lordship of Ruthin to the north.

We know that John Norris of Penllyn was a benefactor of Neath Abbey in the 14th Century. His shield of arms is shown on a floor tile dated to around 1340 found at the Abbey. The cross flory (with fleur de lys) is surrounded by fourteen oblong billets. A seal with a similar cross flory but with twelve billets is reproduced in The Development of Welsh Heraldry[4].

Figure 1. Norris family crest on Neath Abbey Floor Tile (Reproduced courtesy of Amgueddfa ac Orielau Cenedlaethol Cymru, National Museum & Galleries of Wales)

The Norreis tenure at the castle ended in 1429 (and perhaps earlier) when the line failed and this transition is explored by J. B. Davies in the next chapter: "Descent of the Manor of Penllin". The Turberville family then held the castle until 1703, when it was purchased by Richard Seys.

In 1790, Iolo Morganwg wrote "The castle is now in ruin. The north part seems to have lain so for some ages and appears to be of Norman erection by the semicircular and segmental arches, and herringbone ashlar." As can be seen from this 1923 photograph, very little of the original castle now survives. There is no trace of a curtain wall and just the north and east walls of the keep remain.

Figure 2. Penllyn Castle, 1923, north and east walls of Norman keep

Figure 3. Penllyn Castle, 1923, herringbone bricks denoting early Norman construction

Penllyn Castle

What did the original castle look like?

There is no record of any archaeological excavation at the castle, nor has there been a detailed field survey and, without significantly more research, any reconstruction of the castle as originally built must be a highly speculative exercise at best.

However, the Royal Commission on Ancient and Historic Monuments Wales (Glamorgan, Early Castles) advise that the two remaining walls are the north and east walls of the keep *"which was very probably about 12.5m by 8.5m overall and had walls 1.7m thick"*. The RCHAMW also notes that the rectangular keeps of Glamorgan are usually associated with castle ringworks and that *"Penllyn, standing above the cliff as it does, the keep must have stood on the perimeter of any former ringwork"*. Adrian Pettifer[5] also compares the oblong tower to contemporary Ogmore.

For fortification the castle would have been partly reliant on its position on the cliffs of the limestone escarpment overlooking the Thaw Valley. While we do not know whether any fortification predated the stone castle, it is highly probable that Norreis would have built a ringwork, comprising a ditch and bank, upon which the curtain wall would then be constructed, probably out of wood.

The curtain wall would have needed an entrance, itself requiring extra defence in the probable form of a gate tower. Finally the castle enclosure would have had several buildings for family and servants' use. Putting this scant evidence together, and with emphasis on the speculative nature of the outcome, the illustration reflects how the castle might have looked in the mid 12th century when it was first constructed.

In this reconstruction the castle is viewed looking south over the Thaw Valley to Cowbridge and Llanblethian. The stone keep would have probably been 3 storeys high with the sole entrance at first floor level approached by wooden or stone steps. We have shown the curtain wall close to the keep at this point, on the basis that any attackers would be channelled into a narrow killing ground, but the extent and position of the curtain wall may have been very different.

Inside the keep, the ground floor level would have been used mainly for storage. The main hall with defended entrance was at first floor level and the sleeping chambers at second floor level. The Gate Tower is shown on the south side and we expect that the track from the Gate Tower would have led south to the old Roman road (now the A48), a route that would last until the mid 19th century[6], when the Homfrays changed the exit.

Figure 4. Speculative Reconstruction of Penllyn Castle mid-12th century (artist, Paul Jones)

Figure 5. Penllyn Castle: Engraving by Sparrow 1786 (Reproduced by permission of Glamorgan Record Office ref. D49)

The Gothic House

The 1786 Sparrow engraving shows the castle in ruins, with the walls of the keep very similar to the 1923 photographs (Figs. 2 and 3). They also hint at a building to the south though the view is obscured. In 1790 Iolo Morganwg compared this building to the Norman keep and wrote, *"The south part is of Gothic architecture and of considerably later date. Some of the Gothic freestone chimney pieces, door and window cases are of pretty good workmanship. This part was habitable till within this eight or ten years, but the roof is entirely fallen in".*

A second contemporary engraving, by Sandby, shows these ruins much more clearly, and the architectural style indicates a 14th or 15th century construction, possibly reflecting the change in ownership from the Norreis family to the Turbervilles.

Figure 6. Penllyn Castle, Sandby, 1786 (Reproduced by kind permission of Llyfrgell Genedlaethol Cymru/The National Library of Wales)

The Modern House

When Emilia Gwinnett inherited the Castle in 1786 it was with the request that *"she would add to the Castle and reside there mostly in summer"*. The request was observed and, between 1789 and 1804 Gwinnett had built a splendid country house, which survives to this day. The earliest known photograph of the new 'Castle' was taken in 1894, when the Homfray family was in occupation.

Figure 7. Penllyn Castle, 1894

In the two centuries since the rebuild by Gwinnett, changes to the Castle have been minor, mostly to the gardens and internal decoration, though the new tower was added in 1875.

The opulent internal decoration of the Castle is reflected in the photo of the drawing room taken in 1936 (Fig.8). It is said that John Homfray's son, J. R. Homfray, visited the Paris Exhibition of 1861 with his wife and arranged for a French firm to come over and redecorate the drawing room in Louis XV style.

Figure 8. Penllyn Castle, Drawing Room, 1936

The castle was sold to Christopher Cory in 1961 and remains in that family's ownership.

Today, the castle that once dominated the skyline is almost hidden from view by the growth of trees along the escarpment. The only clear views of the castle frontage now are from the south, either from the nearby public footpath[7] or from the slopes of Caer Dynnaf. The Norman keep, with its herringbone construction, remains clearly visible from the footpath through Coed y Castell[8].

Figure 9. Penllyn Castle, as seen from Penllyn Moor, 2003

When the hoarse waves of Severn are screaming aloud, And Penllyne's lofty castle's involved in a cloud, If true the old proverb, a shower of rain Is brooding above, and will soon drench the plain.

Iolo Morganwg

1 'Glamorgan Sheriffs', Patricia Moore, University of Wales Press, 1995

2 'Glamorgan Sheriffs', Patricia Moore, University of Wales Press, 1995

3 After the Norman Conquest all land was owned by William I, who granted much of the land so conquered to his Earls and Barons by a process of enfeoffment, which carried an obligation to provide several mounted knights. In turn they granted knights fees direct to knights. Gradually this process was commuted into monetary payments and was abolished in 1662.

4 'The Development of Welsh Heraldry', M. P. Siddons, National Library of Wales, 1991

5 'Welsh Castles', Adrian Pettifer, Boydell & Brewer, 2000

6 See Parish Map (frontispiece) for original access route and Chapter 7, The Arrival of the Homfrays, for details of the process of the route change.

7 Footpath 29

8 Footpath 27

Chapter 4

The Descent of the Manor of Penllin

The lords of Penllin, which comprised Llangan and Goston (Treoes) as well as Penllin itself and the grange of Llanfihangel, were the le Norris family whose line is said to have ended in four heiresses in about 1400, though some sources seem to favour an earlier end-date.

PENLLYN

No pedigree appears to exist for the family and the entry in *Limbus Patrum*[1] is constructed upon documentary evidence, apart from the account of the four heiresses which is attributed to "other accounts". What Clark has done is assemble all the marriages with le Norris heiresses that he has been able to find in the Welsh pedigrees and attribute them to the heiresses of this presumed last Sir John in circa 1400. We will do well to remember this when deciding what weight to place on Clark's evidence.

At Hugh le Despenser the Younger's death in 1349, a John le Norris was still holding the two fees of Penllin and Llanfihangel, after which we have no documentary evidence for 80 years until 1429. What we then have is evidence, for what it's worth, for the ownership of the manor in 1429, 1546 and at the turn of the 16th century.

A Beauchamp survey of Glamorgan for 1429 survives only in a copy made by the Revd. Thomas Wilkins of St. Marychurch in the 17th Century in his *Analecta Glamorganica*[2]. This shows that Dame Gwenllian le Norris held Penllin manor with Lewis Mathew. At the same time, Goston, which we know was regarded as part of Penllin, was held by Walter Morton and Llanfihangel is listed separately under a lord who appears to be 'Griff. Toli Cappli.

A survey of the Knights Fees of the county in 1546 also survives as a copy in Thomas Wilkins' *'Analecta Glamorganica'*. This shows Christopher Turberville holding the castle and one third part of the manor for which he paid the undivided wardsilver of 13s.4d. Three other parts of the manor were held by Thomas Stradling, Miles Mathew and Thomas Raglan, while James Thomas held the 'manor of Lanvihangel under ye Castle of Penlline'.

By the end of the 16th-century, Rice Lewis in his *Breviatt of Glamorgan* tells us: "...you may note that Penlline is nowe divided between iiii lords namely Sir Edward Stradling, Kt. William Mathew of Landaph, Jenkin Turberville Esq and George Kemes gent & that in the whole ii psh churches & iii Courtes Barons. Langan is the other parische church and William Mathew of Landaph Esq. is patron..."

In considering this evidence, we may discount Llanfihangel as a detached and separate sub-manor and concentrate on Penllin and Goston itself. If Dame Norris's share of 1429 had become Christopher Turberville's by 1546 we may suppose that the two parts held by Lewis Mathew and Walter Morton (Goston), had become the three parts held by Thomas Stradling, Miles Mathew and Thomas Raglan. Beware the thought, however, that Miles Mathew descended from Lewis for he did not.

The Descent of the Manor of Penllin

At this point we must look at the evidence for the heiresses of Sir John le Norris. Clark lists these as four daughters[3]. The square brackets enclose my interpolations.

> *1. Beatrice who m. [Robert] Walsh of Llandough j Cowbridge, and had Edmond Walsh (but she seems to have been an Elizabeth)*
> *2. Maud who m. Philip Morgan of Pencoed (but in fact of Langstone, and some Welsh pedigree sources (see P.C. Bartrum) give her name as Gwenllian)*
> *3. Lucy who m. Tomkin Turberville of Penllin whose son had Penllin.*
> *4. Gwenllian It may be that these were the children of some other John of the same family.*

It is immediately apparent that the two sources of evidence do not tally. Whence came the Lewis Mathew and Walter Morton of 1429 and why was there no Turberville or Morgan share at that date?

Let us take Walter Morton first, for his appearance in 1429 is consistent with Clark's reconstructed pedigree. Lewis D.Nicholl[4] gives us an authoritative account of the Walsh family. Sir Robert le Walsh of Llandough Castle, Cowbridge, married Elizabeth d. & co-h. of Sir John le Norris of Penllin and they had issue (a) Robert Walsh who had died without issue by 1427 and (b) Gwenllian who married Walter Morton who had Goston & Langan manor. Walter died without issue. He was also lord of West Orchard, part of which was held by Thomas Stradling in 1546, which may suggest that the Stradling purchased share of Penllin was that of the Walsh/Morton family.

Before examining the other two heiresses listed by Clark above, let us ponder the problem of Lewis Mathew. The point has already been made that Miles Mathew's share of Penllin could not have come by descent from Lewis Mathew because they were of different branches of the Mathew family. Lewis was one of the three sons of Mathew ap Ieuan of Llandaff, the other two sons being Sir David Mathew of Llandaff who had a great progeny, including Mathew of Radyr; and Robert Mathew of Castell y Mynach who also spawned many branches. Lewis was of Carn Llwyd in Llancarfan and he had but one daughter and heiress.

I will deal with his descent first, because the 1546 evidence coupled with what we know of his descendants rules out the possibility that his share had been purchased by Miles Mathew of Llandaff. His daughter and sole heiress, Catherine, married John Raglan, alias Herbert of Llantwit Major, from whom Carnllwyd descended to his son Robert Raglan and grandson Thomas Raglan who, as we have seen, held a share of Penllin in 1429.

Thomas Raglan sold his estate to one Wildgoose, who presumably sold it on as he does not subsequently appear as a Glamorgan landowner. By elimination the Lewis Mathew/Raglan share has to be the portion which, by 1590, belonged to George Kemeys of Llanblethian, which, according to Rice Lewis's *Breviatt,* had been acquired by marriage with the daughter and heiress of a certain Richard Morgan of Cowbridge who is not identified.

At first sight there appears to be nothing in the pedigrees, and certainly not in the four heiresses postulated by Clark, to explain how Lewis Mathew acquired his share of Penllin and it has not featured in any of the attempts, by Clark, Nicholl and Corbett, to untangle the Penllin descent. But in fact it is accounted for in a pedigree written by Llywelyn Sion, (died circa 1615).[5] This fragment is given by P.C. Bartrum[6] as part of the Fleming pedigree.

Sir John Norris of Penllin, living 1349, issued two daughters and co-heiresses, (a) Efa who m. John Fleming and (b) Gwenllian who m. (1) Tomkin Turberville, (2) Philip ap Morgan. John Fleming and Efa his wife issued Jenkin Fleming of Penllin who m. a daughter of Robert Rayne and issued three daughters and co-heiresses, (a) Sioned, m. Mathew ap Ieuan, (b) Catherine, m. Llywelyn ab Ifor Hir of Alltygawrddu, (c) a daughter who m. Alexander Giles of Gilston.

Mathew ap Ieuan is none other than the father of Lewis Mathew whom we find possessing a share of Penllin in 1429. However, there is another version of this descent given in the Ford Abbey MS[7] which confirms our supposition that the Lewis Mathew/Raglan share of Penllin became the Kemeys share.

Lewis Mathew m. Joneb[b] *ferch Ieuan ap Run and issued Catherine*[c]
b. This Joane was dau. & sole h. to her father and held the mannor of Penllin which afterwards came to the Raglans and by Sir Thomas Raglan soulde.
c. This Catherine was daughter and sole heir to her father and did inherit Carnllwyd and the mannor of Penllyn, now George Kemes, and had the mannor of Lechcastle from Hugh Basset being her brother by one mother which he had forfeited by killing Thos Dy ap Sr Gronwy.

Clearly, the Lewis Mathew share was inherited with the heiress of a Sir John le Norris in the mid 14th century and could not possibly have derived from the co-heiresses of a Sir John who is supposed to have died circa 1400.

In 1376, the abbot of Margam granted land in Bonvilstone to John Le Norris during the nonage of John son of John le Norris of Leche Castle. John le Norris was an executor of Isabel Countess of Warwick, daughter of Thomas le Despenser, but probably he then died for Clark quotes a grant of 1 Henry IV, 1399/1400[8] of "lands and tenements which were those of John Norreys, chevalier, in Glamorgan, then in the king's hands by reason of the nonage of Margaret, his d. and h., with the marriage of the same." Clark adds, "she seems to have married William de Coker of Coker co. Somerset; others wed her to a Turberville". We will pick up this question of Coker below. How are we to reconcile this with Clark's co-heiresses? Surely there were not two Sir John Norrises dying circa. 1400. The most likely explanation is that when Sir John died two or three of his daughters were of age and already married but the youngest, Margaret was not. With this in mind let us now revert to the co-heiresses as given by Clark.

A major problem has always been that one of them married Tomkin Turberville whose descendants certainly held Penllin by 1546, and yet there is no Turberville share of the manor shown in the Survey of 1429. It will also have been noted that the Llywelyn Sion pedigree quoted above claims that Gwenllian, daughter of an earlier Sir John, had m. (1) Tomkin Turberville and (2) Philip Morgan. Such discrepancies we may be unable ever to resolve.

Our next priority is to consider the Dame Gwenllian Norris who held the main part of the manor in 1429. It is interesting that Dame Gwenllian appears again in 1432, with others, giving testimony concerning disputed lands in Peterston super Ely[9]. Amongst the others are Gilbert Turberville, son of Tomkin, Walter Morton, and Jenkin ap Philip Morgan. As Mr Robinson says this deed 'illuminates the social structure of lowland Glamorgan at this date.' It seems to me that *Dame* Gwenllian must be the widow, not one of the daughters of Sir John Norris, though, given that she survives her husband for more than 30 years, not necessarily the mother of all his children. As the widow, however, she would provide a neat explanation for the absence of Turberville and Morgan from the 1429 survey given that their shares of the manor might then have been still her widow's portion.

Where the Turberville connection is obvious, whichever generation to which the heiress really belonged, that of Philip Morgan is not and we will consider this next. The supposed second daughter of Sir John Norris is said to have married Philip Morgan of Pencoed and Langstone in Gwent and the marriage is attested in various versions of their pedigree. Llyfr Baglan has it that Sir John Norris was "of Langstone" with the implication that his daughter carried that estate to the Morgans, but this is clearly an error. The 1429 survey is silent as to any Morgan share and we have already suggested the possibility that this may have been because Dame Gwenllian held it for her life. Other pedigree evidence, suggests that it must have been the Morgan of Langstone share which descended to Mathew of Llandaff as the following shows.

Philip Morgan of Langstone m. Maud Norris and issued Jenkin ap Philip Morgan who issued (a) Morgan ap Jenkin, whence Morgan of Pencoed etc., and (b) Gwilym ap Jenkin who issued two daughters and co-heiresses, (a) Elizabeth, m. Christopher Mathew of Llandaff and (b) Alice, m. Richard John Myners. From Christopher descended Miles Mathew of Llandaff and the Mathew family records are clear that they held the manor of Penllin, Goston and Llangan until it was sold to Lewis Thomas of Betws.

There are Humphrey Edwin Exchequer Bills, temp. James II, that cite the previous ownership of his share as follows: "formerly the estate of Sir Robert Thomas, and before him of Sir Edward Thomas, and before him of Lewis Thomas Esqr. and before him of Thomas Mathew and before him of Miles Mathew, all of them successively lords and owners of the said manor and lordship before your orator came to be seized of the same".

The fourth daughter of Sir John Norris, given by Clark, has no husband attributed to her and we are left with the possibility that the Norris lady who married William Coker was in fact this fourth daughter whose name was not Gwenllian but Margaret. She would have been the daughter under age whose wardship was held by the king. The lack of any survey or other documentary evidence to link the Cokers with Penllin led Lewis D. Nicholl to dismiss the connection but we are left to account for Star Chamber proceedings transcribed by David Jones of Wallington which claim that 'Coker of Bourne in Somerset m. the daughter and co-heiress of Norrys of Penllyn & Llanganna and by her had issue a son, Coker of Penllyn & Llanganna Esq. who m. a daughter of —Walsh of Worle in Somerset, gent.'

Whether this claim succeeded or not we do not know, nor can we tell how well founded it was in the first place. It is always possible that such a share did exist and, confirmed by the above action, was then purchased by Sir Thomas Stradling to add to his other purchased share. But, on the whole I incline to the possibility that this action was one promoted by Sir Thomas Stradling after he had purchased the Walsh share and that it was intended to rule out possible counter claims arising.

In summary, all we can say is that in 1429 there were four parts of the manor. Penllin, held by Lewis Mathew and Gwenllian Norris, Goston held by Walter Morton, and Llanfihangel held by Griffith Tali.

The Descent of the Manor of Penllin

The Llanfihangel share passed in some way that remains obscure to the Thomas family and can be discounted for our purpose. The Goston share held by Walter Morton had descended to him from the Norris heiress who had married Sir Robert Walsh of Llandough was probably that later purchased by the Stradlings. The Lewis Mathew share, which had descended to him from a marriage of an earlier Norris heiress with John Fleming, passed to the Raglans by descent and then, by purchase, to one Morgan of Cowbridge and by the late 16th - century to George Kemeys of Llanblethian. The Gwenllian Norris share, which included the castle itself could, we think, have been her widow estate in 1429 and have been ultimately inherited by Gilbert Turberville, who had the capital messuage, and the Morgans of Langstone whose share descended to the Mathews of Llandaff, who sold to Lewis Thomas of Betws from whom it descended, with Llanfihangel, to Humphrey Edwin. The Coker share remains an enigma but its origin with a marriage to Margaret the heiress under age in circa 1400 is a clear possibility.

This analysis inevitably leaves many unanswered questions, which new discoveries may elucidate in the future. The Margam grant of 1376 makes it fairly clear that there was more than one Sir John Norris in succession to the lord of Penllin in 1349. We might postulate the theory that he left a daughter and heiress who married John Fleming but after providing for her left the greater part of his manor to a nephew whose only son, a third Sir John, was the one who died circa 1400.

J. B. Davies, December 2003

---

1 G.T.Clark, *Limbus Patrum Morganiae and Glamorganiae* (London 1886) (editor endnote)

2 Cardiff MS. 3.464

3 G.T.Clark, *Limbus Patrum*, p. 423

4 Lewis D.Nicholl in *The Normans in Glamorgan Gower and Kidweli* page 75

5 Harley MS 2414

6 P.C. Bartrum, *Welsh Pedigrees* 1400-1500

7 Cardiff SR 5.6 f. 357

8 G.T.Clark, *Limbus Patrum*, p. 424

9 W.R.B.Robinson, "The Testimony of Dame Gwenllian Norris and Others concerning Disputed Lands in Peterston-super-Ely, 13 December 1432" in Morgannwg Vol. XVVI, 2002

Chapter 5

The Turbervilles and Their Faith

The Turbervilles (or de Turbervilles) were a prominent and extensive Glamorgan family descended from Sir Payn (or Pagan) Turberville, Lord of Coity. Sir Payn Turberville was one of the twelve knights to whom Robert Fitzhamon, Lord of Glamorgan, *"distributed divers lordships in reward for their good service"* following the defeat of Iestyn ap Gwrgan in 1090. The Lordship of Coity was held by the Turbervilles for many generations. In time, branches of the family became established elsewhere in the county, one branch being the Turbervilles of Tythegston (near Bridgend), who held lands in Tythegston and Newton.

PENLLYN

Penllyn passed into the hands of the Tythegston Turbervilles by marriage and remained in their hands until the early part of the 16th century when a dispute arose about ownership.

Richard Turberville of Tythegston died in 1501, leaving two sons, John and Jenkin. It appears that Richard had entailed most of his lands to his elder son, John, and then to his male heirs. However, following John's death in 1527 there commenced the *"long strife"* recorded by Leland in his *Itinerary,* between John's only surviving child, Gwenllian (wife of Watkin Lougher of Sker, who stirred up the strife), and her first cousin, Christopher, son of Jenkin, who claimed the estate through male entail. Christopher took possession of the manor house *"quyetly and in peasible manner . . . as lawful was for him to do"* and claimed that Watkin Lougher's son-in-law, Robert Stradling, attacked him and *"... in most ryotous manner came and assaulted the said manor . . . and shotte guns at the same lyke menne of warre..."* Robert Stradling replied that Christopher *"...in most ryotous and forcyble manner accompanied by dyvers ryotous and misruled persons had entered into the said dwelling house..."* and that he, Robert Stradling, had gone to Penllyn to preserve the King's peace *(transcripts of Star Chamber proceedings).* The dispute went to arbitration and was finally settled by two awards in 1535 and 1546, under which Christopher had the manors of Penllyn and North Cornelly, and Gwenllian had the Tythegston manor as well as lands at Laleston and Merthyr Mawr.

Such riots were quite common at this turbulent time. The leading families of the county, such as the Mansels, Turbervilles, Herberts and Carnes all kept small forces of armed retainers who were regularly engaged in local squabbles and disputes. One such affray took place in 1576, when Jenkin Turberville of Penllyn (son of Christopher above) fought the Bassets of Beaupre in the streets of Cowbridge. As was often the case, this affair was referred to the Court of the Star Chamber.

Christopher had twelve children (though probably not all legitimate). He died circa1580 and was succeeded by his third child and heir, Jenkin, who was living at Penllyn Castle in 1593 when the Privy Council sent Sir Thomas Mansel of Margam to Penllyn Castle to search for two priests, Father Morgan Clynnog and Father Fisher. The priests were discovered and, as a result of harbouring them, Jenkin was imprisoned for a period. His wife, Cecilia Herbert, was also charged with recusancy[1]. The Turbervilles had become prominent as protectors of the Roman Catholic faith in Glamorgan and Penllyn Castle was again searched in 1596 when twelve recusants, most of them Turbervilles, were arrested and subsequently convicted.

The Turbervilles and Their Faith

Jenkin died in 1597 and was succeeded by his eldest son and heir, Christopher. Christopher's eldest son, Anthony, inherited the estate, which in due course passed to Anthony's grandsons, John and Thomas. The Turbervilles finally left Penllyn in 1703 when John and Thomas, now impoverished as a result of all the fines, sold the castle and the remaining land to Richard Seys of Boverton. Richard Seys' son, Jevon, sold the castle to Sir Edward Stradling in 1717, thus renewing the link with the Stradling family following the *"long strife"* of 1527.

In the 16th century Glamorgan had few representatives in Parliament. Local government administration was divided into three tiers. The top tier comprised the lieutenants, deputy lieutenants, and sheriffs. Then came the commissioners of peace, forming the second tier, and finally the third tier consisting of those who sat on the bench.

History relates that Christopher Turberville was twice sheriff during the 16th century, though the records show conflicting dates. His grandson, another Christopher, was also sheriff in 1615 but never on the bench. The Turbervilles were steadfast in their determination to retain their faith and their recusancy probably prevented the family achieving the higher standing that might have been expected from their lands and birth. It is known that at least two members of the family entered the priesthood, Henry at Douai, 1635 and Anthony in Paris, 1664. Another relation, Humphrey, had joined the Benedictines at Valladolid in 1602, and two daughters, Cecilia and Margaret, entered convents and became nuns.

The Catholic Faith and the Impact of the Act of Supremacy on the Turbervilles

Christianity came to Britain with the Romans and St Augustine and the faith gradually spread to all parts of the Principality, carried mainly by itinerant monks. Locally, notable monastic communities became established at Llancarfan, Llantwit Major and Llandough-by-Cogan. After the Norman Conquest, Ewenny Priory became the first monastic house in the area, followed shortly afterwards by Margam and Neath. These were all founded by Robert Fitzhamon or by one of his companions, and in the case of Ewenny by de Londres. These monasteries were well endowed with lands from the Glamorgan barons or other landowners. The monks occupied a respected place in the society of those days, farming the land, educating the people and looking after the old and infirm. Generally, a Lord of the Manor would also build his own church near to his castle or manor house. Roman Catholicism continued as the religion of the country right up until the 16th century when Henry VIII's Act of Supremacy in 1534, followed by the Dissolution of the Monasteries in 1536, brought about an enforced change. The majority of people in Glamorgan seem to have accepted the changes and conformed to the new Protestant religion, though possibly with some reservations. Some, such as the Glamorgan poet Thomas ap Ieuan ap Rhys, lamented the liturgical and sacramental changes, claiming that the Protestant teaching was an alien faith imposed upon the Welsh. Most of the people were Welsh speaking and for them the new English liturgy had little meaning. The first Prayer Book in English, which was largely the work of Archbishop Cranmer, was issued in 1549 and it was not until the introduction of the new liturgy in Welsh in the second half of the 16th century that opposition to the new faith began to recede. Even then a brave minority refused to conform, one of the most prominent being Sir Thomas Stradling (1499-1571) who was imprisoned in the Tower of London from 1561 to 1563 and, even on release, did not subscribe to the Act of Uniformity. Pockets of recusants remained loyal to the old faith in the Vale parishes of Colwinston, Penllyn, Llancarfan, Kenfig, Pyle and Newcastle.

The Turberville family were staunchly Roman Catholic and were well known as recusants. They continued to practice their faith despite the penalties incurred for their recusancy. These included fines for non-attendance at the services of the newly established Church of England, as well as confiscation of their property, thereby reducing their wealth considerably over a period of nearly 200 years. In 1650 Anthony Turberville suffered the confiscation of two thirds of his remaining lands.

Eventually, all priests were banished from the country by Parliament. Many fled to Europe, statues were demolished and altars and crucifixes destroyed. Any remaining Catholic priests were hunted down and in 1678 Father John Lloyd, a secular priest, was arrested at Penllyn Castle and taken for trial at Cardiff.

Capture and Trial of St. John Lloyd and St. Philip Evans

During these penal times Catholic priests necessarily carried out their missionary duties in secrecy, so that very little was known of their activities.

In the early part of the reign of Charles II, the death penalty had not yet been imposed on Catholics for their religion. Many were just fined or imprisoned and a list of prominent recusants was drawn up. However, as early as 1670 the Whig, or Country Party, became concerned about the growth of Catholicism in spite of the Act of Supremacy passed by Henry VIII one hundred years earlier. A committee was duly appointed to report on the growth of 'Popery'.

The Turbervilles and Their Faith

In February 1674 the Lord Treasurer was directed to issue warrants against recusants, followed by an order to seize 2/3rds of their lands. Although not much happened initially, in due course the Lord Chief Justice began to issue warrants to search out and charge all priests and Jesuits. Two men in particular, John Arnold and John Scudamore, both JP's and MP's, became determined to enforce the penal laws and during the Autumn of 1678, they pursued the Catholic clergy with a vindictive and relentless energy. Rewards were offered by the King and 'priest-hunting' became a lucrative occupation.

Figure 1. Titus Oates, pilloried.[2] Though he survived this ordeal and subsequent whipping, and was later pardoned by William of Orange, his reputation never recovered. He died in 1705.

Father John Lloyd was born circa 1630 and was the son of an old and established Welsh family from Brecon. He entered the English College at Valladolid in Spain in 1649 and, following ordination in 1653, was sent back to be a missionary in Wales, where he worked until his arrest in 1678. He was known to have said Mass regularly in Llantilio and Penthos (Herefordshire) and Treivor, where there was a large Catholic community.

It is evident from the sequence of events that John Lloyd and a fellow priest, Philip Evans, paid regular and frequent visits to the Glamorgan Catholics, among whom they made many loyal and devoted friends, who were ready to risk all in harbouring them. They took the refuge afforded them by the Turbervilles of Penllyn and Sker. However, in November 1678, Father Lloyd was finally arrested at Penllyn Castle and committed by Richard Bassett of Beaupre to the county gaol, which was then inside the walls of Cardiff Castle. There he was later joined by the Jesuit, Philip Evans, who had been arrested at Sker, another Turberville home, by William Basset on a warrant issued by Richard Lougher of Tythegston. They were confined in the same cell in the Black Tower – an underground dungeon with no light or ventilation.

Here they remained for several months until their trial in May 1679, when they were charged with "returning to work as priests in this country after ordination abroad". No other allegations were made except that they celebrated Mass and gave out the sacrament. Initially, no witnesses could be found to bear witness against them and several men were flogged for refusing to give such testimony. Eventually, an old woman and her daughter were induced to come forward and give the required evidence. Somewhat surprisingly, there was no reference at all to any sort of political activity despite these events taking place at the same time as the Titus Oates' persecution. In 1678 Titus Oates fabricated a 'Popish Plot' supposedly directed at Charles II. When the plot was made public he became a hero for a time but was later found guilty of perjury and was imprisoned.

TITUS OATES

The Turbervilles and Their Faith

At the trial, the grand jury of twelve justices consisted of some of the leading men of the county, many of whom were closely related, and included Richard Basset of Beaupre and Richard Lougher of Tythegston. Both men had been involved in the arrest and confinement of Lloyd and Evans, which hardly suggests impartiality. The petty jury, which included six members of the grand jury, found Lloyd and Evans guilty of 'priest-hood' and they were sentenced to be hung, drawn and quartered.

Sentence entered on the Plea Roll of May 31 1679 per Cardiff Records Vol. III. *"That the aforesaid John be drawn as far as the gallows of Cardiff, and there be hanged by the neck, and alive be thrown to the ground, and his bowels be taken out of his belly and burned while he liveth, and his head be cut off, and that his body be divided into four parts, and that the head and those quarters be placed where our lord and King shall assign them."*

The stained glass windows in St. Peter's Church, Cardiff reflect the last 24 hours of the two priests. On 21st July, they are playing tennis for relaxation, when they are told that their execution will be the next day. That evening Philip Evans was allowed to play the harp. The next morning they were taken to the Gallows Fields by cart.

Figure 2. The Call.
Figure 3. The Eve ▶

ABSOLUTION

◀**Figure 4.** The Absolution

As they ascended the scaffold both priests prayed to God, Father John Lloyd saying, *"I die in the true Catholic and Apostolic faith . . . and I forgive all those who have offended me. Father into your hands I commend my spirit."* Father Evans said, *"This is the best pulpit a man can have to preach in, therefore, I can not forbear to tell you again that I die for God and religion's sake."*

The execution was carried out on 22nd July 1679. Nothing is known of the disposal of their bodies. A plaque commemorating the place of their death can be found at the NatWest Bank in Crwys Road, Cardiff.

A plaque in St Peter's Church reads:

WITHIN OUR PARISH, ON THE 22ND. JULY 1679 FATHER PHILLIP EVANS AND FATHER JOHN LLOYD WERE EXECUTED FOR EXERCISING THEIR PRIESTLY DUTIES. DECLARED SAINTS BY POPE PAUL VI ON 25TH OCTOBER 1970.

FEWN EIN PLWYF, GORFFENNAF 22, 1679, DIENYDDIWYD PHILIP EVANS A JOHN LLOYD AM EU BOD YN OFFEIRIAID. CYHOEDDWYD HWY YN SAINT GAN Y PAB PAUL VI, HYDREF 25, 1970.

Between 1678 and 1681, numerous Catholic priests were executed and, in Wales itself, out of all the priests in the land, only three are known to have escaped martyrdom. Thus with the reduction of the Welsh priesthood and rigorous enforcement of the penal laws against Catholics, the Catholic faith was eclipsed and its adherents reduced to poverty.

Later on, in the 19th century, the Catholic faith returned to Wales, largely through the arrival of Irish immigrants. Both Philip Evans and John Lloyd were beatified in 1927 and were among the forty English and Welsh martyrs to be canonised in 1970.

1 Recusants were Roman Catholics who refused to attend Church of England services following Henry VIII's Act of Supremacy. They were heavily fined and in some cases their lands were sequestered or confiscated.
2 Image from 'Book of Days`, 1st edition, Robert Chambers

Chapter 6

Dr. William Salmon (1790 -1896)

It would be inconceivable to publish any history of Penllyn without any mention of Dr. William Salmon. His former connection with Penllyn remains evident with Salmon's Wood and, of course, Salmon's Wells, the latter described in more detail in Chapter 9. However, notwithstanding what can probably be best described as an unenthusiastic relationship with Penllyn, he is nowadays probably best remembered as its oldest living resident.

PENLLYN

Dr. WILLIAM SALMON 1790 – 1896
(By courtesy of the Chicago Times Herald)
Drawing from the Journal of the American Medical Association
Vol 26 1896

Figure 1. Dr. William Salmon

There are no early portraits of William. All that now remains are images, photographs and sketches, taken when he was in his eighties or nineties. These show a large man who would undoubtedly have had an impressive stature in his younger days.

Although associated with South Wales for many years, the Salmon family originated from Suffolk. William's father inherited considerable debts, forcing the family to leave Suffolk for South Wales in 1796, when William was just 6 years old. They initially settled in a house called Cottrell owned by the Earl of Clarendon. However, during 1802 the family were able to move into number 56, High Street, Cowbridge where William's father continued his medical practice.

Although there is some mention of a sister, no record of her exists and it would seem that William was an only child living at this time with his parents and his father's three apprentices.

The following year William, who was then just thirteen years of age, was also apprenticed to his father to study medicine. He attended the Royal College of Surgeons in London for practical training and qualified at the unusually early age of nineteen in 1809. Fortunately, his father's practice in Cowbridge was flourishing and William briefly joined the practice. In the same year, he enlisted in the Glamorgan Militia in Swansea but was considered too young to join the forces fighting in the Napoleonic Wars. Eventually, in 1815, following the battle of Waterloo, he travelled at his own expense to the battlefields where he treated the wounded.

Following his return to South Wales in 1815 William's life changed rather suddenly. At that time Major Reynold Thomas Deere, a somewhat colourful local character, was the proprietor of Penllyn Court and lived there with two of his daughters, Hester and Susannah. In October 1815, the Major was involved in a fatal riding accident in Swansea. William was asked to ride to Penllyn Court to tell Hester and Susannah. The following year William proposed to Hester, who was seven years his senior, and heiress to her father's estate. They were married in Llanfrynach Church on 17th November 1816.

Dr. William Salmon (1790 - 1896)

Figure 2. Penllyn Court, early 20th century

Following a prolonged honeymoon, which included yet another tour of the battlefields of Europe, William and Hester returned to begin their married life at Penllyn Court. Whilst William initially tried to settle down to life as a traditional country squire, it is clear that the traditional country pursuits of hunting, shooting and fishing didn't appeal to him at all. From the early days of the marriage, he spent considerable time either in London or on the Continent. It is unlikely that Hester accompanied him on these trips, especially since she produced eight children in the first ten years of the marriage!

On 25th April 1818, eighteen months after the wedding, Penllyn Court was advertised for sale or rent and this pattern repeated itself over the next twenty years. We can only surmise why this was the case. Perhaps William felt that Penllyn Court wasn't a very grand country house and it may be that he felt that his Suffolk origins bestowed a higher social status. In any event, by 1816 he had also discontinued his medical practice and resigned his army commission. From this point, he was completely dependent upon the revenue from his wife's estates.

By 1826, the first seven of Hester's children were still alive. The family was no longer living at Penllyn Court although it is unclear where they were living. In 1817, at the somewhat late age of 34 years, Hester had given birth to her first son (William Reynolds Deere Salmon 1817-1858), Thomas was born two years later and Cordelia a year after that. Of their eight children, five died before the age of twenty. When Hester's sister Susannah (who had also lived at Penllyn Court) died in 1830 she specified in her will that all of the considerable proceeds from her estate should be held in trust for her sister and thereafter Hester's eldest son, William. At a time when men retained complete control over the property and assets of their wives, this will provides a clear indication of the concern she had of her brother in law's behaviour.

Hester's third son, Spencer Faulkner Salmon died at the age of four just before Christmas in 1829. This incident appears to have prompted William to return to medicine. He applied unsuccessfully for the post of physician to the Swansea Infirmary and subsequently, the family moved to Eton where the two eldest boys attended school. Repeating his father's pattern, the third William Salmon became apprenticed to his father and by 1841, he was accepted by the Royal College of Surgeons.

By 1842, the family had returned to Penllyn Court. The two older boys were living away from home and the family at the Court consisted of William, Hester and their youngest surviving daughter, Rosa-lany. At this time, perhaps prompted by the onset of middle age, William was taking a far greater interest in local matters and together with Hester raised funds to repair Llanfrynach Church. In 1848, at the age of 17, Rosa-lany married Dr. Stephen Spranger in London and the old family home at 56 High Street, Cowbridge was made over to her.

Although William spent a significant period of time away from South Wales, there is evidence that he continued to keep an eye on what was happening in the parish. In October 1846, a commission set up to examine the 'education of the labouring classes' in Wales, noted that the local school was well organised and that regular visitations were made by the patron Dr. William Salmon. In this role, Dr. Salmon paid the teacher £10 a year extra in addition to the 'children's pence'. He also persuaded Mrs. Ann Homfray to provide material and cloth for the girls to make garments. In 1847, he became a magistrate and sat on the bench at Cowbridge and Bridgend. Few records of the cases that came before him remain to allow us to make any judgement of how well or poorly he served.

Hester died on the 24th April 1858 having been frail for some months. Only a few short months later, their eldest son William, who had become a doctor like his father, died at the early age of 41.

Dr. William Salmon (1790 - 1896)

Figure 3. Hester Salmon and Family plaque, St. John the Evangelist, Penllyn. One of the sad thoughts that springs to mind when viewing a plaque like this, is that William's extreme longevity saw him survive nearly all his family.

We know very little of William's life during the 1860's and 1870's. A naturally private individual, it is said that he left specific instructions that the records he kept detailing his travels be destroyed. We do know that he travelled to France, Italy and Ireland in his seventies and eighties, which suggests that he remained fit and in good health well into old age, as attested by a sketch taken of him by a Mr Lawrence Lowe when he was eighty years old. However, by the late 1870's William's eyesight began to fail and he spent increasingly more time at Penllyn Court tending his garden and vines. His visitors at this time included the renowned scientist Michael Faraday and the writer *Morien.* [1]

In terms of the local 'ruling classes', Dr. Salmon shared influence with John Homfray who had bought Penllyn Castle in 1846. It is fair to say that the men did not become the best of friends. When Homfray created the new road from the main entrance to the Castle, thus denying the villagers their more direct route, and sought to enforce the boundaries of the estate, the villagers objected and William sided with the villagers. Eventually, the matter went to arbitration. This resulted in a partial victory for the villagers although the direct route to Llanfrynach Church remained closed.

The two men had different social origins and professional status. The Homfray family had generations of vast wealth and managerial skills whereas William Salmon had three generations of a professional background but had contributed little to the medical profession during his lifetime.

During the 1890's, the provision of water to the village further highlighted the differences between the two men. A suggestion that a catchment area be set up at the castle for the distribution of water pumped up from the wet marshy ground below, was not well received by John Homfray. For hundreds of years, the two wells situated on land then owned by William Salmon midway between the villages had provided water. William agreed to donate the land to the public and by 1883 the two wells had been roofed with enormous stones and become known as Salmon's Wells. [2]

The 1881 National Census confirms that William Salmon was living at Penllyn Court for the first time since 1851. At this time he was ninety-one, yet records state he had recently visited Ireland. In the following year, his last son (Thomas Deere Salmon) died at the age of sixty-three, leaving Rosa-lany as the only survivor of their eight children.

Towards the end of the 1880's, William approached his hundredth birthday, becoming frailer and in need of constant care. The 1891 census records a Mrs. Emily Morrell, originally from Notting Hill, London, as living at the Court as his carer. However, he had become sufficiently enamoured of her by 1888 to include her in his will, leaving her everything in the event of him not being survived by Rosa-lany. As it happens Rosa-lany did survive her father and because of the foresight shown by her aunt Susanna, the bulk of the lands were left to Rosa, and thereafter her own children.

William died on the 10th May 1896 at the age of 106, leaving £1100 in small disbursements to nine different people. Perhaps not surprisingly, he did not leave anything to local causes or persons, even to David Reynolds, his agent for many years. He left Penllyn Court itself to Mrs. Morrell and the estate was sold by auction through Messrs. Stephenson & Alexander on 2nd May 1899 for £3,060.00, finally severing the Salmon family's connection with Penllyn.

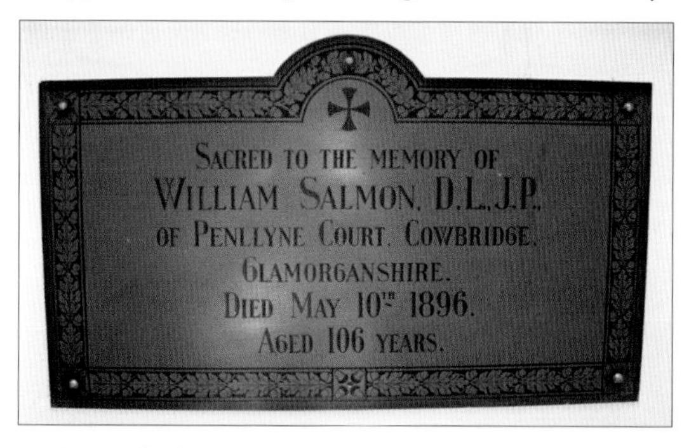

Figure 4. Plaque to William Salmon, located in St. John the Evangelist, Penllyn

Acknowledgements:
David Francis; National Library of Wales; Glamorgan Record Office; Public Record Office; Wickham Market reference centre; Probate Registry York; Berkshire Record Office; Royal College of Surgeons; United Grand Lodge of England; Framlingham History Society; the Archivist, Worcester Regiment; Eton College; Brighton District Council; Lewisham District Council; General Medical Council; Suffolk County Council and Sticks Research Agency

---

1 Owen Morgan (Morien) (?1836-1921) was a reporter with the 'Western Mail' newspaper. He made his journalistic name reporting the Tynewydd colliery rescue at Porth in 1877. His 'History of Pontypridd and Rhondda Valleys' was published in 1903. He had a keen interest in freemasonry, druidism and mythology. (source, Gathering the Jewels, **www.gtj.org.uk**).

2 These wells were used up to 1934, when water was finally piped into the village. Subsequently, they fell into disrepair until a millennium project initiated by the villagers resulted in their conservation and renovation in 2000.

Chapter 7

The Arrival of the Homfrays

A conversation with a resident of Penllyn in this century will probably confirm that they are very happy to live in this lovely part of the Vale of Glamorgan and will proceed to draw a picture of Arcadia, but was it always so? How does it compare with a factual picture of life in Penllyn, as it was in say the early 1840's when the Tithe Survey was produced and before the Homfray family had taken over the Castle and its lands.

The Tithe is the first known available detailed survey that shows the dwellings, fields, roads and people of this Parish. Very little of any earlier plans exist and then only as fragments. When the Tithe survey was prepared for the Church Authorities, with a plan prepared by land surveyors from Haverfordwest (Goode and Philpott), it looked like a meticulously detailed document. However, careful comparison with later documents shows that much of the survey trigonometry is distorted and the compiler has missed out many pieces of information. Nevertheless, it was an honest attempt to value all the land and buildings in the Parish and can form the outline of a picture to which other facts can be added.

The Castle lands, which comprised about one third of the parish, had become rented out in a very haphazard way and 162 acres were still held in hand, that is, they were looking for good tenants. Large areas of unfenced land existed at The Graig and Fistla where the many poor of the parish had erected their hovels and cultivated vegetables, with the odd beast grazed on the moors. The roads were narrow, muddy, stony tracks where the adjacent farmer might throw stone after some field clearance. There was no parish roadman until 1918. The Parish Church at Llanfrynach had fallen into disrepair, the Chapel of Ease was a "whitewashed barn" and the water supplies were of poor quality.

Why had the parish infrastructure deteriorated?

The problems of Penllyn started in the 16th century when, not long after Christopher Turberville was sheriff, the family was arraigned for recusancy. They staunchly held to their faith but after nearly 200 years of confiscation and fines on their property, the surviving Turbervilles sold the estate to Richard Seys in 1703. The property had been described in 1652 as a ruined Castle *'with adjoining it, or in place of it a fair house'*. This was from an account by J. Taylor, a London merchant who undertook a descriptive journey through Wales and called at the house. Seys did start to repair the house but within fifteen years his son sold it on to Edward Stradling. In 1782, Iolo Morganwg described the property as comprising *'apartments all small and low'*. Since this was a contemporary description, we can probably believe it. The 1786 Sandby engraving shows the dereliction of the Castle and adjacent house.

The Arrival of the Homfrays

When Amelia Gwinnett inherited the estate in 1786, she started afresh and built *'a modern house supplying the place of ancient buildings'*, a description in 1797 by Sir Richard Colte-Hoare, the principal Archaeologist of that period and a person recognised for accuracy of description. Miss Gwinnett had also inherited the nearby Cottrell estate from her cousin in 1792, just six years after acquiring the Penllyn estate. She also secured the services of John Franklen as Agent. At that time Franklen was the acknowledged principal agriculturalist of the Vale and Amelia was recognized as one of the top five landholders of the Vale, so she was well able to restore the Castle. Unfortunately, she died within 20 years, a great pity as she evidently had started improving the estate, draining the first part of the adjacent moorlands, (for which she received a medal from the Glamorgan Agricultural Society). The work was then virtually abandoned for nearly forty years whilst the Courts of Chancery resolved the claims of her heirs, her debtors and some curious conditions, which she attached to her will. Lord Clarendon held possession and was occasionally seen visiting in the summer. The plantation of beech trees near the Chapel, probably planted by Miss Gwinnett, was named Lady Clarendon's Plantation in the Tithe Survey of 1842.

William Chute Hayton, of Wistaston Court, near Hereford inherited the Castle in 1839, but he was largely preoccupied with other larger estates that he owned. It took him until 1846 to secure the permission of the Courts of Chancery to remove the conditions originally imposed by Miss Gwinnett on the future use of the Castle, which prevented him selling it. During this time the estate continued to decline.

But what about William Salmon, the benefactor?

Much of what is popularly known about Salmon is gleaned from the diaries of David Jones of Wallington. From these it is clear that in 1881 he met and became a friend of Doctor William Salmon of Penllyn, who was then in his eighties. Jones did not appear to have met the Homfray family, though he referred to some of the changes that they had begun to make to this property. He did give a very detailed account of some of the activities of William Salmon, who he described as a grand old man in his manor house with a scientific laboratory, large gardens and greenhouses, but did not describe much of the history of the Court. He featured the village water supply, which Salmon told him had been a very muddy and unsanitary place, and which he had just seen fit to renovate at his own cost. He failed to mention, however, that Salmon had owned these wells for the previous sixty years, though for part of that time he had rented out the surrounding land. He also omitted to mention that for the first twenty-six of those years, Salmon had been living in the more fashionable towns of Britain and travelling abroad. The Court he had used mainly as a source of money, renting the buildings and farms, selling the timber and leasing the mines for lead ore.

When Salmon returned to Penllyn in the 1840's, he took up residence at the Court and suddenly appeared a model landlord, concerned for the public health and the religious well being of the parish. From the stories in the newspapers of this period, which laud the restoration of the Llanfrynach Church, the Chapel of Ease and the village wells, we get a graphic description of the very poor state into which they had degenerated. It is well to remind ourselves that in 1848 the first Public Health Act was passed, and between 1830 and 1840 the Government virtually directed a complete reform of the Church Establishment. In the same newspapers, there are many accounts of problems of trespass in Penllyn, of the use of spring guns against poachers and of animals illegally removed from the pound and stolen. The only good news is of occasional charitable distributions to the many poor of the village, when the absentee landlord of the Castle, Lord Clarendon, made one of his fleeting visits.

The Arrival of the Homfrays

The Homfray family, long seated in Yorkshire, came to Glamorgan when Francis Homfray of Wollaston Hall, Worcestershire, married Hannah Popkin of Coytrahen (Coetre-hen), near Bridgend, Glamorgan. Francis, a successful iron-master in Staffordshire and Worcestershire, established an ironworks at Penydarren, Merthyr Tydfil. His third son, Jeremiah Homfray (1759-1833) gave up his share in the Penydarren works to his brother, Samuel in 1789. In 1813, Jeremiah was declared bankrupt and he fled to Boulogne to avoid paying his creditors. Jeremiah's son, John Homfray (1793-1877) married Maria, only daughter and heiress of John Richards of the Corner House, Cardiff[1].

In 1846, with legal ties resolved, John Homfray bought the Penllyn estate for £30,000. To judge from the advertisements, the property had been on the market for some time.

From the Tithe survey it is evident that much of the original estate land originally associated with the Castle had become leased to local landowners, fragmenting even the parkland around the Castle. It was to be steadily taken back into the estate by Homfray. He also acquired any other land within the parish that appeared on the market. New roads were laid out to the northern and western boundaries of the Castle parklands, defined by well-built stone walls, suggesting a positive plan of estate landscaping. From a freehand sketch

map of the parish dated 1847, which was among the few family papers rescued in the 1960's and placed in the County Record Office, we can see how Homfray began to plan his new estate. The map indicates the point in time when the driveway, from the front of the Castle to Cowbridge, was removed from the route that had existed since the origins of the Castle.[2]
The formal access into the Castle was via a new road, defined with natural stone park walls and avenues of elm trees, leading around the western boundary and through new large ornate wrought iron gates and sculptured stone gate piers. It continued past the 15th century Chapel of Ease, and then along a winding driveway of brilliant white spar, through new exotic trees and shrubbery, to finally debouch onto the Castle front terrace, with its stunning view over the Bristol Channel to Somerset.

The Yates plan of 1799, scale 1 inch to 1 mile, and that of the Tithe at 1/2500, clearly show the original access as a wide drive, from the turnpike from Cowbridge to Bridgend, leading directly to the Castle on its small hill. It is on a straight line from the Church at Llanfrynach to the Castle then continuing past the old houses of Fistla, Cymle and the Llanharry mines. It crossed the turnpike, now the A48, near the present sub-station, where there is also a stone stile. This had been the main access to the Castle and probably to the village for 700 years and was noted as such by David Jones in 1880.

The 1847 sketch map of the village is interesting, for it is evidently the work of an artistic Homfray, or one of their clerks, with a particular ability for sketching. It is in the style of Saxton with the major buildings in tiny elevation and most of the cottages shown. The tracks are given their local names but are English approximations of their Welsh names e.g. Hoel Gatrog for Heol-y-Gadrawd, obviously by a newcomer to Wales. The map is diagrammatic and has slight errors but shows clearly the well used tracks of the village that were to be considered as parish roads at that time, two of which remain still in their original state as bridleways. The original Castle approach is conspicuously blank and a sketch of the Castle elevation dominates the proposed parkland.

The Castle was still described, in 1833, as elegant and modern by Lewis, in a 'Topographical Dictionary of South Wales' (1833). Homfray did not consider changing the exterior of the house, confining immediate improvements to stables and the water supply. Instead, Homfray proceeded to rebuild the Chapel of Ease and complete the park walls, by enclosing the Chapel within his park, and by closing the route through the Castle parkland. A move to Enclose the remaining 'Common Land' of the parish had been set in hand in about 1856 and involved not only the freehold of Homfray, but also that of William Salmon, Lord Adair, Countess Dunraven, Sir Joseph Bailey and various smaller freeholds of some sixty or so parishioners. This gave virtually every resident of the Parish a direct financial interest, as well as a concern for the amenities of the village, which was virtually their whole world. For all practical purposes the Chapel of Ease, at the rear of the entrance to the Castle, was the centre of social life for the village. When we examine the legal document that authenticated the 1858 Enclosure Award of Penllyn, we see that it defined and authorized new drains and roads. It is particularly interesting to note that this same Bill also included the closure of the route from the Cowbridge road through the original Castle parkland past the Castle to the Chapel of Ease, which was the traditional route from Cowbridge to the village. The 'New Road' provided by Homfray was now the only viable alternative.

It is ironic but just sixteen years before, Doctor Salmon's wife, Hester, had opened a subscription to raise money and had laid the first stone of a new wall to commence the enclosure of the Chapel. At that point the Chapel had been described in the Cambrian newspaper as a whitewashed barn but, following the major rebuild by Homfray, it was now the equal of any newly refurbished church in the Vale and at no cost to the village. Only the main walls were not renewed, they were buttressed and a new vestry added. The windows were reframed in freestone and glazed in stained glass. The old stone tiles were replaced with new Welsh slate.

The villagers did not, however, view all these changes as improvements. Perhaps there was alternative access to Cowbridge but something had gone. Perhaps they did have a much superior chapel but access was restricted and there were concerns that not all of the land now enclosed within the new Castle stone boundaries was really Castle land. It had from time immemorial been open village green, even if it was very untidy with rubbish and quarried holes. This led to formal objections and to the courts.

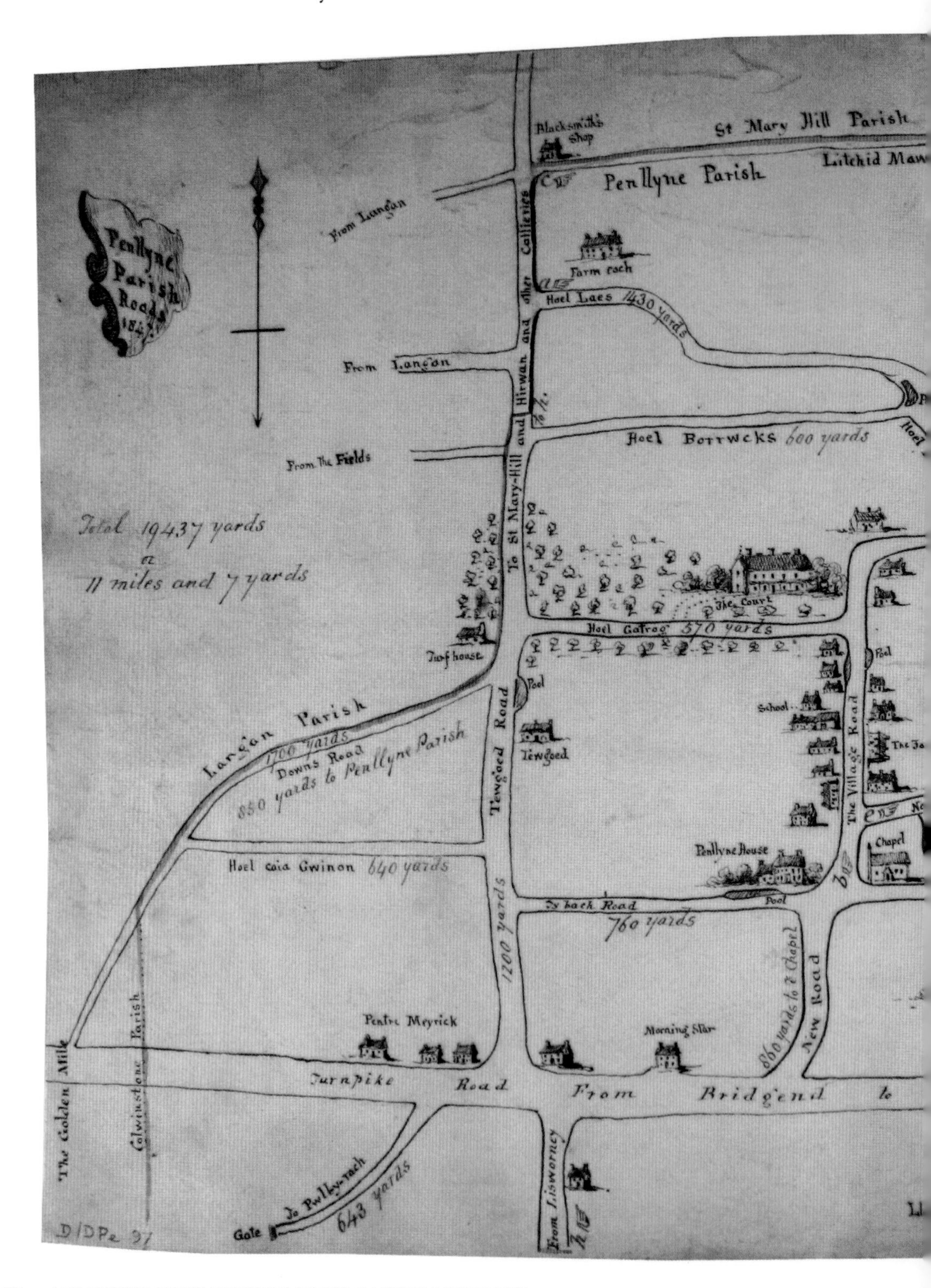
Penllyne Parish Roads 184
Blacksmith's Shop
St Mary Hill Parish
Penllyne Parish
From Langan
To St Mary-Hill and Hirwan and other Collieries
Farm Fach
Hoel Laes 1430 yards
From Langan
Hoel Borrwcks 600 yards
From The Fields
Total 19437 yards
or
11 miles and 7 yards
The Court
Hoel Gafrog 570 yards
Turf house
Pool
Langan Parish
1700 yards
Downs Road
850 yards to Penllyne Parish
Tewgoed Road
Tewgoed
School
The Village Road
Chapel
Penllyne House
Pool
Hoel caia Gwinon 640 yards
Back Road
760 yards
1200 yards
860 yards to the Chapel
New Road
Pentre Meyrick
Morning Star
The Golden Mile
Colwinstone Parish
Turnpike Road From Bridgend to
From Llsworney
Gate
To Pwlly-vach
643 yards
D/DPe 97

PENLLYN

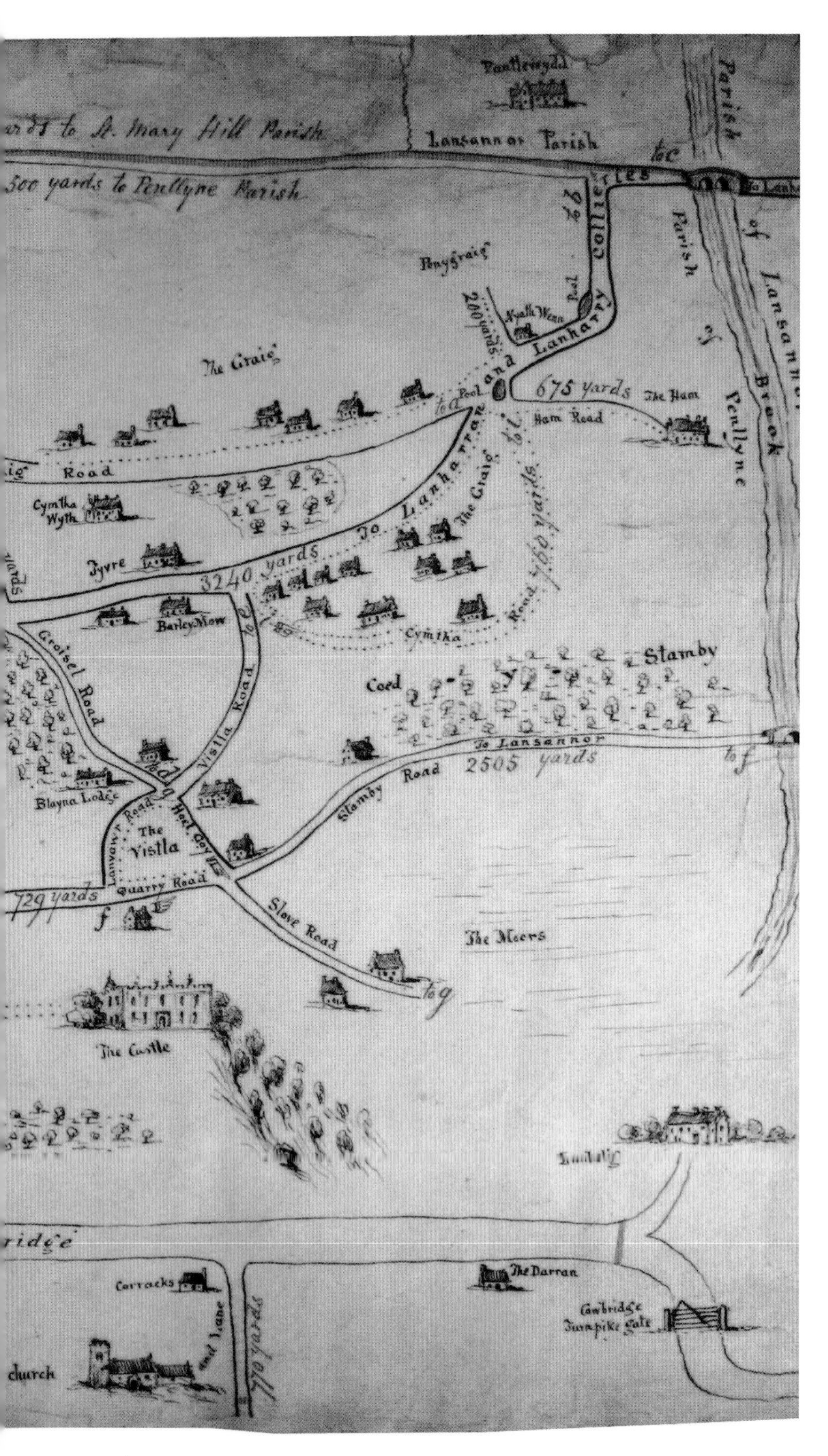

Figure 1. Sketch Map of Penllyn, 1847 (Reproduced courtesy of Glamorgan Record Office DPE 97)

The Arrival of the Homfrays

The decision of the County Court, on the appeal of Salmon and the Penllyn villagers against the enclosure of the Chapel, was inserted into the same Bill with the agreement of the Court. This decision ruled that the Homfray family must provide permanent public foot access to the Chapel and carriage access at Chapel service times, but the procession of the public past the Castle entrance was no longer permitted. With the turmoil of the share out of the Parish Common Lands, and euphoria from all the new employment arising from the construction of the new roads and drains, the decision appears to have been generally accepted and the Homfrays were allowed to retain the enclosure walls and gates. It was certainly a great visual improvement. The open village green and its open rubbish pits had been an eyesore around the Chapel and these had been situated right alongside the newly created driveway to the Castle. John Homfray had reputedly just spent a fortune on refurbishing the old Chapel and had dedicated it to his wife Maria who had recently died. The new estate walls had also involved the removal of the ruins of the priest house and its site being partly enclosed. Homfray had started negotiation with the church, but they were dreadfully slow and so he pushed ahead, such that the church was also involved in the objections, particularly as the access to the Glebe land was involved. Eventually, the church accepted other land from the estate for the priest house ruin and agreed to sell the Glebe land, although the newly created Church in Wales did not finally complete this until 1924. Meanwhile, the 700 year-old access to the front of the Castle had been buried below the parkland and its trees.

The impact of the Enclosure Award, just 12 years after the arrival of the Homfray family with all their improvements to the Castle, its parkland and the village Chapel, is difficult for us to comprehend 150 years after the event. The village must have appeared transformed. The freehold of one fifteenth of the land within the parish was given to the parishioners. Land which they had grazed freely from time immemorial was now enclosed and these individual fields were henceforth owned by them or one of their neighbours. Lucky owners could sell for cash, while others preferred to create larger farms. Gossip and deals would have been the order of the day.

Direct help to the villagers at this point might be considered to have arisen from the Enclosure Award, for ownership of every perch of land within the village, including all lands which by custom had been held in common, was now defined. Even for the poorest there was some consolation, for the Churchwardens were given five acres to hold as gardens and allotments for the use of the poor. After the cost of constructing all the major drains and providing the tracks which would serve as roads were defrayed, along with the cost of the survey and the payments to Lady Dunraven for mineral rights (presumably as Lord of the Manor), the 1,729 acres of land was divided between the freeholders of the parish. Obviously, the Castle estate was the main beneficiary and it was also seen to buy out or exchange many additional parcels not required by the recipients. This considerably reduced the fragmented form of the estate lands taken over by Homfray. Other land transactions must also have occurred, for the fields are enlarged and combined, from the evidence of the Ordnance Survey, and agriculture appeared to be much healthier throughout the parish. The Census also showed a decline in the number of unoccupied houses in the parish.

At this time there were miles of ditches and new roads being constructed across the moors. Both churches were being extensively renovated and with limestone in demand for new walls and mortar and for sweetening the newly drained and fenced moorland, work must have been plentiful and wages high. Coal and lead ore were now being mined at Llanharry and Llangan. Perhaps this was the reason Doctor Salmon decided to remain at home and improve his estate and reorganize his farm rental (for he had also benefited from the share out of common lands). He also floated a new mining company, for much of the old lead mining was on his lands.

At this time also, the wealth arising from coal from the Rhondda valleys was beginning to surge through Barry and Cardiff, and would have added to the demand for fresh food from local farms. The rates for labour in the Vale were the subject of many newspaper articles and labourers at last began to know the feel of money in their pockets.

We know from the 1841 Census that there were about 350 people living in Penllyn in 52 dwellings but of those, over half lived in tiny two or three room crofts or cottages of a Tithe of less than 1s/6d (7p). Of the rest, 13 were cottages or houses Tithed up to 3s/4d (17p) and 11 were houses, including the Castle, Tithed up to 8s/3d (43p). If we compare this with the Parish Rates of the 1920's, we see that of the 73 dwellings, there were 50 rated as small cottages below £4 when a reasonable 3-bedroom house would rate at £10. By the 1860's many labourers and the artisans had begun to move away to the towns and coalmines. Consequently, Penllyn had a pool of poor older people living in the cheap agricultural cottages, mainly around the Graig.

The Arrival of the Homfrays

The 1847 sketch map shows the moorland east of the escarpment, which was clearly impassable (except on foot) before the drainage of 1860, and then only in dry weather. Tracks are shown which pass north to Llansannor and to Llanharry. These had once been used by pack ponies, bringing goods such as iron ore, lead ore and farm produce to the port at Aberthaw, then over the channel to Bristol. Tracks also show major access to St. Mary Hill and Llangan, for they were of greater importance to Penllyn in those days as part of the drovers' routes for cattle to the Midlands and London.

In terms of roads however, Penllyn remained largely neglected, being part of a very poor system of countryside tracks, while elsewhere, new turnpikes and railways were established linking towns with markets. The village roads of Penllyn changed very slowly until the Second World War and private motor transport became more readily affordable. These tracks included the present bridleways that pass direct from Vistla via Court Farm to Red Farm (Fferm Goch) and from Quarry Cottage (Llanmawr) straight down Penllyn Hill to Dan y Coed, a farm on the edge of the moor now demolished (Footpath 19). Walk them today and you will understand the typical trackways that formed the original squalid roads of the village, before the present parish roads were formed in the years between 1910 and 1940. Later road improvements comprised filling the ditches alongside the track, sometimes with open jointed stoneware pipes for drainage, then covering with broken stone to level it and spraying the surface with tar and chippings and only much later with tarmac. It is recorded in the Parish Minutes that surfaced roads only reached the Barley Mow, after much complaint, in 1937. Occasionally, the existing track was too narrow and a strip of adjacent field had to be taken for a new track, such as that just north of Court Farm where the old narrow hollow way can be seen alongside. Within the woodland to the east were once two cottages, some of the many 'lost crofts' that lie within the woodland areas around Penllyn. These lost crofts, which have never been replaced, account for the decline in population after 1800, which dropped from 349 to 275. The problem of the poor remained,

Figure 2. Colonel H. R. Homfray receiving the Freedom of Cowbridge, 1935

as the Parish Records show, though it was much alleviated by government and Estate charity, until commuter owned houses slowly replaced the agricultural cottages of the parish of Penllyn.

The advent of the Homfray family to Penllyn saw an enormous change in the fortunes of the parish from a farming community of many small fragmented holdings, rented from many different freeholders, to one where a major estate established a number of large consolidated farms. It saw the first improvements in the roads and a rapid rise in the patronage for village amenities. The most clearly defined benefit of the coming of the Homfray family to Penllyn was, and is, the manner in which the family identified with the village. Whilst it had no historic or family ties with Penllyn prior to 1846, from the outset the Homfray family accepted a moral leadership, serving as magistrates, militia and local government representatives.

Figure 3. Memorial Plaque to Capt. John Charles Richards Homfray

1 Source, Glamorgan Record Office

2 See Parish Map for original access route

Chapter 8

Church and Chapel

While the prevalence of objects apparently deposited in the marshes and lakes of the Thaw Valley may suggest the worship of other gods prior to the coming of Christianity, it is church and chapel that today provide a lasting testament to more than a millennium of Christian worship in Penllyn.

PENLLYN

Llanfrynach Church (Church of St. Brynach)

Location and Settlement

This church is located 1 km to the west of Cowbridge, adjacent to the 2nd-4th century Romano-British enclosure to the immediate east. It is quite possible that this may have been a holy site before Christianity but, be that as it may, the dedication to the 5th century St. Brynach implies the existence of a Christian church on this site many centuries before the current stone structure. Indeed, local tradition (sadly unsubstantiated) is that St. Patrick worshipped here before he sought tuition from St. Illtud at Llantwit Major.

Figure 1. Llanfrynach Church. Undated sketch, probably of 19th century origin, with the modern castle structure (built circa 1800) in the background

Of more certainty is that the current stone structure is of early Norman origin. Cadw, in its 2002 plaque commemorating a tower restoration, refers to the chancel arch and stone benches as of 12th century origin, which would make the build of the stone church almost contemporary with that of Penllyn Castle, built circa 1135. However, other reports suggest a slightly later, 13th century date for the earliest stonework in the church. The location of the church, a mile south of the main settlement and castle at Penllyn and in the extreme south of the parish, is something of a conundrum.

One local tradition suggests that the isolated position of the church is the work of the devil, who attempted to carry the church out of the parish. Fortunately for Penllyn, he lacked the strength to carry out the task and dropped it where it stands today! The more likely answer is that there was an existing church at the site before the Norman invasion, possibly with an adjacent settlement. An archaeological investigation by Glamorgan Gwent Archaeological Trust (G.G.A.T.) in 1982,[1] in the churchyard area east of the church and adjacent to the road, found remains of two buildings which fell out of use in the medieval period. One building appeared to be for agricultural use, including a flue for corn drying, while the other was a more significant residence.

Church and Chapel

As Margam Abbey formalised the appropriation of St. Brynach's church by Papal Bull in 1384, it would, most probably, have then been a productive asset, raising the prospect that there was either a manorial house, or a church house, at the heart of a small agricultural complex. On the southern boundary of the churchyard is a small stream, with medieval rubble both mortared and un-mortared, indicating the presence of a mill-race. Medieval pottery was also found in the Romano-British enclosure and in several fields to the north of the site. However, without further excavation, the extent and nature of the medieval settlement at Llanfrynach is unlikely to be fully known, nor whether it was a continuation of an (as yet undiscovered) early-medieval settlement, possibly itself a continuation of the known Romano-British settlement. It is interesting to note that both Iolo Morganwg and David Jones of Wallington suggested that a village had existed at this site. Indeed, Iolo Morganwg claimed that the village had been deserted in 1404 as a consequence of the Owain Glyndwr rebellion. However, the G.G.A.T. excavation found 3 silver pennies, dating from the reign of Henry VI (1421-1471) in the destruction deposits of the residential building, which indicates a late 15th century date for the building falling out of use.

The 2002 Cadw plaque suggests that the Black Death wiped out the settlement, which must be a possibility, even though the major plague outbreaks were in the 14th century. Another suggestion is that changes in the water table may have impacted on the viability of the settlement, leading to its desertion. To add further confusion to the date the settlement was finally deserted, Margam Abbey is recorded as being in possession of a tithe barn at Llanfrynach in 1535.[2]

Structure

Figure 2. Llanfrynach Church, south elevation, 2005

Figure 3. Llanfrynach Church, Rood Stair, 2007

The church is aligned west to east and consists of a western tower, with an external or outshoot stair, the central nave with south facing porch and the chancel to the east. There is a rood stair in the north of the nave. The tower and the porch are additions to the original two-cell structure.

Church and Chapel

Particular features of the church include fine late medieval roof trusses and stone pews along the north and south walls. Although freestanding pews have now been introduced, originally the central nave had no pews and the congregation would have stood during the service. For the elderly and infirm, this would not be possible and they were allowed to sit on the stone pews, giving rise to the expression 'the weakest to the wall'.

Figure 4. Late Medieval Roof Trusses, 2007

Figure 5. Stone Pews, 2007

Church and Chapel

That the physical structure of the church survives today is due to the repairs that have been carried out over the centuries but after the desertion of the adjacent settlement, and the later consecration of the chapel of ease in Penllyn, Llanfrynach became increasingly dilapidated and services stopped, although it still remained the burial ground for the parish.[3] Thanks to the efforts of Dr. William Salmon, the church was repaired in 1848 and 'The Cambrian', on 1st September 1848, was able to report the first service at the church for 150 years. In 1851, the religious census reported that the church was used for public services on alternate Sundays in the summer, when attendance averaged 40 persons.

Although the 1848 restoration was the most publicised repair, maintenance of the fabric would be a constant requirement, as can be seen from the 1932 re-pointing. The tower itself originally held four bells, three of which were removed in 1776. The surviving bell, with the inscription SCA MARIA,[4] was cast by the Bristol Medieval bell foundry in 1430.[5] It is now located on the first floor of the tower.

Figure 6. Llanfrynach Church Bell

Figure 7. Llanfrynach Church Tower, during 1932 re-pointing

Today, the church retains much of its medieval simplicity, its simple structure hidden away from the bustle of nearby Cowbridge and overlooked by the ramparts of the Iron Age fort of Caer Dynnaf. Perhaps appropriately, it still has no electricity, heating or modern lighting.

The Coffin Stiles

Figure 8. Coffin Stile on north boundary of churchyard enclosure

Church and Chapel

The main settlement of Penllyn to the north had no burial ground, so coffins would have to be brought to the churchyard at Llanfrynach for burial. Although there is a lane to the church, at times the medieval roads would have been impassable and coffins would need to be carried to the church. To help the bearers traverse the field boundaries, stiles were constructed along the route of the medieval footpath, still way-marked to this day. The bearers were able to rest the coffin on the central pillar while crossing the stile. These stiles are unique in the Vale of Glamorgan.

An alternative version for their construction has entered local folklore. David Jones reported that Reynold Thomas Deere *"had 2 daughters, who were his co-heiresses. As the rank of each of these young ladies was equal, neither was entitled to take precedence over the other and they could not agree as to which, on the road from the castle to the church, first get over the stile. The indulgent father, to prevent any bickering in the family and also perhaps that his daughters should be able to attend to their devotions at church with unruffled minds, had the double stiles made so the co-heiresses might get over together and each maintain her rank undiminished"* and that *"Mr Reynold Thomas Deere of Penlline Court was also a singular character. He had lived apart from his wife who indeed had died an early death. There were four daughters under his roof, two of whom were of legitimate birth and two were not. When he and his two daughters were received into Society events to stay at any of the neighbouring houses, the careful father always saw the daughters to their chamber himself and locked the door upon them taking the key with him."*

His daughters, Susannah and Hester, were duly grateful and a plaque is erected in the church with the inscription: *"This poor tribute of gratitude is erected by two most afflicted Daughters to the memory of their beloved Father REYNOLD THOMAS DEERE their best and most dearest friend A man endued with sound sense and acute judgement with brilliant but inoffensive wit and an elegant taste Unshaken courage the tenderest the noblest feelings that ever adorned humanity with truth as bright and integrity as clear as the day in Heaven."*

St. John the Evangelist Church

For centuries this church, located on the north side of the entrance road to the castle, was a chapel of ease to the parish church of Llanfrynach but, when Penllyn became part of the Rectorial benefice of Cowbridge in 1995, the church was dedicated to St. John the Evangelist.

Figure 9. St. John the Evangelist Church, 1923 postcard

Church and Chapel

The original chapel was possibly 15th century, built by the Turbervilles. In the late 1840's, John Homfray completely refurbished the Chapel and dedicated it to his wife, Ann Maria, who had died in 1846. It was reputed that he spent a thousand pounds on this work at a time when wages were about eight shillings a week for a labourer. The new estate walls enclosed the previously open Chapel, which led to a County Court confrontation with the villagers. Finally, the Homfray family was allowed to retain the walls but with a permanent pedestrian access to the Chapel – hence the kissing gate. They were also allowed to close the driveway through the parkland but were required to allow access for carriages to the Chapel for services.

Figure 10. St. John the Evangelist, south chancel window, 2007

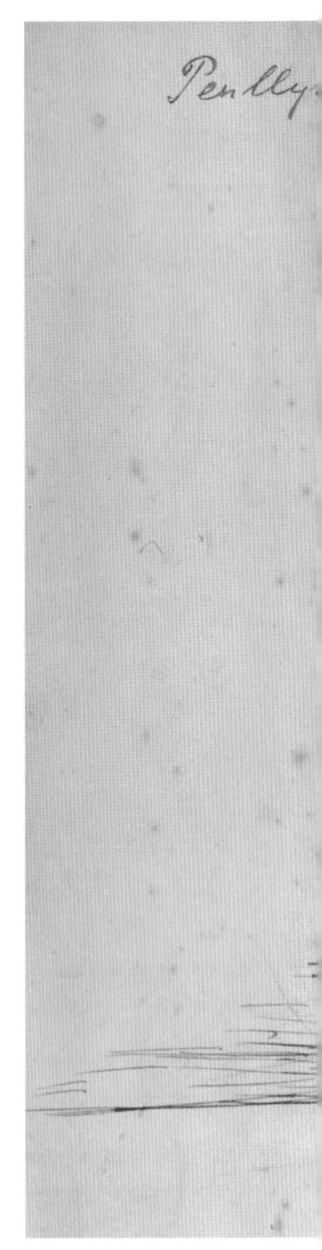

The stonework of the chapel walls is nearly all original, the post 1840 alterations being the addition of the porch, vestry, corner buttresses and new windows and stonework surrounds. The roof timbers were replaced and roofed with slate tiles. Recent structural repairs to the roof, necessitated by dangerously rotten roof timbers, led to the discovery in the roof space of some stone tiles, suggesting that the chapel used to have stone roof tiles prior to the refurbishment.

Figure 11 St. John the Evangelist, 1846, prior to Homfray refurbishment (Reproduced courtesy of Glamorgan Record Office ref DPE 114)

Church and Chapel

The religious census of 1851 refers to the Chapel being consecrated in about 1700 *"because the church is situated far apart from the residences of the inhabitants."* The date of the consecration coincided with the sale of the Penllyn estate by the Turbervilles to Richard Seys of Boverton, in 1703.

Morning attendance in 1851 averaged 80 people, including 20 scholars, while afternoon attendance was just 10 Welsh. William Llewellyn, the Minister, noted, *"the Welsh congregation would be more numerous were they not deterred by great echo of Chapel."*

One surviving tradition involves marriages. When the wedding service is completed, and the bride and groom seek to leave through the castle gates, village children tie the gates shut with a ribbon, to be removed only when the groom has paid an appropriate toll!

Figure 12. St. John the Evangelist: window dating from late 1840's

Figure 13. St. John the Evangelist, Bell Turret above west gable end. The bell was cast in Bristol in 1380

Figure 14. St. John the Evangelist, November 11th 1923, dedication of new carved oak panelling (reredos) to rear of altar

Church and Chapel

Other interesting features of the church, as listed by the benefice, include:

- the stone font on a stone plinth and pedestal adjacent to the South Door. An inscription dates from 1682 and has the letters "W. I. T. R. CHURCH W".

- the organ, probably dating from the late 19th century, built by H. Farrant of Brighton. George Osmond of Taunton rebuilt this in 1884. Dedications are to Francis Richard Homfray who died 10th April 1888 aged 25 years and to Albert James Wood Newton, organist, 1920-1984.

Recollections

(A.N.) When the Colonel[6] got on that organ it was very hard. I don't know whether you were here at the time but my father, he played the organ as well. But when the Colonel played, he needed a lot of pumping. He only played on big occasions when the Bishop came or something like that. And I used to be able to pump well enough to suit my father but when the Colonel really got moving it was a job to keep up. He would put his head around the corner and say, 'Blow up my boy'.

- A good array of well-designed and carved oak furniture including the altar, pulpit, stalls, 20 pews, lectern, credence table, and two Glastonbury chairs.

- A number of memorial tablets on the north and south walls of the chancel, mainly dedicated to members of the Homfray family of Penllyn Castle, and Salmon of Penllyn Court, long associated with the church.

The Methodist Chapel

1851 Religious Census: NEBO. CALVINISTIC METHODIST
Erected: October 1831
Space: free 400; other 48; standing 400
Present: aft.120; even 100
Average: general congregation 100

Extract from a lease dated 17th June 1833

Made the seventeenth day of June in the year of our Lord 1833 between Evan Williams of the Parish of Penlline in the County of Glamorgan – Farmer, on the one or former part and (1) Richard Thomas of the Parish of Llysworney in the said county, - Minister of the Gospel, (2) William Evans of the Parish of Llantrisant in the said county, Minister of the Gospel, (3) David Howell of the town of Swansea in the said county, Minister of the Gospel, (4) Benjamin Evans of the Parish of St Fagans in the said county - Minister of the Gospel (5) John Morgan of the parish of Laleston in the said county, - Preacher of the Gospel, (6) David Roberts of the town of Swansea as aforesaid – Preacher of the Gospel, (7) John James of the Parish of Coity in the said county – Preacher of the Gospel, (8) Elias Bassett of the Parish of Llantwit Major in the said county – Gentleman, (9) William James of the Parish of Coity as aforesaid – Farmer, (10) Thomas Morris of the Parish of Llansannor in the said county – Shopkeeper, (11) Edward Jenkins of the Parish of Pendoylan in the said county – Farmer (12) David Davies of the Parish of Llanblethian in the same county – Maltster and (13) David Reynolds of The Parish of Penlline – Cordwainer of the other or latter part.

Whereas a Chapel or Meeting place hath on the faith of an agreement dated the 26th day of April 1831 and made between the said Evan Williams of the one part and the said David Reynolds of the other part, been erected on the parcel of ground herein after demised at the expense of the Members of the Welsh Calvinistic Methodist Connection and divers persons piously disposed to promote the Gospel of Our Lord and Saviour Jesus Christ at Penlline aforesaid who have contributed thereto and in compliance with such agreement as aforesaid the said Evan Williams hath consented to grant the said parties hereto of the latter part a lease of the said for and during the term of 987 years.

Church and Chapel

Curiously, it is not until the 1877 Ordnance Survey map that the chapel is identifiably mapped at its location opposite the Barley Mow in the Graig. In 1883 new trustees of the Welsh Calvinistic Methodist Chapel were appointed and in 1888, the 'Central Glamorgan Gazette' reports *"Penllyne, a new chapel. The Calvin Methodists are shortly to build a new Chapel. Sir J. L. Spearman of Llansannor Court has kindly given land gratis for the purpose, local subscription amounting to £130 have already been promised. The friends of the cause at Penllyne are particularly grateful to Mr Griffiths of Is-y-Coed for his handsome donation."*

A stone plaque on the side of the chapel, laid by Lady Spearman, is dated 13th July 1888. But a question arises over the gift by Sir J. L. Spearman - was this additional land or land already subject to a long-term lease? Evan Williams, the original lessor, was himself a tenant of Sir Joseph Bailey. If the land was gifted to the new Trustees as reported, it may be explained by the prior marriage of Sir Joseph Bailey's daughter, Ann Bethan, to a son of Sir Alexander Spearman and the possibility of the land being included in a marriage settlement. Further research is required to investigate this link.

The last major service to be held in the chapel was the Harvest Festival in October 1951 and, on the 30th May 1957, the Glamorgan Presbytery East accepted a minute that the Calvinistic Methodist Chapel at Graig Penllyne had closed.

Figure 15.
The Methodist Chapel, 1915

In October 1957, the Communion vessels were received from Mrs. Roberts of Vistla Farm and Mrs. Williams of Graig Farm and in April 1958 the building was closed up.

On 6th July 1973, the 'South Wales Echo' reported that the windows had been smashed and glass covered the well-preserved pews and floors. Also that *"the graveyard is overgrown and a boundary wall crumbling away"*.

Finally, on 10th October 1980, the chapel was bought for £3,100 by John Vincent, who also acquired the graveyard in 1982 for an additional £100. Mr. Vincent converted the chapel into a private house on three levels and the headstones[7] in the graveyard were moved to the side to create a Garden of Remembrance. The rest of the land was converted to garden and a new garage built.

People

One of the new Calvinistic Chapel Trustees in 1883 was Manoah David, a farmer at the Graig. Born in Ystradowen in 1830, he was by then married to Mary, and had three daughters and one son, Robert. Robert's daughter, Gwyneth, remembers the Chapel and the gatherings of ministers afterwards, at Winchfield House.

Recollections

(M.T.). And you used to get big meetings? **(G.D.)** We used to have the Reverend so-and-so, and the Reverend so-and-so **(M.T.)** At the little chapel? **(G.D.)** Yes, it was a big event, a big meeting and of course it used to be who preached the best sermon, really, and they all used to come to our house, between the services, during the interval **(M.T.)** Did they stay over the weekend? **(G.D.)** The Sunday ministers used to come and make a weekend of it and I can remember walking into what we called was our parlour and the room was full of smoke and they did used to say which was the best minister, among themselves, which was very wrong.... Once, a weekend minister was staying with us, and my father thought Lloyd George was wonderful, and this man thought Kier Hardie was wonderful, so of course two personalities clashed. The end of it was the poor minister was out on the front lawn pacing up and down. I don't know what happened to him, whether he came back...

Church and Chapel

Figure 16. Llanfrynach Church service, 1969. Rear (L-R) Albert Newton, Reverend Dodd, Reverend Voyles, Anthony Powell. Front (L-R) Jonathan Powell, Christopher Smith, Peter Francis (standing behind), Simon Hargreaves, David Harris. The service celebrated the 1969 landing on the moon.

Recollections

What were the Sunday congregations like? **(A.P)** Well early days they were big. We used to have a Cymry'r Groes[8]. Started by the Vicar, and in those days we had to cycle. There were a lot of Cymry'r Groes clubs in lots of places. Like St. Mary's Church. We would cycle from here to St. Mary's Church for a social evening. **(H.G.)** Reverend Rees started them. **(K.H.)** So when we are talking about you going to church when you were younger, was that the church up in Penllyn, and not the chapel[9] where Bryan Gillard lived. **(A.P.)** Yes, that was going and that was good. If it was harvest festival or something like that the church people would go to the chapel and the chapel people would go to the church. **(N.J.)** And we had Sunday School outings. **(A.P.)** And not only that but we would walk from here over to Llansannor church and go past your place **(The Ham)**[10] and go across the fields that way. Or if it was mucky we would go around the roads. **(K.H.)** So it was part of your social life then, as much as anything else? **(B.P.)** Yes and with the Chapel I can remember people coming from St. Mary's Hill in a pony and trap. **(A.P.)** Yes and horses and where [Terry]Turner lives[11], there was a place underneath, a stable where they would put the horses. And they would go up the steps because there was a room above like a vestry. And there was one chap called Davies who would cycle from Bridgend. He would take the service.

Figure 17. Sunday School outing, 1924

Recollections

(G.D.) And about the 1904 revival, he told us that, they all gathered together. Of course, in those days, it was a great thing, the Sunday School outings, a great event, so anyway they all gathered together in a little vestry in the chapel to decide about the Sunday School outing. And not a word was said about the outing, they all fell on their knees and prayed. And that was during the 1904 revival.

1 Parkhouse and Robinson preliminary report, Glamorgan-Gwent Archaeological Trust, Annual Report, 1981-2

2 Valor Ecclesiasticus, 1535

3 Llanfrynach monumental inscriptions can be found at: **www.genuki.org.uk/big/wal/GLA/Penllyn/Llanfrynach**

4 SCA is an abbreviation of Sancta.

5 'Medieval Churches of the Vale of Glamorgan`, Geoffrey R Orrin, 1988

6 Colonel H. R. Homfray

7 The location of the gravestones and their inscriptions is shown in Appendix 1.

8 Cymry'r Groes literally means Welshmen of the Cross. It was a Church youth organisation, whereby candidates were admitted after making a promise in church to abide by a "rule of life" involving prayer and following Jesus (source, Church in Wales).

9 Methodist Chapel

10 Ham Farm and Is Coed, Craig Penllyn

11 Merida

Chapter 9

The Village Wells

Access to fresh water is essential for the existence of any settled community. A study of the sources and the development of the water supply to any ancient settlement can reveal rarely studied aspects of a community's history. This proposition was neatly illustrated by the decision of the present residents to investigate and restore to a useable condition, the group of springs covered by masonry wellheads in the centre of the parish. These had become almost completely overgrown since the Second World War when they fell out of use. Marked as Ffynnonau-y-Pentre on the Ordnance Survey and all other known maps but locally known as Salmon's Wells, they are clearly remembered by the older residents as the centre of village life, but were virtually unknown to the majority of new families.

In June 1997, a few late-come residents with an interest in history noted these lost wells and the fact that they appeared unique and decided the site should be Listed. It took some months to convince Cadw but on 9th April 1998, the site was Listed and Penllyn Community Council agreed to support the Residents Association who had resolved to make the Wells restoration a 'millennium project'. It was seen as a means of restoring village awareness of its history and it was realized that it would be a classic example of early village development for educational use. When this was explained to appropriate charity funding groups, promises of financial support were given for the scheme though the residents had already undertaken to underwrite the initial cost. Professional help was available from a few retired residents and the Vale Conservation officer gave enthusiastic encouragement. Thus the scheme was launched.

Figure 1. Salmon's Wells, post restoration, Wellhead 1 to left, drawn by Eric Evans, conservation architect

The Landscape

Since late medieval times, the most populated part of the parish has been the crescent shaped high ridge of limestone running north to south to the west of the River Thaw Valley, as illustrated on the Parish map (see frontispiece). The parish itself is leaf-shaped, some two and a half miles long and one and a half miles wide with the ridge as the rib of the leaf. The River Thaw forms the eastern boundary and illustrates the antiquity of this settlement, for this was a Welsh commote[1] boundary prior to the Norman occupation. Between the settlement on the ridge and the River Thaw is a steep escarpment of limestone and a wide area of marshland. Until the mid-1800's no hard trackway crossing existed so there was never easy access to fresh water from the river. The limestone below the settlement is pitted by sinkholes so all streams disappear very quickly into deep underground waterways.

The Village Wells

Only two wells[2] have been successfully sunk (over 20m) to locate the underground streams and these wells are known not to have been dependable. Both are located on the edge of areas known to be village waste or common land and probably served to water commoners' cattle[3]. The only dependable sources of fresh water are the natural springs, now covered by wellheads, and known locally as Salmon's Wells.

The first known survey of the area is the Tithe Map of 1840 but this is known to be a very inferior production and does not include any reference to water sources. It was not until the 1858 Inclosure Map[4] that a plan detailed enough to include water sources was made. This appears to be based on Ordnance Survey data although the official OS sheet was not published until 1890[5]. The Inclosure Map shows the site of two springs within a boundary identical with the present and also shows the two deep wells previously mentioned, but no others within the parish. From the geological survey[6] of the area, it can be seen that the site coincides with a geological upward ripple (anticline) in the lower Carboniferous Limestone which at this point has a strata of clay like shale, which acts as a natural water trap and conduit. At the surface, there is a glacial hollow which exposes this strata and the natural syphonic flow of water which trickles out from here, goes northward for some two hundred yards, then disappears into a sinkhole and via underground streams to the river to the east. It is part of the Cardiff/Cowbridge anticline which gives rise to a number of prolific springs within the Vale of Glamorgan[7]. Largest of these are the Schwyll Well near Ogmore Mill which since 1869 supplied Bridgend with piped water. By 1921 the Mid Glamorgan Water Board abstracted five and half million gallons a day for the Vale but it was not until 1934 that this included Penllyn.

History

An indication of early problems with the water supply is given in the report of Parkhurst and Robinson (1981-2) on work associated with Llanfrynach Church[8]. The report refers to a stream, which still exists adjacent to the churchyard wall, and notes *"at present the stream flows intermittently but may have carried more water in the mediaeval period"*. Studies of Lay subsidy returns of 1543[9], the Hearth Tax returns of 1660 and 1670[10] and Tithe redemption records all indicate the existence of between 60 and 80 occupied dwellings in this parish from medieval times to the 20th century. All these would require a supply of fresh drinking water. Further enquiry has established that every surviving early dwelling of consequence within the parish has, or had, extensive facilities for storage of rainwater. Penllyn Castle still has extensive cisterns, and these were in regular use until the 1890's. Great House, a Georgian period house near the church, also has cisterns, *'in which a man can stand'*, and in the 17th century 'Village Farm' the cisterns are still visible. In the late 19th century, many of these cisterns were surmounted by cast iron pumps, some of which still survive and serve to confuse the fact that there are so few true wells in the parish. The overall situation was summarised by a letter reported in the Parish minutes for August 1896. It came from Mr. Page, a Civil Engineer in Cardiff who was appointed by Cowbridge Rural District Council to report on the water problem of Penllyn. He found only two deep wells together with the two village springs within wellheads. He concluded, *"the greater use of Dr. Salmon's Wells with the provision of a storage cistern near the well of a capacity of 60 days at 6 gallons per head of population and a 3" cast iron main laid to the lower end of the village with cast iron standards as necessary, is required. For the upper part of the village a request could be made to the owner of Penlline Castle, Capt. Homfray, who is currently installing a large water tower and pump to raise fresh water from the Penlline Moors."* (This would be springs from the underground streams feeding the River Thaw). *"Alternatively a pump or ram must be provided at the Salmon's Well".* He emphasised the need to ensure that the well water was used only for domestic purposes. Unfortunately, the Parish Council decided the capital cost of the proposal was too great and Capt. Homfray was unwilling to agree to the considerable enlargement of his private supply. Subsequently, the Council decided to deepen the northern of the two sunk wells (in Winchfield at the Graig) and to provide a new hoist. Meanwhile they exhorted every freeholder to provide adequate cisterns for rainwater. The two deep wells did continue to contribute to the supply and in 1897 they were fitted with new doors to cover them. Of the two, the Winchfield well was evidently the more important, for in 1901 it was arranged to fit a hand pump and to renew the stonework but it was not successful and later references mention the fitting of a new rope. It is of interest to note that for 700 years the servants at the castle had to carry fresh water from the wells, a full half-mile, and there was a direct footpath from the castle to the wells and from the wells to all groups of dwellings in the parish. In living memory, Great House servants collected water from these springs using a yoke and buckets and this continued to 1934. Repairs and maintenance of all the parish wells are detailed in parish records and in 1901 the Cowbridge R.D.C. accepted the care and maintenance of them. The last recorded public use of the Salmon's Wells site was for an open-air thanksgiving service after V.E. day in 1945.

The site of Ffynnonau-y-Pentre is traditionally accepted as part of the manor house lands of Penllyn Court. This lies between Penllyn Castle and the large area of common land to the north of the parish know as the Graig. It is around the Graig that virtually all the small, low rated cottages in the parish were built on poor quality land with its one deep sunk, but not dependable, well. The land is generally very steep and wooded here and comprises the remains of the waste or common land of the parish. There is a general fall to the north but it should be noted that there are no permanent long streams. All rain water and ground-water drains quickly into sinkholes.

The Village Wells

David Jones recorded in his diaries[11] that Dr. Salmon *'provided two wells for domestic water supplies'* on his land. It is evident from this that in 1875 there were two wells only and they were in an extremely poor state of repair. Dr. Salmon was stated to be concerned for the welfare of the village community. At that time, the site of these wellheads was separate from the grounds of the Court, and was part of a farm which from the 1840 Tithe Survey, was rented by David Williams who lived at the farmhouse Tŷ Fry[12] at the Graig. Between 1840 and 1880, Dr. Salmon evidently repossessed the land and improved both the Court grounds and the village wellheads. A stone marked 1883 is recorded as the keystone in the arched head of Wellhead No. 2, which suggests the legendary restoration by Dr. Salmon or a subsequent one, for the detailed drawing of the stonework showed evidence of many repairs. This stone is now missing. It is also recorded that a summer drought could cause severe problems in the whole area. In 1887, Queen Victoria's Jubilee year, the drought was so bad that scores of people from the villages of Llansannor, St. Mary Hill, Llangan, Treoes, Colwinston and Llysworney queued with pitchers to collect water from the Penllyn wells. This is of interest because in a future extract from the same diary is a description of the well at Llysworney, where it is noted that it has an extremely strong spring never known to fail in the driest season.

The Site

There are now three springs within the site. Numbers 1 and 2 are covered by masonry wellheads and No. 3 is an open pool. Recent archaeological work has allowed the surviving construction of the wells to be examined in great detail. Wellhead No. 1 was originally a basin hollowed into the clay/shale strata approximately some 2.0m diameter and 0.5m deep. Large limestone blocks are laid as a foundation for a masonry superstructure approximately 0.5m thick forming three sides of an oblong surround averaging 1.5m high. The oblong is irregular and approx. 1.5m x 1.2m with the opening on the short side. It is roofed with some massive limestone slabs, some corbelled at the rear and finished with one very large slab approx 1.4m square. The front opening is surrounded by similar masonry to an imposing curved facade. Wellhead No. 2, which is upflow (west) about 18m, cuts into the shale strata some 0.8m and again is hollowed to a similar basin. The foundations and masonry surround construction is similar to Wellhead No.1 but slightly larger. The roof cover is a shallow arch with about 120mm rise in roughly cut local limestone. Careful examination of the walls of both wells shows a series of major repairs but no complete rebuild.

Figure 2. Wellhead 2, post restoration, drawn by Eric Evans, conservation architect

The roofs of the wellheads are probably as originally built. Wellhead No. 1 has a single limestone slab 1.2m long and 150mm thick as a front sill. It is worn by considerable usage at the top (120mm deep in places) and a later rebuild to maintain support to the roof has built over the wear. It is also perforated with a circular hole to form an overflow and to maintain the water 150mm below the top of the sill. Wellhead No. 2 has a niche, which may have housed a saint's image, constructed as part of the original rear wall. This is outlined by small slabs and is 280mm wide and 280mm deep with a triangular head 280mm to 400mm high. Both wellhead interiors have been given repeated coats of whitewash to create a substantial skin.

Excavation has revealed that both had paved stone aprons. Wellhead No. 1 has an area 3.0m x 2.0m of irregular slabs of limestone averaging 20mm thick neatly fitted together. These have been laid over a similar type of paving which must be badly worn. The perforation in the vertical kerbstone to the well front which acts as an overflow, discharges through a stone lined conduit 300mm deep and 150mm wide, covered by the paving, and passes into the roadside ditch which is similarly lined for 2m before it is joined to modern pipes. Wellhead No. 2 has a neatly cobbled area of paving 4.60m x 2.40m overall, laid to falls. A paved channel from the centre of the well conducts the water from a small weir, constructed below the flat slab, 0.6m wide 200mm deep, which acts as a step to the well entry. The generally smaller slabs of foundation stones, different details of construction and the fact that it is constructed upflow of Wellhead No. 1, all argue a later date of construction for Wellhead No. 2.

Between the road boundary and the stone paved aprons fronting the wellheads, broken shale has been regularly spread to cover the mud that accumulated around the Wellheads in this damp hollow. About 1920 the Rural District Council, which was then responsible for the water supply, spread a thick layer of imported hard limestone chippings above the muddy shale. It was to this level that the site was cleaned so that the stability of the underlying deposits was not disturbed. However, much broken pottery and rubbish had naturally worked its way to the surface of the mud and much was accumulated in and around the stream overflow,

The site as restored by Dr. Salmon between 1840 and 1880 was bounded on the east by the road and a masonry wall with a stone stile. There are a large number of stone stiles of identical form in the parish. Most are on boundaries of land once owned by the Homfray estate and are attributable to their improvements of the 1860's - it appears to be the local masons' style. The southern boundary of the site is a bank perforated by earlier paths, remnants of the 'hollow ways' that preceded the present roads. The northern boundary is a stream, which is the ditched overflow from Wellhead No. 2, and connects with the roadside overflow of Wellhead No. 1. The north edge of this stream is revetted to an average of 1.0m above water level. This is partly due to the natural hollow but also to regular stream clearance, evidently over a long period. Adjacent to Wellhead No. 2 was originally a shallow revetted bank, though the site mapped in 1858 extended west of this, following the glacial hollow.

Twentieth Century Changes

After his death in 1896, Dr. Salmon's Penllyn Court was sold in 1899 to a Mr. T. L. Evans, a retired publican and property speculator from Clydach. In 1911, it is recorded in the Parish Council minutes that a Mr. Evans had dug a well on his property adjacent to the parish wells and residents were afraid it would tap off the flow of water. The archaeological work shows that Well No. 3 was created by removing part of the original stone revetment adjacent to Wellhead No. 2 and extending the stream overflow west, almost certainly following a natural waterflow, and then opening a further ground spring in the natural shale some 9m west of Wellhead No. 2. This cut deeply into the shale and

Figure 3. Wellhead 3 post restoration, drawn by Eric Evans, conservation architect

required revetting and retaining walls. It produced a flow of water sufficient in wet weather to form a waterspout. First hand accounts state that the flow was sufficient to wash out the intestines of locally killed pigs! The well was opened out and lined to create a basin 1.4m x 1.5m with an approach by steps from the east and a wall set to the west. The steps connected to a cobble path laid over the top of Wellhead No. 2 and joined the traditional access between wells by a flight of stone steps alongside Wellhead No. 2. These had collapsed not long after construction and a slippery path had since been worn alongside the stream overflow as it had been cut into the shale. Clearly, the village had reached an understanding with Mr. Evans and was using the well he had dug. From Well No. 3 a neat stone bridge leads over the outflow to a path leading to the landscaped garden of Penllyn Court. This does raise one puzzle - for recent work by the present owner in the gardens of the Court revealed not only foundations of earlier buildings but also a shallow well dug down into the same shale some fifty yards east of the village wells, but never shown on any maps.

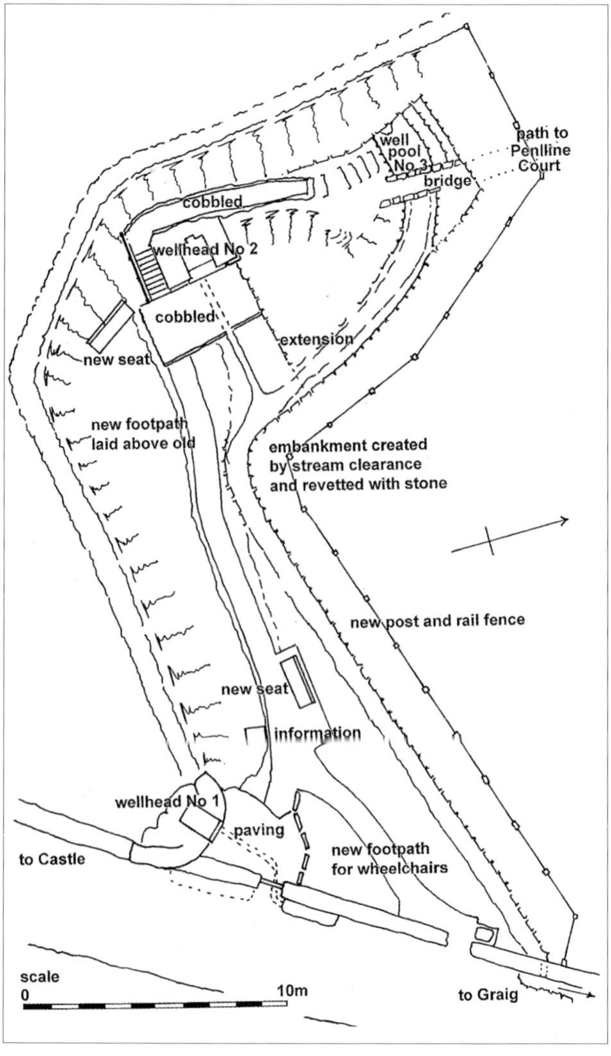

The Wells fell into disuse after 1934, when mains water was laid to the village and people were discouraged by notices posted by the R.D.C. suggesting the water should be boiled before use, as the R.D.C. had discontinued regular cleaning and whitewashing of the wells. By 1990, the wells' site was only visible by the portion of Wellhead No. 1's masonry adjacent to the main road with its marble 'tombstone' style inscription 'Dwr - Rhodd yr Hollalluog Dduw' (Water – Gift of the Almighty God). This inscription, a nice example of Victorian piety, has no known attribution. The present inscription is a replacement by the Parish Council in 1966 of an identical one, vandalised and lost.

Figure 4. Plan of restoration works

The Restoration

When it was abandoned, leaf mould and silt accumulated quickly in this dell surrounded by trees, and saplings soon grew rooted through the paving. By 1999, only drastic removal of scores of small trees and some 250mm of black soil and roots could reveal the site. Tree roots and ivy infested the masonry and parts of the wellheads' masonry had already tumbled from this neglect.

The Village Wells

The clearance of the site was carried out to archaeological standards and there now exists a detailed survey of the site and of the upstanding masonry. The excavation of the accumulated debris within the uppermost levels of the site resulted in the collection of a good sample of material broken in use or discarded as domestic rubbish over the later period of use. It includes approximately 90kg of pottery with, naturally, a very large percentage of 19th century material. However two sherds were noted from the medieval period and there were small quantities of pre-industrial fine and coarsewares showing continuous use. The glass gives a date range from the 17th century to the 20th century. Dateable clay pipes that date from the late 1600's, coins from George II and an almost perfect pewter spoon from 1700 came from the stream. Material in and below the original loose stone footpaths of the site was not disturbed. This suggests people were collecting water from the site from at least the 14th century to the 20th century, for the volume of breakage and loss would be proportional to the material wealth of the population at any period.

Figure 5. Queen Anne Spoon, circa 1700, now deposited at National Museum and Galleries of Wales, Cardiff

The range of materials found in the surface clearance of the site (see Appendix 2) would show that the Wellheads Nos. 1 and 2 were in use many centuries before the arrival of Dr. William Salmon and his philanthropy did not include providing the wells. The earliest spring must be the lowest and therefore that covered by Wellhead No. 1. This is adjacent to the track, which was reputedly part of the packhorse route between the mines of Llanharry and the town of Cowbridge and the port of Aberthaw. The use of massive corbel stones to form the roof of the wellhead could very likely be attributed to the 13th century. Contemporary accounts of building of Norman castles and townships do include the provision of wellheads. We have shown that this is the nearest water source to the castle and other medieval buildings nearby. The marble inscription, which was added to the wellhead in Victorian times, only confuses its history. Its original erection date must be inferred from its crude form, the material associated with its use and its relationship to the village.

In periods of dry weather, the flow of Wellhead No. 1 is seen to slow down much earlier than the others and it would seem reasonable to infer that this was the same in times past. It would appear sensible to have sought improved water flow higher up in the strata which seeps water and this would produce Wellhead No. 2. Its construction above the basic hollow cut into the shale is different to Wellhead No. 1. It illustrates a better technique in masonry and a greater knowledge of building design; a bucket of water is more easily removed. The rear masonry and the rear of the arched roof appear to be original. The rear wall incorporates the niche described, which we suggest could only be constructed for religious safeguarding of the water whether Christian or pagan. The suppression of the Catholic faith following the Reformation of 1534 would make the construction of a wellhead with a 'Saint's niche' very unlikely and this would certainly be true following the edicts of the Commonwealth 1640-1660. Whilst Penllyn in the period of Elizabeth was notorious for its recusancy, it would not exhibit public display of its beliefs, so the wellhead must precede this date.

Surviving local legend does not attribute any healing or magical powers to these wellheads or spring and Francis Jones' extensive survey of Welsh Holy Wells[13] has no mention of Penllyn. No similar niche is known in other wellheads in Wales but enquiries continue and we would provisionally date this wellhead to around 1600.

Well No. 3 is clearly constructed in 1911 and attests to the serious problem arising from the increased consumption of water with improved hygiene starting in late Victorian times. The population of the village had been stable for 500 years, yet the Parish Minutes reflect increasing concern with water shortage only from 1896. Evidently, Mr. T. L. Evans endeavoured to carry on the example of Dr. Salmon by improving facilities and flow at the wells, though he does not appear to have been thanked for it in the parish minutes. However, it was 1934 before the Parish Council could persuade the Rural District Council to provide a piped water supply.

Figure 6. Wellhead 1, July 2000, Cleaning being undertaken by Bryan Gillard (left) and Ray Caple (right)

1 Commotes were districts under Norman rule, lying west of Offa's Dyke. They were subject to Welsh Laws and Customs, but outside the jurisdiction of the Hundred. These units were assessed for taxation and military service in carucates rather than hides. Due to the retaining of Welsh Law and Custom, it is a possibility that these districts were created much earlier

2 Marked "W" on the Parish Map

3 Glamorgan County Record Office; 1840, Penllyn Parish Tithe Survey, document dated 18/1/1839

4 Glamorgan County Record Office; 1860, D/D Pe Item 102 Copy of Inclosure Award, missing Map, 1858, Inclosure Map found in vestry of Penllyn church

5 Ordnance Survey, 1890, Sheets XLI 14 and XLV 2, scale 1/2500

6 IGS Sheet 261/2

7 Randall, H. J., 1961, *Vale of Glamorgan Studies in Landscape History,* 46, John R. J.

8 Parkhouse, S. and Robinson, D M, 1981-2, *Excavation and Survey of Llanfrynach,* Glamorgan Gwent Archaeological Trust Annual Report 1981-1982, 36-37

9 Griffiths, 1982, Bulletin of Board of Celtic Studies, 29 iv

10 Parkinson, E., 1994, *The Hearth Tax Survey of 1670,* South Wales Record Society LD 336/278

11 Cardiff Central Library Ref. 2.358

12 RCHAMW, 1982, *An inventory of the Ancient Monuments in Glamorgan, volume 3, part 2, Medieval Secular Monuments, Non-Defensive,* Cardiff HMSO

13 Jones, F., 1954, *The Holy Wells of Wales,* Cardiff University of Wales Press

Chapter 10

Farming and Daily Life

The Land in Penllyn

At some time between 1450BC and 900BC, the soil of the Glamorgan uplands deteriorated due to woodland clearance and climate change and this established the major differences between the agricultural patterns of the Vale and the Valleys. Along the Border Vale, as this area of northern Vale has been termed, there is still open limestone downland, but also good agricultural land. Penllyn, Llangan and Treoes (Goston) were recognised as good fertile lands by the Normans, who established corn growing manors in the area (Francis, 1976). Between 1600 and 1800, inhabitants were almost entirely dependent on agriculture or related craft pursuits for their livelihood and this determined the way that life was organised.

Crops

In the mid 19th century, the acreage in Glamorgan devoted to wheat, barley and oats was roughly equal, at between 12-13,000 acres. This quantity was considered by W. Davies (1815a, p.481) to be in excess of that needed by the local population, and the excess was sold to the neighbouring 'populous iron works and collieries'.

By the end of the 19th century, both wheat and barley acreage had fallen (6-7000 acres) due to increased imports of wheat and a resulting fall in price.This fall in price led to a decline in the eating of oat and barley bread, in favour of wheat. Wheat was imported from early in the 19th century; a passage in 'Cowbridge Tracts' (1831, p.11) states *'if our wheat crop fail, the granaries of Poland and America make up the deficiency at an advanced price certainly'*.The acreage devoted to oats at this time however was maintained at 13,000 acres.

Further changes in cropping patterns for these cereals occurred in the 20th century, with increases during both World Wars, but a different pattern could be seen by the mid-20th century, with wheat on 4,000 acres, barley on 11,000 and oats on 2,000 acres only (Williams, 1985). These changes reflect major shifts in imports and utility of these crops. The reduced acreage devoted to cereals was paralleled by an increase in the production of milk.

Potato cultivation spread quickly after its introduction in the mid-18th century, so that by the middle of the 19th century, 2,500 acres were under potato cultivation, presumably in addition to those grown in individual gardens (Williams, 1985). The 'Cowbridge Tracts' (1831, p.7) however warned *'we advise you to abstain from a potatoe diet as long as you can... because potatoes are cheap... if you live habitually on the cheapest food, the more expensive kinds will cease to be cultivated but for the use of the rich... eat therefore wheaten bread in good season and help out bad seasons with potatoes'*. It was commonplace for landowners to grant space in their fields for potatoes to be planted, in exchange for labour at harvesting. A row of 80 yards of potatoes was allowed for a day's work at harvesting time. This was well established by the end of the 19th century, and continued in places to 1939 and even beyond (Freeman, 1980).

The success of crops was dependent on the vagaries of the climate, and in the last decade of the 18th century, there was a series of poor harvests, with a resulting increase in prices. The situation was exacerbated by war with France, as crops and livestock were sent to feed the soldiers.

Later, between 1831 and 1841, there was a succession of unproductive seasons. Tithes, rent and rates charges were high and incomes from sheep, cattle and butter were low. The small farmer suffered and *'lived on brown barley bread and potatoes'* (Parry Lewis, 1960). Farmers were also however keen to improve their output, and the Cowbridge Farmers Club, established in 1862, concerned itself with issues such as *'sheep management, pig feeding and the cultivation of the potatoe'*. Mechanisation of many aspects of the farming process was encouraged by competitions with substantial prizes. The resulting benefit in terms of farm output increased farm revenues in the early 20th century (Scourfield).

Penllyn Farming

Farming has changed considerably from these earlier times. When John Homfray bought the Penllyn Estate in 1846, it comprised a small Home Farm and 13 separate farming businesses. Now the Estate consists of Home, Great House and Darren Farms only.

Over the last century, there has been a consistency in the names of some of the families who have occupied the properties forming the Estate. Elderly residents of the village remember the following - no wonder they used to say *'kick a Thomas on the shin, and the whole Vale limps!'*

Brynawel:	Williams
Court Farm:	Thomas, then Chatterton
Cross Farm:	Thomas, then Harris
Great House Farm:	Williams, Griffiths, then Llewellyn
Ham Farm:	Thomas
Llwynhelig:	Thomas
Moorlands :	Llewellyn
Tŵgoed Farm:	Vaughan, then Bassett, then Harris
Ty Fry Farm:	Thomas
Village Farm:	Roberts
Village House Farm:	Matthews
Vistla Farm:	Thomas

Captain H.C.R. Homfray bought Penllyn Court, together with its small estate, in 1920 for £500. Almost all the residents of the upper village either farmed on their own account as tenants of the Estate or worked for the Castle (Homfray) or the Court (Deere, Salmon, then Homfray). Each tenant farm would employ one or two outsiders, who usually lived on the holding more or less as a family member. For example, the Castle would have employed the following: Head cook, Kitchen maid, Scullery maid, Laundryman, Chauffeur, Butler, Footman, Parlourmaid, Lady's maid and 6 or 7 gardeners.

PENLLYN

The Home Farm was quite small and well kept, but fulfilled most of the needs of the community at the Castle. Livestock would have included 8-10 cows, 2-3 sows, hens and ducks. These would have been tended by a cowman, a forester and a haulier/ploughman. A mason, mason's lad and a carpenter were also employed.

Typically, farms in Penllyn would comprise between 20 and 100 acres. They might each have 8-10 cows milked by hand, 3 or 4 horses for ploughing and hauling, a single furrow plough and a binder. Because of the enormous cost of new equipment, very few could justify owning a baler, combine harvester or grain drier. There were no artificial fertilisers and no sprays to protect crops. Hoeing and weeding were done manually and yields were low.

All winter fodder depended on the hay cut. A horse-drawn mower cut the grass, a shaker turned it and it was also often turned manually, over and over again with pitchforks. It was then picked up by hand into cocks, and each heap was then forked onto a trailer. The advent of the Hayloader mechanised this last stage of lifting the hay onto the trailer.

Figure 1. Frank Gane, with 'Farmer' and 'Duke', cutting hay 1938

Farming and Daily Life

Figure 2. Gathering Hay,
Lodge Field, 1929

Figure 3. Building the Haystack, 1933

Figure 4. Successful Hay Harvest, 1935

Farming And Daily Life

Harvesting the corn was also exhausting. The crop was cut with a binder, which used a propeller to push it out the other side in sheaves, left 6 to a stook. The stooks were placed in ricks in the field where the corn had been grown. Each rick was thatched with last year's straw to keep off the rain. When these were dry, they were loaded onto a wagon and taken to the barn where they awaited threshing. This was carried out by a steam-powered threshing machine, which was hired for the day, to separate out the grain. This was a major task, and involved cooperation between several farmers, while their wives saw to the provision of food.

Co-operation was also needed in other activities, including the annual pig slaughter. Each winter, one or more pigs (depending on the size of farm) would be killed on each farm, and salted for between five and six weeks. The carcasses would be hung in the farm kitchen. Nothing was wasted, brawn was made from the head, faggots from the liver and lights, and the fat melted down for a variety of household uses, as well as cooking.

Figure 5. Washing sheep at the Moors, 1929

Recollections

(H.G.P.) As you know, I was born & brought up in a farming family at Ystradowen - well, between Ystradowen and Welsh St. Donats actually -- and we used to drive our sheep from there to Newton moors to be washed. For us as kids it was a cracking day out. Neighbouring farmers would arrange the day, following consultation with Noel Llewellyn who farmed Moorlands as a tenant at the time, and who was the Czar of the 'sheep wash'. On the agreed day we at Bwlchgwyn, the Jenkins family at Tal y Fan, and one or two others would gather all of the sheep together and drive them to Newton moors where Noel would previously have put a barn door across the north side of the stone bridge so as to hold the water back to form quite a large pool. The sheep were driven into the field on the Moorlands side of the river, then made to swim through the water to emerge on the Newton side. Now sheep are not the quickest animals, so the whole process took from early morning until lunchtime. By that time, both farmers and sheep were knackered, so sandwiches, thick slices of fruit cake, and flasks of tea were consumed in a leisurely manner, with jokes and stories - gossip and reminiscences enthralling us kids. Eventually, the sheep would have more or less 'drip dried', and they were driven home again, but left all together in one field overnight to be sorted into individual flocks the following morning. Of course, there was not much traffic in those days -- can you imagine driving 200 - 300 hundred sheep along the lanes these days? Anyway, as I said, the reason for doing this was to clean the wool a bit (you'd be amazed at the amount of "grime" this simple process removed from the fleece) so as to get a better price for 'washed wool' from the merchants. As you know, the shearing of sheep takes place in late spring/early summer, so the washing was only a few days prior to shearing, and of course, in my memory, the day was always sunny and warm.

On one such occasion, Noel Llewellyn's son, John, fell off the bridge at the age of 5 and was rescued just in time, as the damming of the Thaw created a fair sized pool, which was surprisingly deep.

Trade in Farm and Other Produce

Access to markets and fairs provided an income if goods were sold and also enhanced the variety of the diet. Goods traded were very diverse and included dairy products especially butter, which was taken by water from Aberthaw to Bristol. The 'Welsh Back' in Bristol was the site of the main market. Poultry, pigs, fruit, wheat, oats, barley, beans, deer and rabbit skins were all sold to English traders. Large amounts of cheese were sold to Bristol and Somerset, from as early as 1662. The Vale population obtained salt, Spanish wines, brandy, tobacco, oil and vinegar from the English traders (Williams, 1959).

Farming and Daily Life

Women and children contributed by making stockings and drapery as well as selling yarn and wool. Stockings in particular were an important item, with a woman able to make 4 pairs per week, which sold at 4d each. The market in Cowbridge, originally held on Saturdays in the 17th century, but which had moved to Tuesdays by the 19th century, was an important meeting place for the exchange of news and the sale and purchase of goods and livestock. Butter, cheese, eggs and poultry were the main items traded, but a whole variety of hardware and domestic necessities were also available.

Most of the farms in Penllyn were very self-sufficient. All were mixed farms, producing milk, butter, cheese, bread, bacon, sausages, eggs, fruit and year round vegetables. The items bought included tea, salt, sugar, flour, currants and rice. Very little fresh fruit would be purchased. Butter was sold between 7am and 9am, corn from 12noon - 2pm and butchers' meat from 9am - 3pm, *'so that some of the most sober farmers may be home for dinner'*. (Davies 1815b, p417)

Figure 6. Mary Ann David, Winchfield House, famous for her butter at Bridgend Market

Annual fairs, such as that at St. Mary Hill on 26th August would be an opportunity for further exchange of goods and gossip. After the War, farm produce was also sold in the weekly Producers' Market in Bridgend, and the farmers' wives would take their goods for sale on the bus which came round the villages on Saturdays.

Recollections

(M.T.) When they got married they had that house built? **(G.D.)** In Penllyn **(M.T.)** What was it called? **(G.D.)** Winchfield House, because we had a large field that's there now in front of it, and it had a winch, or a well, I suppose it's there now. So we used to go there for water **(M.T.)** That's where you got your water? **(G.D.)** Oh no, we got our water in this well-built house. No bathroom. **(M.T.)** So there was water piped to it? **(G.D.)** No, we had a big back kitchen, and a huge cistern in the back kitchen and we put a cover on it, and a pump in the back kitchen and we used to put this huge big deal table over the covering and when we wanted water we used to pump and get the water. Then we had a big range in the kitchen, one side of the range had a sort of miniature tank with hot water in it and the other had an oven. And during the summer, when my mother used to make butter, and it was very hot, no deep freezes thank you then, they would put all the butter in a huge bath and lower it into this sink, into the well in the back kitchen, our drinking water, and to keep it cool before taking it to Bridgend.

The quality of produce sold in Cowbridge was strictly regulated. For example the Assize of Bread laid down the weight of a loaf of bread and its cost, based on the price of wheat at the time.

In 1771,	a penny wheaten loaf	had to weigh 9oz 11dr.
	a penny household loaf	had to weigh 13oz 1dr.
	a sixpenny wheaten loaf	had to weigh 1lb 13oz 1dr.
	a sixpenny household loaf	had to weigh 2lb 7oz 2dr.

(Hopkin-James, 1922)

Trade in food goes back for many centuries, and an inspection of the accounts book of a country gentleman from the Vale of Glamorgan (Matthews, 1900) gives a surprising insight into both the range of produce that could be bought, and the relative price of these goods. Between 1721 and 1731, a man could earn 6 shillings per week carrying hay, and could spend it on the following if he wished:

Quarter of mutton	1s 3d.	Butter (1 lb.)	3 ½d	A quart of syder	4d
Shoulder of veal	8d	2st 3lbs cheese	5s 1½d	Wine	1s 6d
Beef steaks	8d	Eggs	2d	Ale	3 ½d
Goose	1s 2d	Bread	½d	Small wort	3d
Couple of fowl	10d	¼ cwt salt	2s 3d	¼ lb tea	3s 3d
Beef (44 lbs)	5s 6d	Jamaica pepper	1d	Coffee	5d
Side of kid	9d	Saffron	1d	Treacle	1d
Tripe	2p	Bushell of pease	7s	Sugar	3d
Fish	6d	Parsnips	1d	1 lb hops	5s
Musles	1d	Potatoes	1d	2 bushells malt	16s
Barrel of pickled oysters	8d	Onions	3d	Barm (yeast)	½d
Laver bread	2d	Spinage	1d	Sweetmeats	9d
Oatmeal	3d	Radishes	1d	1 lb Chocolate	3s 6d
Sagoe	3d	Asparagrass	6d	Halfpenny cake	½ d
Currants	1 ½d	Leeks	½d	Prunes	3d
Apples	1d			Lemons & oranges	3s

Farming and Daily Life

Twentieth Century

Life did not get much easier for the majority of people in Penllyn at the start of the 20th century. There was no mains water supply until 1934. Children were expected to help with milking in the mornings, or scrubbing the kitchen, and again with farm work after school. One girl recalls helping to churn butter from as young as 5 years of age, and learning to press cheese. Cooking was still a slow process, with few gadgets – a mincer perhaps being the only 'aid'. Milk from Penllyn was taken by van to Cowbridge where it was loaded on to the train to Pontyclun.

Data from the 1930's indicating who lived where, provides a vivid snapshot of how the community continued to depend to a large extent on its residents to meet its needs:

Keeper's Cottage	Estate Gamekeeper
Church Cottages	Chauffeur, Coachmen
Castle Lodge	Head Gardener
Great House	Farmer
Pear Tree Cottage	Farmworker at Great House Groom at Penllyn Court
Mead Cottages	Estate forester, Estate gardener
Penllyn Cottages	Butler at Castle
Forrest Cottage	Groundsman at Castle
School House	Headmaster, Llangan School
Rose Cottage	Home Farm manager
Tyle House	Roadman
Village Farm	Farmer
Village House	Farmer

Beyond these, there was Court Farm, and about 12 houses in Craig Penllyn, besides Tŷ Fry and Ham Farms. The residents of these were either smallholders, or they worked either in the iron ore mine at Llanharry or one of the two coal mines at Heol y Cyw. These workers would have cycled to work, as cars were a luxury only the wealthy could afford.

Villagers recall that many deliveries were made to the village in the early post war years: groceries from Ewenny, the Sionni Onion man, the baker from Bridgend, a man from Llanharry or Pontyclun with a horse and cart selling fruit and vegetables, Williams the Grocer from Pencoed and a fish seller from Llantwit Major, who also sold ice cream. In addition, the Post Office that was on the Graig was a shop (now Copse Edge), but was particularly remembered as selling sweets.

The Gane Family

Although much of the history of Penllyn concerns itself with the wealthier and more privileged land-owning classes in Penllyn, many ordinary families have a story to tell. One such is the Gane family. The name isn't common and may originate from the Norman *enguine* meaning ingenuity or trickery. The word was also used to describe a stratagem or device, particularly a trap. Engaine, or Ingaine is mentioned as a Northamptonshire family name in the Domesday Book.

This local family can be traced back to an Albin Gane born in approximately 1807 near Glastonbury. He was employed as a farm labourer and married Mercy Scott in 1837. Mercy gave birth to five boys and four girls. One of the sons, Frank, married Emily Masters, the daughter of a Glastonbury innkeeper and they moved initially to Pontypridd. This appears to have been an unhappy time, since it seems likely that seven of their children died there, some at least, from diphtheria. The 1881 census records just two of Frank and Emily's children at home, one of whom was Albion Gane. However, by 1891, there were eight children and a further daughter was born after this. There were three sons in all, one of whom was also named Frank (b.1884).

At this time, Frank and Emily were living in a cottage close to the Barley Mow, possibly known as Glyn Cottage, now extended and known as Little Acre. The precise address is difficult to pinpoint, as the deeds were split and lost when the Barley Mow and a series of outbuildings were sold off as separate plots in 1940. Emily died in 1922 aged 71 years at Pwllyomper Farm, Peterson super Ely and Frank, whose occupation was recorded as haycutter died in 1933 at Pleasant View, Pencoed.

Farming and Daily Life

Frank and Emily's son, Frank, married Mary Kate in Bridgend in 1910. Frank was involved with horses from a young age and it is said that at the age of 12 he was horse ploughing with a light plough. Later, he worked at the top of a pit with horse drawn drams. His occupation in the census is given as haulier. Frank and Mary Kate lived at Rosedew, where all of their six children were born - Minnie, who died in 1988, Emily, Mary, Francis Richard, Leslie Wilfred and Herbert John.

In 1925, Frank went to work at Penllyn Castle, and as a house came with the job, the family moved to Mead House. All six children were born before Frank went to work for Colonel Homfray. When Frank retired at the age of 70, he went to live in Pentre Meyrick, and later in Llanmaes, where he died in 1966. Mary Kate lived on until 1972. Both are buried at Llanfrynach Church.

Herbert and his wife Elizabeth are the only remaining Ganes still living in Penllyn, at Ayres Cottage, which is now surrounded by new houses. Francis (Frank), a bachelor lives in Cowbridge and Leslie Wilfred lives in Cirencester.

The world that Francis was born into, and the world of his childhood, are bound up in the recent history of the village. At the age of five, living at Rosedew, he started school, walking the mile or so to attend Llangan School. Francis left school in 1929 aged 14 years and went to work for Mr. Griffiths who kept Great House Farm. He remembers when working on the farm before the war that he used to take a horse drawn water tanker down to the wells to collect for water for the cattle. The water in the first well wasn't flowing very quickly so sometimes he had to carry it from the second or third well.

Later, at the start of the Second World War, he worked as a builder's labourer and as such his call-up was delayed. However, in April 1940 he found himself in the Welch Regiment and after some time was sent to India. After demobilisation in 1946, he was employed on the airfield at Llandow breaking up old Lancaster bombers.

At that time, there were only five houses in the village with telephones. One was at the Castle, one at Penllyn Court, one at Village Farm, another at the Post Office and finally Frank Grant, who ran the livery stables from the Old School House, had a phone - with number Cowbridge 257.

Life in the village improved after the war, with the arrival of electricity in Penllyn. There was a reading room in a hut on the site of the current village hall. There were books, and newspapers used to come across from the Castle. Interestingly, even the 'Fox' used to have a small library that would lend books. The reading room was more like a man's club and in 1937 Francis was paying 6d a month to be a member. There were table skittles and small bore shooting. The hut had a good floor and every Friday there was a 4d hop. Once a month, a band from Cowbridge called the Cowbridge Night Hawks would visit. The cloakroom was at one end outside the main building, and was reportedly handy for a bit of courting!

Thanks to Mrs. Morgan of Old Breach Farm for invaluable material and the reminiscences of the Gane Family, without whose help, this section could not have been written.

Cowbridge Tracts (1831) (Society for the improvement of the working population in the County of Glamorgan) On the Principle of compensation as respecting the condition of the working class at different periods. No. 2. Cardiff: Wm Bird

Davies, W. (1815a) General View of Agriculture and Domestic Economy of South Wales, Volume I, London

Davies, W (1815b) General View of Agriculture and Domestic Economy of South Wales, Volume II, London

Francis D. J. (1976) The Border Vale of Glamorgan. Barry: Stewart Williams

Freeman, B. (1980) First catch your peacock. Gwent: Image Imprint

Hopkin- James, L. J. (1922) Old Cowbridge, borough, church and school, Cardiff

Matthews, J. H. (Ed) (1900) Thomas Morgan's Commonplace Book 1708-1736, Records of the County Borough of Cardiff, Vol. II

National Museum of Wales: oral archive, Nos. 8689/1, 8172/1, 6052/1, 6019/1, 6043/1

Parry Lewis, J. (1960) The Anglicisation of Glamorgan. Morgannwg, 4, 31

Scourfield E. Glamorgan County History Vol. 6, (Ed 66) Rural Society in the Vale of Glamorgan, 225-243

Tibbott, S. Minwell (1985-6) Liberality and hospitality: food as communication in Wales, Folk Life, 24

Williams J. (1985) Digest of Welsh Historical Statistics, Vol 1, Cardiff: Welsh Office

Williams M. J. (1959) Some aspects of the economic and social life of the Southern region of Glamorgan 1600-1800, Morgannwg, 3, 21-41

Chapter 11

Education

The earliest positive record of any formal education in the parish of Penllyn is the existence of a schoolmaster, Lawrence Richards, who with his wife Frances recorded the baptism of a son, Jabez, on 4th November 1818.

PENLLYN

While records can be found of other religious groups in the Vale offering basic education to children in the late 18th century and before, nothing records an actual group in Penllyn. The incumbents of the Parish Church in Penllyn from 1747 are mainly resident in either Oxford or Cornwall, whilst the church at Llanfrynach was reported in 1823 as in ruins and its chapel of ease at Penllyn was a whitewashed barn.

From the 1820's the established Church in Wales awakened to the problem of ruined churches and the lack of schools and took active steps to create and establish primary schools throughout Wales. However, none of this affected Penllyn. Organised non-conformity was not established in the village until 1830 and Sunday schools did not exist until the 1840's.

It was in the 1840's that Dr. William Salmon became increasingly interested in both the local church and the school. This occurred at a time when increased wages and improved economic trends arose from the demand for food and timber, as a result of the newly developed coalmines. The arrival of the Homfray family in 1846, and their enormous improvements to the Penllyn Estate, would appear to have stimulated Dr. Salmon. It is from this date that the first Dame school was established on Homfray land with Dr. Salmon providing payment to the teachers.

The 1847 Blue Book of Enquiry into education sets out much detail of the schools in use at that time in South Wales. It has been extensively quoted, sometimes without qualification, as an indicator of the social and economic conditions common at that period, but it produces a biased and distorted picture. In truth Penllyn, in comparison with the rest of south east Wales was well served for education from 1840 onwards, possibly as a result of the competitive social rivalry between Homfray and Salmon.

Notes from the Blue Book of 1847 relating to Penllyn reveal the following:

• Dr. Salmon guaranteed the dame £10 a year in addition to the penny a week she took from the children, which amounted to £5 and four shillings in 1846.

• The schoolroom was 7ft. high and 14ft. square with insufficient furniture but in good repair.

• There were 9 girls and 15 boys aged between 5 and 10 years, and 10 girls and just 4 boys above 10 years old.

• Average attendance for the previous year had been 30.

• No scholars lived more than one and a half miles from the school.

• Pupils were taught the Holy Scriptures and the Catechism.

• Instruction was given with English books, although Welsh was spoken when explaining them.

Education

The teacher was a married woman who also kept a small shop. The 1851 census shows there was a grocer's shop in Penllyn at that date. She was a *'pleasing woman who spoke English very well. Her class read the 119th Psalm with perfect ease, but did not seem to question what they had read. All sorts of vague and random answers were made to questions asked.'*

In 1823, Lawrence and Frances Richards had a second child Silas, but the family do not appear in the 1841 census. The census does include a schoolmaster in Penllyn called Edward Munden, a 60 year old father of five. Frances Richards, in the 1851 census, was recorded living in School House as a widow aged 65 and acknowledged as schoolmistress. She is possibly the unnamed Dame recorded in the 1847 report, despite a 5 year diference in recorded age. Born in Oxwich in 1786, she appears to have devoted her life to the school in Penllyn, first as the wife of Lawrence, then mother of two boys and a girl, and then as schoolmistress as well as operating a village shop. David Jenkins took over from Frances as schoolmaster and they are both recorded in the 1851 census. He was a local boy born at the farm called Tŷ Fry, opposite the Barley Mow. In 1851, Silas Richards appears in the census as landlord of the Barley Mow. In 1861, he was a local estate agent and in 1871, the innkeeper of the Commercial Hotel in Cowbridge.

The Munden family also remained in the village, Edward presumably serving many years as schoolmaster. He died in 1855 aged 79, having been married and widowed twice and having produced six children. His eldest son, Edward Thomas (1822 - approx.1920) became agent to the Homfrays at Penllyn Castle. He lived at Ivy Cottage, then Rose Cottage which was later demolished and replaced with High Beeches in about 1960. Edward had four children, two of whom, Margaret and Catherine, became teachers. Catherine married Thomas Hughes, a schoolmaster at Pencoed, and when he died she became headteacher there. They produced two daughters, Dulcie and Lilliam, both of whom became teachers. Lilliam married William Abbey, a groom at Penllyn castle, and she also taught at Penllyn.

In 1870, W. E. Forster, the son-in-law of Dr. Arnold of Rugby, introduced the Elementary Education Act. This was the Act that sought to end the scandal whereby only half the children in England and Wales attended school. School Boards were set up to ensure that, where voluntary provision of schools was insufficient, new schools were established. They were financed by central government and levies on ratepayers. One such board was created at Bridgend and, despite the existence of the school financed and operated between Homfray and Salmon, a Board School was built in 1872 to accommodate 80 pupils. It was sited on land adjacent to the Fox and Hounds on land purchased from Homfray. The school opened in 1874 with Mr. E. A. Harrison as headmaster. Average attendance at the school until 1912 was 53 pupils. With the creation of the School Board, the interest of Dr. William Salmon and the Homfrays ended. The Homfrays arranged for the vicar, the Rev. William Llewellyn, to represent the Parish on the Board. From the 1881 census we know that David Williams became schoolmaster at Penllyn, while John Rees Llewellyn (possibly the son of the farmer at Moorlands Farm) had the post in 1895. Mr. E. A. Harrison had moved to St. Mary Hill to take charge of a new Board school established there in 1876.

The Mountain School, Llanharry

In 1859, the National Society for Promoting the Education of the Poor in the Principles of the Established Church (1811) built a school at Llanharry, to take up to 70 pupils from the Llansannor, Llanharry and Ystradowen areas. The first recorded teacher was Mr. T.J. Batchelor who started teaching there in February 1874 at a salary of £20 per annum. This Church School, or Mountain School as it was known locally, still flourishes today, having been extended in 2000 to accommodate 180 pupils from a wider catchment area. Many children from Penllyn have attended this school over the years. Further details of this school are to be found in *'A Short History of Llansannor'*, published 1990.

Llangan School

Figure 1. Llangan School

Education

The Bridgend Education Board had ambitious plans and in September 1911, after 11 years of negotiation, they built and opened a much larger school for 123 pupils, sited in Llangan. The schools at Penllyn and St. Mary Hill were closed. The new school at Llangan was necessary because from 1880, education was compulsory for all children up to the age of ten. For Penllyn pupils, this meant a journey to Llangan of up to 3 miles. These paths were often flooded, and this continued to be a problem until well after the last war, as many older residents can testify.

The average attendance was 93. The first headmaster was Mr. Ernest Augustus Harrison who was transferred from St. Mary Hill. Mr. Harrison was the first to sit at the old master's desk still present in the school library. Other head teachers were Mr. E. T. Griffiths 1931-1939, Mr. A. Price 1939-1965, Mr. H. Bown 1965-1981, Mr. Keith George 1981-1996 and Mrs. Jean Hunt 1996-2003.

Recollections of Llangan's First Head teacher, recalled by Mr. Illtud David, a pupil at the School until 1922

Mr. Ernest Augustus Harrison, originally from Shrewsbury, was headmaster at St. Mary Hill old school and then became headmaster of Llangan when the school opened in 1912.

Being a former army man; an instructor in the use of the Lewis gun; he was at all times a very strict master with his pupils as well as with parents. He patrolled the yard during playtimes smoking his pipe. He was always sympathetic when parents were ill and was willing to let the children stay at home if necessary.

He took us on walks, even as far as Llanblethian Castle, and then treated us all to sweets in the little shop in Penllyn, which in those days were one penny each. We were taken to many places of interest such as the old lead mines in Llangan and various churches, and he explained the history of these places.

While he was in hospital during the war, we collected eggs for Mrs. Harrison to take to him. He was a lovely personality and was loved by all who knew him. We were sorry to leave at 14.

Mr. Harrison was taken very ill and when he recovered he came back to Llangan School. When he retired, he had a presentation from present and past pupils, and he went to live with his daughter in Bridgend. He suffered a stroke and when he died was buried in St. Mary Hill Churchyard.

Figure 2. Infants, circa 1935, Mr. E. T. Griffiths (Headmaster)

Figure 3. Juniors, circa 1935, Mr E.T. Griffiths (Headmaster) and Betty Williams (Teacher)

Llangan School, Punishment

Extracts from Llangan School's punishment book (previously the punishment book for St. Mary Hill) show the range of corporal punishment meted out for bad behaviour.

1906	Fred - Smoking in playground - one stroke of the cane
1907	Howel, David, Thomas - beating girls on way home from school - two strokes each
1909	Fred and Joe - smirking in lesson - two slashes across the shoulders
1909	William - broke two pegs in cloakroom, ran for home, brought back screaming
1930	Jack - standing on toilet seats - one stroke
1930	Tom - threw apple core at Miss Evans - two strokes

The last recorded punishment in the book was in 1942 for imperfect and faulty work and that child received two strokes across the buttocks.

Llangan, Sanitation

The old school toilets were outside. This comprised a plank of wood with a hole in it and underneath this was a bucket. There was no running water so the children were unable to flush the toilets. A man from Penllyn was paid 8 shillings (40p) to empty the buckets twice a week. He emptied these into trenches dug in the ground. There were no inside toilets for the teachers so these facilities had to be shared. The infants had five toilets and there was also a urinal for the boys.

Recollections

(J.B.) And we had a run of latrines you know. We didn't have a flush, Mr. Hughes used to have to empty it.... Obviously you had to run down the back to empty them. He (Owen) twigged this now you know. We'd look and we'd get a nettle....!!

As rainwater was the only water available, pipes were connected to the gutters, which led into a tank where water was stored. Hand washing water was dirty and the toilets were smelly with lots of flies. They were a health hazard that led to disease. Children at Llangan died of diphtheria, the last outbreak of which was in 1935. Fresh water first came to the school in 1936 and the old toilets were finally knocked down when modern toilets were built in 1968. Teachers today enjoy separate toilet facilities!

Llangan, Heating and Lighting

In 1911, open fires heated the school. There was a fireplace in each classroom, the office and the hall. The caretaker was paid an extra 75 pence a year for each fire he lit. It was hard work carrying coal to all the fires. The grates also had to be cleaned out every day and the chimneys had to be swept every year. James and Sarah Thomas' great grandfather of St. Mary Hill Farm was paid to do this job.

Every classroom also had two oil or paraffin lamps, which the Caretaker had to look after. The lamps had to be filled with oil and the wicks trimmed. The lamps were made of brass and were kept well polished. These used to hang from strong hooks in the ceiling, which can still be seen today, as can the oil lamp in the photograph, located in the school hall. The oil lamps and coal fires were used until 1958, when electricity was connected.

Figure 4 Oil Lamp

Llangan, a well equipped School!

A search through the old stock inventory at Llangan makes for interesting reading. Very few of these items would be required to teach the National Curriculum at Llangan today.

1916	
4 zinc baths	1 pail
18 flat irons	1 flue brush
1 set black lead brushes	6 lbs soda
1 lb borax	1 pkt blue
3 lbs starch	1 lb ammonia
2 oz salts of lemon	1 quart vinegar
1 pt turpentine and can	1 pt linseed oil
6 bath bricks	1 tube Seccotine
1 bar salt	1 quart bottle of black ink
1 quart bottle of red ink	1 tin ink powder
1 doz. ink wells	1 ink jug
1 ink stand	1 gross penholders
½ gross rulers	
1925	
1 baby's bottle – boat shaped	
1928	
¼ lb gum Arabic	2 wicks for lamps
1 pkt chloride of lime	
1936	
1 Dutch oven	permanganate of potash

Llangan, the Second World War

During the Second World War from 1939-1945 a large number of evacuees arrived from the London area. In all, 173 evacuees attended the school. Extra space was needed and the Settlement Hall was used as a classroom. The school logbook records that on 1st July 1940, a system of 'double shift' lessons was started with local children being educated from 9am to 12.30pm and evacuees, from 12.45pm to 4.00pm. This was the time of German air raids and every time the air raid siren sounded, the children would rush out of the school and shelter along the lane leading to Llangan. In 1942, the school railings were removed for salvage as part of the war effort.

Llangan's Recent History

Since 1911, the school at Llangan has been responsible for educating in excess of 3000 pupils. In the 1970's more space was needed and the first outside classrooms were built. The first Parents' and Teachers' Association was formed in 1972.

In 1986, the school's 75th anniversary was celebrated. Two trees, an oak and a sweet chestnut, were planted in the grounds as a memorial. A time capsule with letters and newspapers depicting school life was also buried and awaits discovery by a future generation of pupils.

A nursery enrolling pupils aged 3 opened in 1997. The nursery building arrived at the school in two large sections on the back of an enormous lorry. Millennium celebrations in 2000 included an open day when many past pupils visited the school and shared their many interesting memories with pupils and staff.

Figure 5. Llangan School pupils and staff, 2000

Education

Mrs. Jean Hunt retired in July 2003 and Mrs. Mary Noyes was appointed as the new headteacher. There are 115 pupils on roll at present. In 2006, work started on an extension to the school buildings.

What happened to the old schools?

Figure 6. Dame School, Penllyn (now known as The Old School House). This reverted to the owner, John Homfray, and became part of Penllyn estate. It is now privately owned.

Figure 7. Board School, Penllyn (now known as The School House). This reverted to a private residence, which Mr. Harrison occupied after his promotion to Llangan.

Schools Today

With the opening of Llangan School in 1911, there was no school situated in the parish of Penllyn, a situation which continues today. Now, primary age children usually attend school at Llangan, the Mountain School (Llansannor) or Y Bontfaen (Cowbridge), while the principal secondary education provider is Cowbridge Comprehensive School. The lanes and footpaths are now considered too dangerous to use, so instead of children walking to school, they catch the school bus or are driven to school by parents on 'the school run'.

Recollections

(K.H.) So how did all of you, as children, get from this village to Llangan School then? **(Group)** Walked, Cycled, Shanks' Pony. **(K.H.)** So when you were walking home at the end of the day, it must have been dark then? **(A.P.)** That's right, and in those days, we didn't even lock our doors, if you went out to visit a neighbour, you left the door open.

Figure 8. Board School, St. Mary Hill, (now The Old School House, 1995 photo, with Charlotte Hemingway and her granddad). This building was converted into a house in the 1950's. It had not actually been used as a school since the new school was built in Llangan. Locals remember the old school building being used for concerts and dances and recall it being cold and draughty, as the room was open to the rafters. Subsequently, it was used as a grain store before it was sold for house conversion.

Acknowledgements:

We are indebted to Mr. Keith George for his recollections of the school and also to Mrs. Jean Hunt for allowing access to the school log books and other historical records, to glean much of the information used in this chapter.

Chapter 12

Diet and Health

Recollections

(G.D.) Oh yes, I was four years of age. My father, and I can remember that now, was coming down the old rough road, with a huge iron roller with 'Blossom', our horse. I can remember I was a little girl with curly fair hair, running up to meet him, and he could feel something bumping under the roller. He stopped the horse, and there was me and if it had gone few inches further it would have gone right over my head. So he had the presence of mind to back the horse back, and the roller back, over my body. I can remember them taking me into the [*Winchfield House*] kitchen in Penllyn and putting me on this table. And my head was going round and round and round. And my father had I suppose to cycle to Cowbridge, to see old Doctor Meller, and he fainted on the doorstep. I was in bed then for a long time at home, with a Bryant splint[1], and a pulley and the holes could be in that ceiling now!

Because only a few early records from the South Wales area specifically relate to the village, as in the recollected account of a near fatal accident in the Graig in 1911, a number of inferences will be made based on more general information from the area. Within this type of traditional rural community, the food available is dependent on the land as well as trade links and so reference should also be made to the chapter on farming and daily life.

Crops and Plant Foods

In 1188, Gerald of Wales described the Welsh as living on the produce of their herds, with milk, butter, cheese and oats being staple articles. *"They serve the food on large thin cakes, baked daily"*. Oats had been the predominant cereal crop grown and eaten in Wales for many centuries. Both wheatbread and oatbread were specified as part of the food-tythe paid to the king. In Elizabethan Wales, country folk are reported as eating oatcake, peascake, ryebread and boulted (rye and wheat) bread, although the poorer class continued to produce oats, even on land suited for wheat and rye.

Barley was also an important cereal staple, and in 1801 accounted for 60% of the overall cereal crop in Wales, with 20% coming from oats and only 15% from wheat. Barley was of course used for making malt for brewing. Wheat cultivation was only suited to better soils and consequently became more widespread in the Vale, although oats were still regarded by many as the main staple.

The 'General View of Agriculture and Domestic Economy of South Wales: Volume I' by W. Davies reported that in the Vale very little bread was consumed. What was eaten was made from pure wheat, except in seasons of scarcity (1800 and 1811), when barley was brought in. Interestingly, Davies also comments on the nutritional value of using the whole of the milled wheat, noting that the *'nutritious aliment'* is found in the inner coat next to the bran, and is lost when the inner core only is used from the bolting mill. Clearly, healthy eating was making an early appearance.

The introduction of the potato to Wales in the latter part of the 17th century had an important impact on the diet. Primarily, the potato was a cheap, readily cultivated food that could be stored over the winter. From the nutritional point of view, it provided valuable vitamin C and prevented the development of scurvy, which had been commonplace in winter months.

Gardens were an important source of food for those with access to some land. Root vegetables, such as carrot and parsnip were particularly important in hard times. The association of Wales with leeks goes back many years. John Worlidge, writing in 1688, comments on *'the constant use of leeks by the Welsh, who propagate an abundance of them...the greatest part of the garden stored with leeks and part of the remainder with onions and garlick.'*

A garden might provide early potatoes, yellow turnips, early and winter cabbages, greens, peas and beans, carrots, onions and other alliaceous plants, broccoli, cauliflowers, seakale, asparagus and rhubarb, as well as currants, gooseberries and raspberries. Freeholders might have an orchard with a variety of fruit trees, including apples, pears, plums, cherries, as well as peaches and walnuts. Penllyn Castle had vines, and on some estates, melons and pineapples were also grown. For the cottagers, fruits and nuts (such as hazelnuts) were more likely to have been picked in the wild.

The Normans had planted fruit trees, such as apple, cherry, medlar, pear, plum and quince on the edge of woodland, so that the peasants could easily get to the fruit while the open-field system of cultivation was in operation. Boundary hedges, formed when areas of former woodland were cleared, still contained semi-wild fruit trees. Flowers were also used in cookery to add colour and flavour. For example, marigolds were used to add flavour to cawl and colour to cheese, butter and custard, while violets were used in puddings and creams to add flavour and colour and elderflowers were added to jam to add scent. Honey was used widely as a sweetening agent.

Free food was an important contributor to the diet. The hedgerows and sea-shore were, in season, sources of a variety of 'greens'. Iolo Morganwg (1802) in his travels through Glamorgan comments on up to 15 items commonly picked by the local population, including '*sea cale, laver, wild rape, water cress, wild spinage, nettles, alisanders, wild mustard, meadow purslane, meadow and wood sorrel, stone cress, rhamsons and mushrooms.*' Many of these were used as greens, 'sallat' or pot herbs.

Livestock and Animal Foods

Many households kept a pig, which provided an important source of both protein and fat for the household. Killing of pigs would be staggered within a community, between early October and late March, so that help would be available. Helpers would usually get a piece of fresh pork in return. Produce was made from the offal, mainly faggots from blood and lights, and brawn from the head. These would be eaten fairly soon, or sold at market. The main carcass was salted and thus preserved to last for the best part of the following year, providing bacon for many meals. Fat was rendered and stored, for use in cooking, sealing preserves and health care.

Recollections

(N.J.) And then the butcher would come up and carve him up and put him on the slab. **(A.P.)** And that was the time then to have faggots. Faggots and peas, oh lovely! **(H.G.)** Oh don't talk about that, it would be lovely it you had them on the cook now. **(A.P.)** They would kill a pig and they would make faggots and peas and then they would go around the houses. Mrs. Jones would have some and that, you didn't keep it all yourself. **(H.G.)** I used to like the brawn as well. One thing I couldn't stand was the black pudding. **(A.P.)** Oh I love black pudding. **(E.P.)** And me! **(K.H.)** So, no freezers of course **(Group)** No. **(K.H.)** But of course kitchens were cold. **(A.P.)** Yes and if you went around haymaking you would go into some kitchens and there would be legs of pork hanging up.

Other livestock were also kept, including cows, sheep, goats and poultry (geese and hens). Beef (from a bullock or barren cow) and mutton were salted in brine, but took more salt than pigs, and were thus seen as less economical. A cow might be shared between two or three households. Very little of the meat would be eaten fresh. Eggs were mainly collected for sale, and although hens were widely kept, eggs were eaten very sparingly. Only when the price of eggs fell, were more available for home use. Goose feathers were used to make bedding, and were also used in the kitchen, for sweeping, or as a brush in baking. A goose would be killed usually at Christmas.

For freeholders, any animal caught on their land was considered to be theirs. Tenant farmers had a greater dilemma, as the rightful ownership lay with the landlord. Inevitably this was not a guaranteed source of food, and the literature mainly discusses game as appearing on the table of the wealthy landowners, who shot and hunted for game such as hare, rabbit, duck, partridge, snipe and even rooks. However, when times were hard for the poor, the occasional game would have been a welcome addition to a meagre diet.

In 1894, the Royal Commission reported that the Penllyn Castle estate was suffering serious crop losses at this time due to rabbits. Benjamin Maddy, a rabbit catcher living in Penllyn, describes how he could trap 800 rabbits on 30-40 acres of land. He would be employed by tenant farmers, at the rate of 4s. per dozen rabbits, but often found that the keepers would undermine his efforts by destroying his traps.

The acidity of the soil in Wales meant that cows' milk was mainly suited for the production of soft cheese, rather than the hard, fully mature type. Ewes were also milked as this produced a harder cheese, more suitable for roasted/toasted cheese (caws pobi), which had been popular in Wales from Tudor times. In poorer households, or when times were very hard, the cream was taken from the milk to make butter, and cheese was made from skimmed milk. This produces a very thin, brownish cheese. In the Vale, ewes' milk was added to skimmed cows' milk to make a better quality cheese.

Butter was always heavily salted, to improve preservation, although even this did not prevent it becoming rancid towards the end of the winter months. Salt for all the preservation processes was obtained either from sea water or salt springs. Salt workings had been established around the Welsh coast from the early Iron Age.

Fish was not a major item in the diet. Most people would not have travelled more than five miles from their home, but itinerant sellers (often widows) might bring produce to the area to supplement their income. Thus salted herrings, cockles and oysters might very occasionally feature in the diet. For the wealthier landowner, with a greater likelihood of visiting friends, the gift of a fish caught further afield may be recorded.

Food Preservation

The preservation of all food for as long as possible after harvest, or slaughter was a high priority. In addition to the storage of grain and salting of meat described above, vegetables were stored either in clamps (in the case of root vegetable), or salted, bottled, pickled or dried. 'Catchups' were made from walnut, cucumber and mushrooms. Eggs were preserved when the price was too low to sell. Fruits were made into jams, both vegetables and fruit may have been made into wines. An 1894 recipe book (W.F.M.) lists the following wines: apple, apricot, blackberry, cherry, cowslip, currant, damson, dandelion, ginger, orange, parsnip, raisin, raspberry, and turnip.

Recollections

(K.H.) Was food preserved for use over the winter? And if so, how was this done? **(A.P.)** Well, bottled fruit of course. **(N.J.)** Yes, a lot of jam was made, nearly everybody had jam in the pantry in the country didn't they? **(A.P.)** Yes and carrots, we used to keep them in sand didn't we? We used to have boxes of dry sand and we used to have pickled eggs.

Beverages

The common beverages of the 21st century did not feature greatly in the lives of people in earlier times. Although tea was drunk, it was considered to be 'special', as it involved spending money to buy the tea leaves, whereas many drinks could be made at home with whatever was available. Coffee was expensive and, as such was not a common or popular drink, maybe also because of the way it was prepared.

The 1881 book, '*Cookery and Household Management*' by S. A. Edward, gives this recipe for milky coffee for one person:
'*Take 1 dessertspoon of coffee and 1 pint of milk, boil together for 15 minutes; add eggshells or isinglass to clear and boil a few more minutes.*'

More common drinks were buttermilk, sour milk and various 'homebrews' such as beers based on hops, ginger, amber malt and even chilli, as well as cider made from apples grown in local orchards. Lemonade was made at home, and sometimes served with milk. The 'Cowbridge Tracts' recommend tea over spirits, and beer drunk by the fireside, rather than in the public house. Drinks based on honey, such as mead, metheglen and bragot were also made. Bragot was made by brewing honeycomb with malt and spices. Various wild berries, such as rowan were also made into drinks.

A variety of spirits were also available, including rum, brandy and gin and drunkenness and brawls were features of life in the vicinity of public houses, especially on market and fair days.

Daily Food

Edward Smith, on behalf of a Government Commission, completed an extensive dietary survey of parts of South Wales in 1863. Although he did not visit Penllyn (keeping instead to the railway), he noted that the typical adult consumed 14lb of breadstuff per week, a few vegetables, but mainly potatoes, 3oz of butter per week and buttermilk. Cheese was eaten, perhaps on Saturday and fresh meat was exceptional in the diet – mostly the meat was salted beef or mutton. The diet of both labourers and tenant farmers was characterised by sameness and monotony, with a general deficiency of food *'not more than sufficient to maintain health'*. In the late 19th century, the diet of small farmers and tenants was based on home cured meat, home grown vegetables and potatoes, dairy products and cereal based porridges.

'Cooking on the Open Hearth'
by M. S. Tibbott, describes a typical day's eating at the turn of the 19th/20th century.
Breakfast: Oatcake/ oatmeal or coarsely cut bread in beef or bacon stock, or milk. This may have been boiled, or soaked overnight, and milk or buttermilk and sugar may be added (to the milk based dishes)
Dinner: (eaten at 12 noon) was the main meal of the day and invariably based on boiled bacon or salted beef. This would be served as cawl (broth) in the winter, with the meat boiled in a cauldron with potatoes and vegetables, or as 'stwnsh rwdan' in summer, with potatoes and fried bacon, or boiled ham with mashed swedes. On Sundays, there would be a roast dinner, including fresh meat from the local butcher, followed by rice pudding (or apple suet pudding / boiled suet pudding).
Afternoon Tea: Bread and butter, cheese or home made jam, with tea. Special cakes on birthdays and Sunday, generally baked on a bakestone. ***Supp****er*: Porridge or broth, as for breakfast.

Diet and Health

Food and Special Events

During the year, food was used in various symbolic or special ways to mark particular occasions. Hospitality was important, and visitors would be given 'the best'. This might include drop scones, perhaps a boiled egg; even tinned salmon or yeasted buns might be bought.

Catering for helpers during harvest or shearing involved much effort. Haymakers would be fed a cold oat jelly (sucan), made from soaked oat husks and leavings, prepared overnight and taken out to fields at mid-day. This was 'a quivering brown blancmange' and was served with cold milk or beer. Bread and butter or roast potatoes would supplement this meal. Beer, ginger beer or water laced with oatmeal would be available to drink during the day. Home cured ham, kept especially for harvest, new potatoes and vegetables, followed by rice pudding and apple dumplings would be offered in the evening.

Sheep shearing would be important opportunities for a social gathering, and up to two days would be spent preparing food for the shearers. Cold roast beef, potatoes, peas, rice pudding, bread and butter, cheese and jam would be offered, together with rich yeasted fruitcake and gooseberry pie. Sometimes, food would be needed for up to 100 people. On a smaller scale, help with harvesting might simply be 'paid for' with bread and cheese.

At Christmas, the main meal might be goose or beef, followed by rice or plum pudding. Christmas tea included a rich yeasted fruitcake. Hot spiced ale and cake were traditionally provided before funerals, as the procession set out from the house. This continued to the mid 19th century, but later became the funeral wake, eaten after the burial. Bread and butter, home boiled ham, pickled onions and fruit cake were the traditional items. Mourners might bring food to help with the meal.

Food was also used to raise money, in much the same way as it is now, with parties being organised and people invited to take part in beer and light refreshment, for a small charge. In this way social support, for example for a bereaved family, could be provided.

A newly delivered mother might receive gifts of bread, butter, tea and sugar, but the guests and the midwife would then expect to eat this. At weddings, the present 'list' might include items of food, for example, cheese, potatoes, butter. Food might also be sold at the wedding feast to raise money for the couple.

On New Year's Day until noon, children would go round collecting food, usually bread – especially white, which would be a change from their normal whole grain family loaf.

Cooking

The basic method of cooking was using a cauldron over an open fire. A variety of fuel was used, with different fuels producing varying heat and therefore being suitable for different cooking needs. Peat, wood, fern or even cattle manure were used in turn. Earlier cauldrons were earthenware. Later, brass and iron cauldrons were used with the cauldron either being suspended from a chain or pot hook, which gave greater flexibility to control heating as the pot could be swung closer or further from the fire, or rested on a tripod.

Other utensils included a skillet for making sauces and possets, copper or cast iron saucepans and frying pans, often with very long handles of up to 3 feet. Bakestones were important, and were made from sandstone in the Cowbridge area. These could be suspended over the fire, or later rested on the iron grate or range. A Dutch oven was a popular cooking device, which incorporated a semicircular hinged back, supported on a trivet that increased the heat around the food being cooked within. The implements and utensils used were generally of wood, and were scrubbed as white as ivory with brass and copper pans polished to mirror perfection.

The traditional wall 'bread oven' was usually only fired up once per week, so that a supply of bread was baked. This then had to last for the following week. It is little wonder that so much bread was consumed crumbled into milk or broth. Daily baking was done on the bakestone and involved flat breads, or scones. These were diverse in their ingredients and far more varied than the traditional 'Welsh cakes' with which we are now familiar.

When cast iron ranges were introduced in the early part of the 20th century, the oven was largely used only for the weekend joint and pudding. Mid week cooking was still done largely on the open fire, using the cauldron, saucepan, frying pan and bakestone, together with the Dutch oven. This continued well into the second half of the 20th century.

In the years between the First and Second World War, a substantial breakfast for the whole family became more likely, with bacon and egg, fried potatoes or fried bread. Meal patterns were repetitive, with a roast, fry up, stew, chops, and fish featuring regularly through the week. Puddings were generally still rice pudding and variations on suet puddings (with apple, jam or currants).

Villagers recall having Horlicks in school at Llangan, although school meals did not appear in Llangan School until after the war. The years of the Second World War were associated with rationing, although it is likely that food supplies in the countryside were affected less than in the towns, with more opportunities to keep animals and grow vegetables. Workers who came to help with harvesting and threshing would be paid in coupons, for cheese, sugar and butter. Sometimes, there were extra luxuries, for example chocolate from the American GI's stationed in Penllyn.

The Health of the Population and Medical Care

Early health care in Wales is allegedly based on texts from the 13th century ascribed to the Meddygon Myddfai,[2] who practised herbal medicine and advised on exercise and hygiene.

By the end of the 18th century, medical care was provided by a variety of practitioners, with diverse qualifications. Various doctors from Cowbridge are mentioned in the local papers of the time: in 1740, Dr. Bates treated smallpox in Cowbridge, between 1788 and 1801 'Dr John Walton and Bevan the doctor', and in 1814 'Dr. William Nicholl and Lewis the apothecary'. Of course, the Salmons of Penllyn were originally medical practitioners based in Cowbridge. It is interesting to note the distinction in the titles given, reflecting the status of these individuals.

Although university medical education was in existence at the turn of the 19th century, not all practitioners had completed this. It was not until the formation of the General Medical Council in 1858 that medical education became more uniform throughout Britain. Early in the 19th century voluntary dispensaries were established, providing 'outpatient' facilities, and many of these developed into Infirmaries, which then appointed 'House Surgeons'. By 1861, there were 253 medical practitioners in Wales, of whom 69 were qualified to MD level, 52 were physicians, but the remaining majority were apothecaries without formal training.

Life-threatening diseases were the focus of most attention, and patients with psychiatric disorders were 'contained', often in part of a prison. Eventually, an asylum for '150 lunatics' was established in 1856, after almost 50 years of discussion and effort. This became Glanrhyd Hospital, and was partly funded by a donation made from the estate of Sir Jeremiah Homfray in 1834.

Those diseases prevalent in the 21st century, such as heart disease and cancers were not recognised at this time as separate clinical entities.

Orthodox practice included the use of leeches, bleeding and strong laxatives. Water from local wells was believed to have great curative properties for many disorders, such as palsies, rheumatism and consumption. The ineffectiveness of these remedies is underlined by some of the more desperate measures that were taken. For example, it was believed that erysipelas,[3] also known as 'blast', was caused by sitting near a hot fire, and was to be treated by covering the head, regardless of which part of the body was actually affected. Animal food, hot rooms and an overabundance of clothing was thought to cause measles. Typhus was treated by washing the patient early in the disease in cold vinegar and water, and later by bleeding, blistering, emetics and purgatives.

Sometimes 'mild' cases of smallpox were used to produce a vaccine, although in some cases the recipient developed the disease and died. This practice was made illegal in 1840. In 1898, the Vaccination Law was passed which aimed at universal coverage with free vaccination for smallpox, although the vaccination had been introduced as early as 1800, but at a cost. The coverage by 1901 was 79.7% of births in Glamorgan.

Information about treatments for ailments was passed between friends, and recipes for 'home cures' can be found in a number of diaries. These include those passed on by word of mouth, as well as some cut from newspapers and journals. 'John Perkins of Llantrithyd – the diary of a gentleman farmer in the Vale of Glamorgan 1788-1801' gives a series of examples of such recipes for *'heartburn, rheumatism, stone and gravel (constipation), cholick, hysterick and epileptick fits, dropsy, coughs and palpitations.'* Other instructions are for making sticking plaster, lavender water and how to treat a sore breast in a breastfeeding mother. More unusual recipes describe how to treat drunkenness and how to make someone drunk, as well as how to lose fat (clearly a problem for some even in those days!).

The following adverts, appearing in the 'The Cambrian' newspaper in 1804, promised a number of remedies:

- Pectoral Balsam of Honey for coughs, colds, asthmas and consumption
- Dr Taylor's Remedy for Deafness – 1 bottle will completely cure the most obstinate deafness even in a person deaf for 40 years
- Barclay's Original ointment – never failing cure for The Itch (does not contain the smallest particle of Mercury)
- Barclay's Asthmatic Candy – an effective preservative from the ill effects of fogs and damp air
- Dr James's Analeptic Pills – for rheumatisms and colds, for bilious and other disorders of the stomach and bowels, for headaches occasioned by indigestion and for preventing palsies and apoplexies
- Dr Solomon's Cordial Balm of Gilead – for those debilitated by premature or excessive indulgencies, weakness of sight, vertigo, loss of appetite and mental decay
- Betton's Only True British Oil – for the cure of internal and external bruises, lameness, swelling, sore legs, rheumatic and leprous disorders and coughs, inflammation of the lungs and consumption

Diet and Health

Sadly, mortality rates were high. The 'Cowbridge Tracts' in 1831 comment, *'a century ago the average mortality was 1 in 30.... at present it is 1 in 58'*. Infant and child deaths were commonplace, and school registers would starkly record *'Left...dead'*. Schools were closed due to epidemics of smallpox, diphtheria and measles, especially in the latter part of the 19th century. Dr. Rice Morgan wrote in 1906, that schools mix the sick and the healthy together in over-crowded rooms to obtain high percentage attendance.

Management of Infectious and Other Diseases

Recollections

(K.H.) What illness and diseases were feared most? **(A.P.)** Well I suppose it was diphtheria. Diphtheria was the one that got a lot. We had two cousins we lost from it. **(K.H.)** What about T.B? **(Group)** Yes, there was that. **(K.H.)** What was the hospital over here at Crossways? **(A.N.)** That was a hospital for babies and children under the age of 8 or 10 with T.B. of the bones. **(H.G.)** I worked in one and I used to have to go through the wards with my job. I was there for a couple of days and the children they would be saying 'what you doing Mister?' It was pitiful. **(A.N.)** Yes, you would hear that there was a new baby coming and it was pitiful, for the first three days you would hear them crying, but they would eventually settle down all right. Oh it was upsetting.

The types of infectious diseases recorded in the area include smallpox (1740 and 1840), cholera (1849 and 1866) and diphtheria (1840). Scarlet fever was the most common. An outbreak of typhus fever was contracted at a ball held above stables in Cowbridge in 1854, and a further outbreak was recorded in 1894. Means of managing infectious diseases such as typhoid, scarlet fever and puerperal fever included burning all the bedding, and recommending the use of disinfectants, although there was no obligation to do this. In point of fact, there was then no means of disinfecting bedding or clothing other than by burning.

Infectious Disease Notification was empowered in 1889, but there was no Isolation Hospital available in the area until a temporary hospital was set up in Bridgend in 1895 during a smallpox epidemic and a permanent building in Pontypridd. By 1902, there was a joint 12 bed smallpox hospital in the Bridgend and Cowbridge District.

Tuberculosis mortality exceeded that from all other infectious diseases. In the Cowbridge Rural District it was 2/100 in 1895, one of the highest figures in Glamorgan.

Mortality rates rose during 1914-18, probably as a result of poor diet, and again from 1922 onwards associated with high levels of unemployment.

The awareness of a need for inspection of milking herds, testing and heat treatment of milk gradually increased from 1927, but this 'better' milk was rarely available to the poor, who remained at high risk of tuberculosis. Agricultural Colleges and University departments were directed to assist farmers in testing their milk. However, there was no significant reduction in contamination from milk until after the Second World War.

Recollections

(A.N.) Talking about health, well I had to have my tonsils out. And the doctor came from Cowbridge, Dr Callaghan and he also had a brother who was a doctor in Cardiff Royal who was a consultant surgeon. Well one Sunday morning I had to have my tonsils out and they arrived at Rhyd house and took my tonsils out on the kitchen table. Of course I didn't have my breakfast and my father had taken me out to play football, out in the field to distract me. And I saw the car coming up and we went in and I got up on the kitchen table, chloroform and that is the end of my story anyway.

Bigger operations, such as removal of the appendix, were carried out at the cottage hospital in Merthyr Mawr Road, Bridgend. Dr. Meller and his daughter Dr. Kay Meller provided medical care from Cowbridge during the latter part of the 20th century. Prior to the introduction of the N.H.S., medical care was paid for by insurance subscription. Doctors prepared prescriptions themselves.

Social Welfare

The Poor Law was introduced in 1834 to reduce the financial burden of providing relief for the poor, mainly in the form of rent payment to allow them to remain in their own homes, and subsidising wages of low paid workers. Consequently, unions of parishes set up workhouses. The Bridgend and Cowbridge Union was formed in October 1836. The Guardians appointed a medical officer for each of the 3 districts within the Union, who was paid an annual salary of £65, to cover the medical and surgical expenses

A typical workhouse diet:

Breakfast: Able bodied infants received 7ozs bread and a pint of gruel

Dinner: On 3 days: 4ozs meat and either ¾ lb of potatoes, or ½ lb rice and 4ozs vegetables

On 2 days: 1lb of pudding

On 2 days: 4ozs bread and one and a half pints of pea soup

Supper: 7ozs bread and one and a half pints of broth and 2ozs cheese and bread on two nights

Diet and Health

In the last quarter of the 19th century, Friendly Societies were established to provide members with money allowances during incapacity from work, resulting from sickness or infirmity, as well as making provision for death expenses. These attracted local craftsmen, farmers, tradesmen and farm labourers. Lodges in the Vale included the Grand United Order of Oddfellows with the Loyal Mountain House Lodge at the Barley Mow. The Lodge often organised local festivities, or revels, although the rowdiness associated with these may have contributed to the disapproval expressed by the Temperance movement.

Sanitary Conditions

The Public Health Act of 1872 required that Medical Officers of Health be appointed, and Bridgend and Cowbridge Rural District became a Sanitary Authority. The aim was to improve access to light and air and cleanliness. It was reported in the 'Glamorgan Observer' in 1873 that Edward Bates, the Medical Officer of Health and Watkin Bevan the Sanitary Inspector undertook energetic measures to the north of Cowbridge.

These measures were intended to eliminate possible centres of fatal malaria, fevers and death. Disinfecting agents included permanganate of potash, carbolic acid and chloride of lime. Disinfectant agent depots included the Barley Mow in Penllyn, and, when required, disinfectant was supplied free. In addition, careless causes of nuisance to the water supply were identified, such as ill-drained pigsties, dung heaps and cesspools.

William Williams became the Medical Officer of Health (M.O.H.) in 1893, and undertook a major survey of the sanitary conditions in Glamorgan. This was the first of its kind in any county in England and Wales. He commented that labourers' dwellings were totally unfit for human habitation, with small windows, defective roofing and sunken floors. The Report of the Royal Commission on Labour (1894) supported these findings about the poor quality hovels that many lived in, with no attempt at upkeep. Water supplies came from springs and deep wells sunk in the limestone, but also some shallow wells. Few of the wells were lined or had proper copings and all water supplies were prone to pollution from the soil and cattle. Dr. Meller in an M.O.H. report of 1893 mentions water supplies at Llangan and Graig[4] as sorely in need of protection from surface contamination.

Lavatories were only available in larger houses and the majority of people used pails and privies, with a hole in the ground, which could also then contaminate the water supply. There was also no provision for the disposal of refuse or ash. Slop water ran into gutters, highway drains, ponds and together with farmyard waste formed stagnant pools. If these could be managed, the M.O.H. states *'much illness and discomfort would be prevented'*.

Recollections

(K.H.) What about water for loos? **(A.P.)** Outside. Tŷ Bach. And you didn't have water, you had a bucket and when the bucket was full you dug a big hole and buried it.

The years 1933-34 were affected by drought and there were very poor water supplies in the Cowbridge area. Piped water was first brought to Penllyn in 1934. Despite improvements in the water supply, typhoid fever continued to be a problem. Milk, butter and itinerant travellers were all suspected as sources.

Improvements in the physical environment during the 20th century, such as the provision of clean water, sewage and refuse disposal together with better housing and working conditions improved the mortality rate. The introduction of enquiry and services relating to malnutrition in children, better training for nursing staff and improved maternity services were becoming established by the 1930's. In 1888, fewer than half the infants born in Glamorgan survived to the age of 40. By 1974, over half lived to over 70.

Health care has improved substantially and sickness and death from infectious disease is largely only a memory. Nevertheless, new causes of sickness have afflicted the population of Penllyn in the 21st century, often associated with having too much of the food that our predecessors worked so hard to produce, without having to exert the considerable physical effort involved in producing it.

Diet and Health

References:

Cowbridge Tracts (1831) (Society for the improvement of the working population in the County of Glamorgan) On the Principle of compensation as respecting the condition of the working class at different periods, No. 2, Cardiff: Wm.Bird

Davies, T. G. (1988) Lewis Weston Dilwyn and his doctors, Morgannwg, XXXII

Davies, T. G. (1993) An asylum for Glamorgan, Morgannwg, XXXVII, pp 40-55

Davies, W. (1815a) General View of Agriculture and Domestic Economy of South Wales, Volume I, London

Davies, W. (1815b) General View of Agriculture and Domestic Economy of South Wales, Volume II, London

Dewar, I. (1967) George Clive and the establishment of the New Poor Law in S. Glamorgan 1836-38 Morgannwg, 11, 46-70

Edwards, S. A. (1881) Cookery and Household Management, Corwen

Francis, D. J. (1976) The Border Vale of Glamorgan. Barry: Stewart Williams

Freeman, B. (1980) First catch your peacock, Gwent: Image Imprint
Glamorgan Observer and Monthly Illustrated Journal, June 1873

Hughes, R. E. (2003) Dysgl Bren a Dysgl Arian, Nodiadau ar Hanes Bwyd yng Nghymru (Wooden Bowl and Silver Bowl, Notes on the History of Food in Wales), Lolfa

Jones, I. G. (1992) Mid Victorian Wales – The Observers and the Observed, Guildford: Biddles

Linnard, W. (1987) John Perkins of Llantrithyd – the diary of a gentleman farmer in the Vale of Glamorgan 1788-1801, Morgannwg, XXXI

Local Government Board, Annual report, Vol. 32, (1902-3)

Mabbitt, J.H.L. (1973) The Health Services of Glamorgan, D.Brown & Sons

Owen, G. D. (1962) Elizabethan Wales, Cardiff

Report of the Royal Commission on Labour, 1891-94, London

Royal Commission on land in Wales (1894), Volume II, London: HMSO

Thomas J. E. (1974) Morgannwg 18 The Poor Law in West Glamorgan, 1834-1930

Tibbott, S. Minwell (1982) Cooking on the Open Hearth, National Museum of Wales

Tibbott, S. Minwell (1985-6) Liberality and hospitality: food as communication in Wales, Folk Life, 24

Welsh Folk Museum manuscripts (1894), recipe book 3494/1-9

Williams, W. (1895) A Sanitary Survey of Glamorganshire

1 This applied traction to the limb, which would be held vertically, in this case suspended by hooks from the ceiling. Also known as gallows traction.

2 The Physicians of Myddfai or 'Meddygon Myddfai' were a family of physicians who lived in the parish of Myddfai, Carmarthenshire. They are thought to have been related to Rhiwallon Feddyg and his sons, Cadwgan, Gruffudd and Einion, who were physicians to Rhys Gryg, Lord of Dinefwr in the thirteenth century. It is believed that their descendants continued to practice as physicians in the area until the eighteenth century. The gravestones of the last physicians in the line, David Jones (who died in 1719) and John Jones (who died in 1739) are to be seen in the parish church of Myddfai today.

3 An acute streptococcal skin infection

4 Presumably the deep well in the Winchfield

Chapter 13

Law and Order

Penllyn's relative safety and distance from lawlessness and disorder is a major appeal to many of its residents. Indeed, Penllyn is able to boast one of the lowest reported crime rates per head of population in Wales. But just occasionally the peace has been disturbed, sometimes with tragic consequences.

PENLLYN

The earliest record of major crime dates back to 21st June 1487, and is noted in the National Library of Wales ISYS database:

"FINAL CONCORD made by William Flemynge and Jankyne gelez touching the inconvenience that was betwixt John ap Thomas ap rogger vaughane and his kin and the kindred of Thomas Nycholl of Seynt Tathane who was slain by great unfortune by the said John that the said John must give a sack with 45s. of money at Penllyne is gren' the Sunday following St Barnabas' Day[1]; with a bond in £10 to observe the covenants by William Nycholl son of the said Thomas, Harre Nycholl, William Nycholl, Richard Nycholl, Will Thomekyne, John Thomekyne, and Thomas Nycholl for themselves and all their kin except Richard Nycholl, brother of the said Thomas who dwells at Bannewyll, to the said John and Robert Gameg."

The Star Chamber[2] Proceedings listed in the table below also indicate that violent crime in Penllyn has a long history:

Star Chamber Proceedings relating to Penllyn

Monarch	Complainant	Defendant	Accusation
Henry VII (1485-1509)	Christopher Turberville	Sir Edward and Robert Stradling	Murder of complainant's servant and dispute as to the manor of Penllyn
Queen Elizabeth (1558-1603)	Thos Morgan of Penllyn (Gentleman)	Antony Griffith and Richard Robert (JPs and Deputy Lieutenants)	Maintenance by defendants of murderers and the rescue of a murderer, their man, from the constable of Cowbridge; illegal imprisonment of complainant in Cowbridge prison, using their office for self enrichment, publicly saying that "it was common policy as the world went now"

Law and Order

In the early part of the nineteenth century David Frederick, the Penllyn blacksmith, paid the price for his antisocial behaviour. In January 1823, he was indicted at the Quarter Sessions in Cardiff, for breaking open the parish pound[3] and taking his cattle out. He was found guilty and sentenced to two months imprisonment and hard labour in the Bridewell[4] at Cowbridge.

Subsequently, Frederick's horse trespassed on Dr. Salmon's plantations and was taken to the common pound. Frederick broke open the pound and called upon his neighbours to witness the act and instigated them to follow his example. For this offence he was convicted at the Quarter Sessions in Cardiff and imprisoned in the county gaol at Cardiff with hard labour for two months.

Though not an incident of living memory, High Lanterns (previously Castle View and The Croft) has an interesting story to tell. Two brothers lived at the house and one was said to have emigrated to Australia. However, when the remaining brother died, a skeleton was reported found in the chimney.

Recollections

(B.P.) Well I remember that the first lot of soldiers that came there were a Welsh regiment and there were black, coloured Americans after and there were also white Americans. The roads here in the evenings were full of them walking about. My father would be here in the garden in the evening and they would stop and he would talk to them. This one night a Mexican soldier stopped to talk to my father and asked my father if he could borrow his 'wheels' to go to the pub, he meant his bicycle. My father said, well, yes but you must bring it back by 10 o'clock. Anyway, I was in bed now and apparently there was a fight between him and this American, near Rhyd cottages, you know those two council cottages, by the furthest one, you know, Mr. Pembridge's. He heard the commotion outside, and a shot apparently. Anyway my father went at 10 o'clock to look for his bike you see and he heard groaning in the gutter out there and when he went to look it was an American soldier bleeding and somehow he got him back here to the house. I was in bed and didn't see anything but my mother was bathing his wounds and all the rest of it and soon the house was full of military police and officers.

I didn't see a thing, but all I can say now is that there was a court martial and my father and Mr. Pembridge had to go to Barnstaple for the Court Martial and they were treated very well, with all expenses paid. I know that the American was called Peter Fanning and he did come back, I don't know after how long, to thank my parents for saving his life really. **(K.H.)** He didn't die then? **(B.P.)** No no, and after he went back to America he used to write to my parents.

Policing at that time was provided from the Police Station and house at Pentre Meyrick, at the time a strategic location along the busy A48 Fishguard to London trunk road. The station closed in the late 1960's following the retirement of P.C. Sheppard to a civilian post at the Police Headquarters in Bridgend. Policing since has been provided directly from the larger station in Cowbridge.

Figure 1. The former police station at Pentre Meyrick, now a dwelling house named "Crosswinds". This house may have been used as a pub in the mid 19th century

Recollections

(A.P.) The other thing that was one of the other questions was the policing in the village. Well the first one that I can remember was Tarr – wasn't it? (Others agree). **(A.N.)** I remember him, they were very hot in those days on the carbide lights. My father had a big motorcycle combination – one of the biggest around and that had carbide lights and P.C. Tarr, he would be hiding somewhere near the A48, not so much traffic on it in those days – well he would be hiding there waiting to pounce on somebody, whose lights had blown out.

(A.P.) Anyway, Tarr was the policeman and then George Cosslett[5]

(A.N.) He was the one that got me into the Police Force. **(A.P.)** Coslett was the policeman at Pentre Meyrick during the war and there were three special policemen, Dick Hinton – he lived where Mrs. Homfray lives. **(E.R.)** Sorry Anthony, when you said that there was a policeman at Pentre Meyrick – was there a police house there? **(A.P.)** Yes, where Shepherd lived – that was the police house. Police station then. Tarr was there, then Coslett and then they had three special policemen,[6] and they covered the Cowbridge area as well. Richard (Dick) Hinton, where Mrs. Homfray lives. There were two houses there. My father down in the Graig, Jonathan Powell, or Jack Powell as he was known. Betty's father down here and William (Bill) Thomas, who received the Queen's medal and they were the three special policeman during the war. **(A.N.)** Cause of course he used to come through the village, George Coslett on his bicycle and he knew us all by our Christian names you know, and I was quite tall then and he used to say "Albert you want to join the Police Force" and I'd say no, I don't want to join the Police Force and he would say, "Well when you decide that you do want to join the Police Force, you come up to the station and we will give you a cup of coffee and we will chat about it". And of course he won didn't he.

Figure 2. P. C. Tarr, 1927

In most murder cases the victim knew his or her assailant. This was the case when, in the early hours of 1st January 1960 at Pear Tree Cottage, Penllyn, George Carter, a man in his 40's, slaughtered his wife Ruby and left for dead their baby son, Alan. Miraculously, Alan was found alive several hours later and survived his terrible injuries. George Carter was later arrested, charged, convicted of murder and sentenced to life imprisonment. He died several years later after his release from prison.

However, not all murders touching the village have been detected. In October 1979 Jack Armstrong, a Cardiff taxi driver, collected a fare from a public house in Pentrebane, Cardiff. His destination was unknown but it proved to be his final journey; his body was found on Stalling Down near Aberthin several days later, his car having been driven through the bottom of Craig Penllyn on the day of his probable murder. For one Penllyn resident, Robert Evans, then a young Police Cadet, it was his first experience of working on a murder enquiry, involving many painstaking hours of finger-tip searching over open countryside for a possible murder weapon. Mr. Armstrong's killer remains at large today.

Thankfully however, not all crime has been of a tragic nature, indeed one act was said to be fortuitous to the good wives of the village. Following a decade or so of very sociable (but not always sober) years of sporting enjoyment, changing demographics within the male population of the village resulted in its cricket club suspending activities, pending an influx of the next glut of volunteers. Kit, pads and bats were put away for safe storage (so it was thought) in the garage of Dave Llewellyn. That is, until a dark winter's night when the whole lot was stolen from beneath the noses of the players, who all lived within a stone's throw of the crime. Conspiracy theories abounded, but only the men-folk seemed crestfallen on hearing of the crime!

Recollections

Q. Who did the school children regard as the 'bogey man' of the village? The squire, the parson or the chapel elders? **(A.P.)** Well the only one I remember was the policeman (all laugh). Here he is coming up the road. **(H.G.)** I remember we used to play one game. He would be wanting to go home and two of us would be holding the back wheel of the bike and he would be pedalling like mad and going nowhere!

---

1 11th June

2 The Court of the Star Chamber was named after the star-shaped ceiling decoration of the room in the Palace of Westminster, London, where its first meetings were held. It was set up by Henry VII and abolished by the Long Parliament in 1641.

3 The parish pound would be used to impound stray animals which were then released on payment of a fine.

4 Prison

5 During the war the police were responsible for ensuring the safety of the public when unexploded high explosive bombs (UXBs) were found. P.C. 539 George Coslett, based at Pentre Meyrick, was specially trained as a Bomb Reconnaissance Officer to be sent to the site to inspect the UXB and confirm its position.

6 Under Common Law every able-bodied person in Great Britain has a duty to go and help a police officer when required. This duty has been embodied in the Special Constabulary, an auxiliary police force made up from members of the public trained in police duties, and hastily sworn in by local magistrates to help the police if required. The legal statutes for the Special Constabulary have been in place since the seventeenth century, however it was not until the two World Wars of the last century, that the Special Constabulary finally achieved the recognition it deserved as a valuable and integral part of the permanent police. (source: South Wales Police Museum)

Chapter 14

Mining and Quarrying

Penllyn's economy has remained principally rural over the centuries and mining has not dominated local industry as it did in many parts of South Wales. Penllyn has, however, experienced periods when mining or quarrying played a part in its social and economic life.

Coal

The parish of Penllyn lies well south of the geology of the South Wales coalfield and there are no coal workings in the parish. However, the proximity of mines in adjacent localities meant that Penllyn people often sought work in the pits.

Figure 1. Sinking the shaft at Wern Tarw colliery, circa 1920 (Reproduced courtesy of Pencoed Town Council)

Recollections

(E.P.) Who was the Village Coal Merchant? **(N.J.)** Well, miners had their coal delivered. **(A.P.)** A lot of the people living here worked in either the collieries or the Iron Ore. My father went to work in Wern Tarw[1]. **(E.P.)** Were they collected then, Anthony, or did they have to find their own way? **(A.P.)** Cycle. My father used to cycle to Wern Tarw. Seven miles there and he would work a full shift on stoking and cycle all the way home and then he would have to bath when he was at home. **(E.P.)** My father was a stoker as well. **(A.P.)** And that is how the miners got their coal, it was brought in a lorry and tipped outside your door and you would have to carry it in.

Figure 2. Jonathan (Jack) Powell shifting his allowance of coal[2] outside Tŷ Canol. He noted at the time that he had worked a full shift as a stoker, and then had to start again when he got home!

Mining and Quarrying

Lead

The annals of Tewkesbury make reference to lead mining at Llangan in the 12th century but not at Penllyn. Lead ore (galena) still exists as crystalline deposits within calcite, both deposited by hydrothermal action in the cracks and faults in the limestone, which underlies the parish. These thin seams have been followed across the parish landscape, mined where rich enough and where the price of ore was high enough to warrant the gamble.

Usually ore from mid Wales, the Mendips or even overseas was more easily mined and at less cost. The only mining records are from the early 1800's, coinciding with a fever for the exploitation of the mineral wealth of Wales to meet demand from the newly emergent industrial revolution. In the previous 200 years, there are only occasional references in private letters to the export of ore from southeast Wales to Bristol with the ore travelling by packhorse and coastal barge[3].

An outcrop of faulted rock with traces of ore can be followed from the holes and adits[4], which are shown up by the bright white calcite waste from which was sorted the shiny grey galena crystal. A thin seam might lead to a thick one, though usually it just petered out or ran into an underground stream.

Figure 3. Filling in lead mine workings at Mount Pleasant, 1928. The exact location of these abandoned workings is unknown, though presumably they lie on a rise near Mount Pleasant farm just north of Cowbridge.

PENLLYN

In 1841, the 'Cambrian' Newspaper reported:
'It seems somewhat extraordinary, that in this speculative age, when such vast sums are sent to seek - and often to sink - their fortunes in a far distant regard, that our home treasures should be so disregarded, even our own county of Glamorgan. Lead ore, of the purest quality, which can be scraped up by the side of the road, in ditches, and abundantly a few feet beneath the surface of the soil, still continues to be dormant – science, capital, the gigantic power of the steam engine, all alike, dormant.

Can there be a finer field for science and capital combined, than offers itself in this our highly-gifted rich mineral county of Glamorgan? St Hilary, Colwinstone, Llangan, Penlline, and other parishes abound in lead ore. Take up a handful of earth near any of the old pits and it is full of lead ore. Twenty five years ago it was asserted by the oldest persons then living, that the workings of the Lead Mines on the Penlline Court Estate was suspended (from 80 to 100 years ago) in consequence of the overwhelming pressure of water, years before the steam engine, with its gigantic power, came into play, and that the main vein of ore at that time was thirty seven inches in thickness. The ore was then carried about half a mile to be washed, and taken back again to the smelting house, which adjoined the pits.'

In December 1851, a prospectus was issued for Penllyne Court Lead Mines[5], such mines being described as: '*very extensive, and are situated in the parishes of Penllyne and Langan, near Cowbridge, Glamorganshire; they are held under lease direct from the freeholder (William Salmon Esq. of Penllyne Court) for thirty-one years, at a royalty of one-fifteenth for the first eleven years and one-twelfth for the remainder.*'

The prospectus refers to large piles of lead slag[6] scattered around. A recent walk at the site produced no slag, but clinker (the fused silicate residue from burning coal) was found, presumably from the smelting house.

Figure 4. Clinker found near site of Penllyne Court Lead Mine

The prospectus also carried a report by Captain[7] Matthew Francis, described as the most eminent lead miner of the day, as follows:

"I find the ground covering a very large tract of country, on which traces of ancient mining exist to a considerable extent, as well as remains of a smelting establishment, and a barbarous attempt at supplying steam power; all this however, was evidently a failure, as the miners only succeeded in pumping the works dry to a depth of ten or twelve fathoms…

I went back over the back of the principal lodes for a length of 300 to 400 fathoms, and I have never seen more beautiful veins… The lodes may honestly be described as being full of gozzan and lead … And from two to four and six feet wide."

Mary and Gordon Tucker published an article[8] on the mine and extracts are printed below:

'Operations began in May 1852. The old workings of three shafts were "cleared up, timbered and sunk upon". The sinking of the middle and lower shafts was hindered by the presence of water. Capt. Curry recommended the use of two horse whims[9] to get the water out. These cost £34 and were working by the end of October but were hampered by extreme wet weather, so one whim was removed to the upper shaft on higher ground where they were troubled to a lesser extent and work was concentrated there.[10] In January 1853 a new shaft was opened about 80 fathoms East of the upper shaft. By then an improvement had taken place in the West branch of the upper shaft – two men took out half a ton of fine lead ore in seven hours[11] and at the June 1853 meeting of shareholders a stone of ore weighing 228 lbs[12] sent by the resident agent was exhibited on the table.'

In June 1853, it was agreed to use a steam engine to drain the mine's deeper level: '*In December 1853 the agent Lewis Williams reported the arrival of the engine at the mine as well as still larger stones of ore … one weighing 483lbs*'[13]

'*The engine, a Medwin and Hall portable, was started on 26 February 1854, pumping up 50 gallons of water per minute*[14]. *John Griffiths, the new agent*[15] *appointed in January 1854, reported on 1 April: "from everything I see we shall soon have a paying mine"*[16] *but there is no mention of very large stones as found by Lewis Williams and in November John Griffiths disagreed with a consultants recommendation as to the future working of the mine.*[17] *Griffiths opposed the deepening of the engine shaft on grounds of time and cost, and wished to know more about the lodes before further capital investment was made. No agreement seems to have been reached and at the beginning of August 1855 a special meeting was held where resolutions were passed confirming the dissolution of the company.*'

Figure 5. A simple horse whim. One or two horses would be connected under the wheel that was then revolved to lift and lower buckets. It was common to have two buckets connected. Where possible the buckets would help to counter balance each other. The two whims at Penllyn were covered rather than open as illustrated (drawing courtesy of Heathcote Public School, New South Wales).

Mining and Quarrying

'The Tithe Awards (N.L.W.) of 1841 show the main site, where the shafts are, as TEWGOED BACH COED in the ownership of Wm. Salmon, and the piece of land to the north, where the stone wall stands, as TŶ COCH OLD BUILDING, *in the ownership of the Earl of Dunraven.*[18] *This therefore leaves no doubt as to the identity of this site, which must also have been that of the 18th century Tewgoed Mine.'*

Figure 6. Location of Penllyne Court Lead Mine (courtesy of Bulletin Peak District Historical Mines Society)

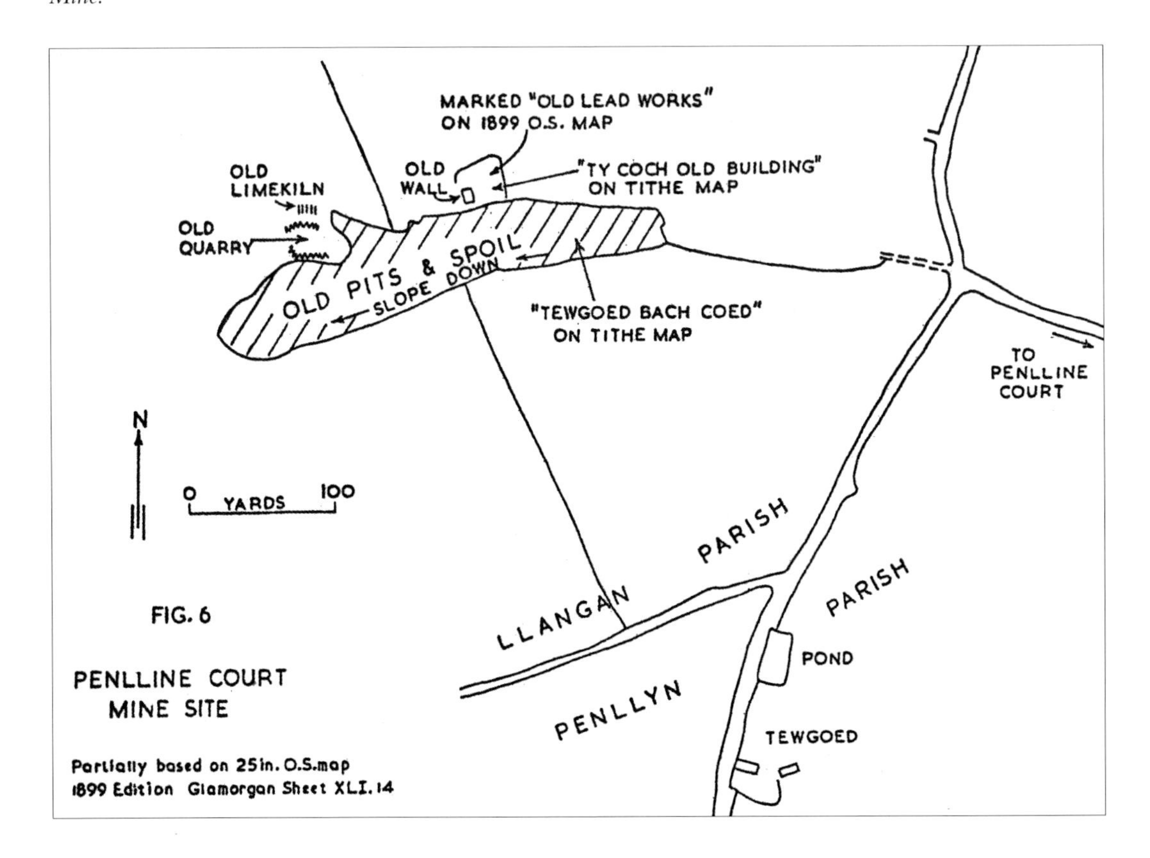

The Penllyne Court or Tewgoed mine, which in the 18th century reportedly employed 500 people,[19] never reopened. It is ironic, given the mine's name, that the mine buildings were located just across the parish boundary in Llangan parish, where traces of the buildings and spoil mound can still be seen as shown on the location map.[20] Eventually the lead miners went into the coal pits opening up after 1850, though many families

Figure 7. Remains of Penllyne Court Lead Mine buildings

Figure 8. Spar (or Calcite) $CaCO_3$ Reproduced courtesy of Barry Marsh, School of Ocean and Earth Science, National Oceanography Centre, Southampton

Spar

Recollections

(A.N.) As I said, I worked for a mason there on the estate. **(H.G.)** Do you remember the mortar mill there then? And the carpenter's shop? **(A.N.)** Yes and they had their own roller to put the spar down on the drive and they worked the spar from down underneath the Castle there. I have seen the spar down there and when things were a bit quiet for the workmen, no matter who they were they would have to go down there and mine the spar. **(S.W.)** Is that the white stuff that they put on the castle driveway? **(A.P.)** Yes, it got to a state that they had to fill in the holes.

Figure 9. Spar Mine in woods near Penllyn Castle, 1932

Figure 10. Frank Gane, with 'Farmer' and 'Duke', hauling spar from the mine to repair the castle drive, 1932

Spar was used to line the drive leading up to the castle from the grand entrance gates next to the Church of St. John the Evangelist. This practice had been a feature of the castle for many years. The result was a dazzling white drive, no doubt intended to impress visitors to the castle. Pieces of spar can still be seen locally, thrown up in the molehills on the Parish Field, but the castle drive has long lost its sparkle.

Figure 11. Castle Driveway, 1894

Limestone

The limestone ridge that underlies Penllyn and the Graig provided the raw material that was used both for construction[21] and agriculture. Limestone blocks could be used for walls, while burning and slaking the lime created lime putty, lime powder, lime mortar, render and limewash. The method of manufacture of these products is shown in the lime cycle diagram.

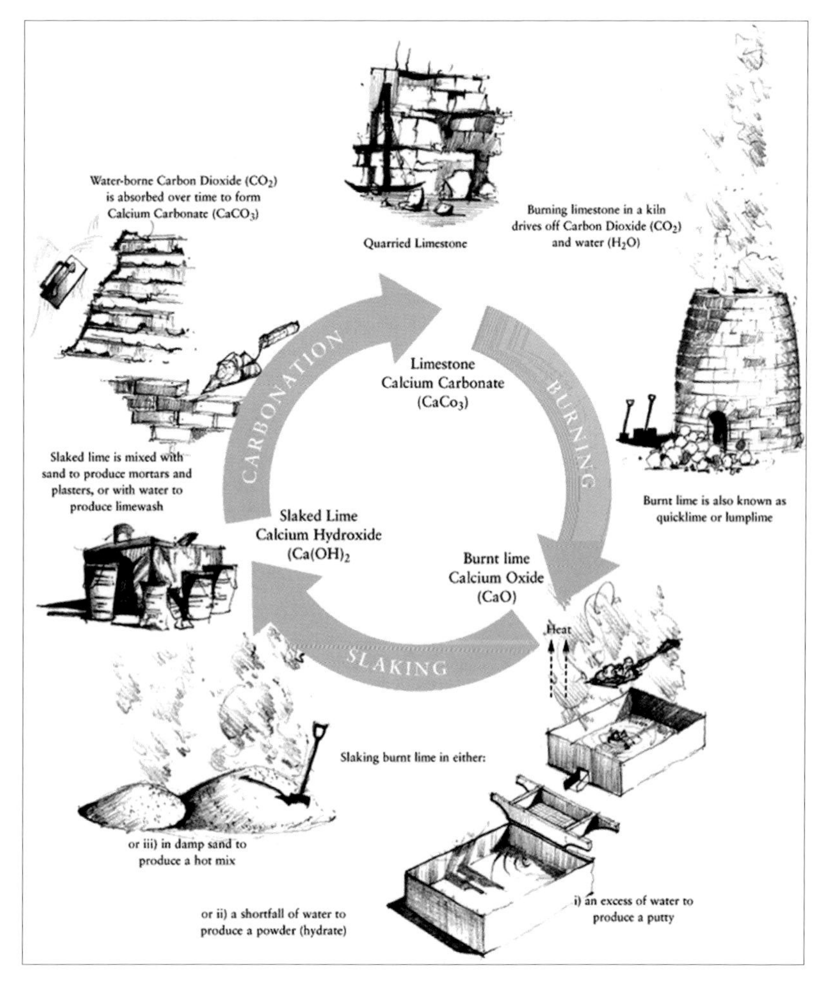

Figure 12. Lime Cycle (courtesy of Tŷ-Mawr lime, Llangasty, Brecon, who still supply lime products for historic building repair and restoration)

Mining and Quarrying

Walter Davies, in his 1814 book: 'General View of the Agriculture and Domestic Economy of South Wales,' wrote:

'*In the extensive limestone tract of the Vale of Glamorgan, there are but few public kilns for the sale of lime: every farmer is a lime burner; raising the stone in the field to be manured; so that there is scarcely an arable field to be found without having, either at present or formerly, a limekiln within it. The stones are too frequently raised, and the kiln erected, in the middle of a fine field; some indeed raise the stone and erect the kiln on the side of the high road, where it is over-broad; and thereby convert a private eyesore into a public nuisance. In many instances, kilns might be made, with equal feasibility, in the more useless corners, or on the slopes of small dingles, places inaccessible to the plow, but more accessible to the limestone strata. Of late, landlords have very properly interfered.*

These kilns, built of limestone, require to be rebuilt or repaired frequently; once in a season, where the farmer useth much lime: one new kiln is about two days work for a mason.'

The enclosure awards of 1860 meant that the Thaw Valley moorlands, with their acidic soils, would be drained and cultivated. Hydrated lime would have been essential for spreading on the land to neutralise soil acidity and create optimal PH values for crop growth.

Given Davies' comments above, it is perhaps surprising that a number of these kilns still survive in the parish,[22] albeit in a partially ruined state. The example (Fig.13) is on the hill near the Castle, while a larger kiln can be seen on the public footpath near Ham Farm.

Figure 13. Lime Kiln, ruin,
Penllyn Castle Woods

1 The mine referred to was Wern Tarw near Pencoed. Wern Tarw was the last deep coal mine in that area until 1964 when an underground fire forced it to close.

2 This was a long established perquisite of all coal miners in Wales and recognised by the National Coal Board in 1946 and formed an official payment.

3 'England's Improvement by Sea and Land`, Andrew Yarranton, 1677

4 The earliest speculative holes and adits stretch in a line along the eastern escarpment of the Thaw Valley from the Castle and northwards. There is no written evidence associated with these, only tracks and levelled floors. The later deeper shafts with buildings and written evidence of lease and in the Mining Journal lie on the western parish boundary and the buildings are mainly in Llangan. There is no evidence that the two series of faults meet. The two areas appear to have remained in distinctly separate ownership and no evidence has been found linking the Homfray family with lead mining.

5 Also known as Tewgoed Mine, but not to be confused with nearby Llangan Mine, which was operated, by Llangan Silver Lead Mining Co. Llangan Lead Mining Co. and Glamorgan Consolidated Lead Mining Co.

6 The slag is mostly found adjacent to the chimney stacks.

7 Captain in this context is the chief engineer/manager of a mineral mine. Most learned their profession in Cornwall and contracted to come to Wales.

8 'The Lead Mines of Southeast Wales`, Mary and Gordon Tucker, Bulletin Peak District Historical Mines Society, Vol. 6, No. 1, pp 15-27, May 1975

9 See horse whim drawing

10 Mining Journal 1852, p525

11 Mining Journal 1853, p46

12 Mining Journal 1853, p348

13 Mining Journal 1853, p814

14 Mining Journal 1854, p170

15 Mining Journal 1854, p25

16 Mining Journal 1854 p 496

17 Mining Journal 1854, p766

18 Penllyn Court Lead Mine subsequently obtained a lease of land adjoining the Salmon land from the Countess of Dunraven.

19 'Lead Mining in Wales`, W. J. Lewis, p263

20 Take Public Footpath 10 to view workings.

21 The limestone of the Penllyn area produces inferior hydrated lime mostly suitable for agricultural uses and rough mortar.

22 A recent survey of the Thaw Valley revealed ruins of over 70 kilns.

Chapter 15

The Hunt and the Races

The influence of the Homfray family in Penllyn has ensured a long association with hunting and racing. Numerous photos from the early 20th century show the Homfrays, and other Glamorgan gentry, attending races, the hunt, hunt balls and parading the hounds. Newspapers record their involvement as race stewards and horse owners. Indeed Colonel H. R. Homfray is described as belonging to the genus '*homo rusticus*' and as '*a warm hearted squire to whom horn and hound were almost as important as public life.*'[1]

Glamorgan Hunt

The Hunt's website[2] records: '*The history of hunting in Glamorgan can be traced to the late fifties of the 18th century. No less than five packs were kept by local squires for their own and neighbours' amusement. The Cowbridge harriers hunted mainly hare, but after Christmas fox was hunted. For many years these harriers were the property of the Traherne family and were kennelled at Llandough.*

In 1863 Mr. Theodore Mansell Talbot of Margam, hunted a pack of harriers. It is believed that this was the pack owned by the Traherne family, with which he continued to hunt Mr. Traherne's country and use the Llandough kennels (the old kennels near the village, not the present site now occupied by the Glamorgan Hounds).'

In the 20th century, the Hunt would meet twice or even three times a week, well attended by the gentry and local farmers.

Figure 1. Meet at Boverton, 27th February 1927

The Hunt and the Races

Glamorgan Hunt records list the masters as follows:

1863 - 1877 T. M. Talbot

1875 - 1886 J. S. Gibbon

1886 - 1897 Col. R. T. Bassett

1897 - 1906 The Mackintosh of Mackintosh

1906 - 1914 Col. H. R. Homfray (Penllyn), who hunted the country three days a week until the outbreak of the war

1914 - 1934 R. H. Williams of Bonvilston House

1934 - 1960 Capt. H. C. R. Homfray (Penllyn)

1951 - 1962 Lady Boothby

1962 - 1967 John Cory

1961 - 1991 A. S. Martyn, who hunted hounds for 26 seasons and established the kennels at Llandough where hounds are kennelled today. He was the last master to carry the horn in Glamorgan and, from 1986, a professional huntsman hunted the hounds, namely:

1986 - 90 G. Sales

1990 - 91 C. Shillam

1991 - 95 R. Newton

1995 - present Neil Burton

The longest serving professional huntsman was Frank Grant, **1909 - 1934** who, when he retired, kept livery stables in Penllyn.

Figure 2. 5th February 1926. Presentation to L. G. Williams, of Bonvilston Cottage, 28 years Hon. Secretary and Treasurer, Glamorgan Hunt (and who subsequently served another 8 years!). Left to right, R. H. Williams, The Mackintosh of Mackintosh, L. G. Williams, H. C. R. Homfray, H. R. Homfray

When the Homfrays were Masters of the Hounds, the hounds were paraded at the Vale of Glamorgan Show. The diet of the hounds would be supplemented by fallen stock, a practice that continues to this day. During the Second World War, the hounds were taken into Penllyn Castle and cared for and fed by Captain Homfray, Mrs. Evelyn Homfray and Miss Serena Boothby. The Captain would organize a meet of the hounds when a former subscriber was home on leave.

Capt. Homfray had great difficulty obtaining feed for the hunt horses but, despite this, he formed a mounted unit of the Home Guard, known in the Vale as "Homfray's Cossacks", to which many local farmers belonged. This mounted unit would meet at Court Farm, where Reg Chatterton had two horses, one of which was a large beautiful black that he used to ride. One day the horse, objecting to being controlled, reared back and fell, trapping him underneath. He needed a long spell in hospital, and bed-rest at home, to finally recover. Anthony Powell used to take the horses down to Rhyd Forge to have them re-shod, which he remembers as a great day out.

Figure 3. Hounds at the Vale of Glamorgan Show, 1936

Figure 4 Grassy John, aged 86, 1926

There were many Hunt characters, not least of whom was Grassy John, who started with the Hunt when he was 14. Grassy John was a terrier man. His grandson, Arthur John of Cardiff, remembers his popularity with the gentry and that the Mackintosh of Mackintosh once came to his house to visit. In 'Cowbridge and District Remembered'[3], Arthur John recalls:

"I was brought up by my grandparents, John and Miriam John. He was known as "Grassy" or Gras-y" as he had been brought up by his Aunt Grace, in a cottage on the Aberthin Road, next door to the Edmondes Arms in Cowbridge."

Jeff Alden,[4] a local historian, recounts:

"Johnny Grassy had seven daughters and three sons, and died in 1932 at the age of 92. He was quite short, but a jaunty character and a great horseman. He rode frequently and attended all the hunt meets. When not on horseback he used a thumbstick, and always wore a bowler hat and breeches.

He was also well known for taking part in the Mari Lwyd celebrations. Until the custom was revived in recent years, Johnny had been considered to have been the last person to have gone around from house to house 'under the horse's head' - it was he who wore the horse's skull set in a dark cloak. This was at a time when the challenges were sung in Welsh - and he used to sing the responses in the Glamorgan dialect of Welsh."

Hunt Races

From the late 19th century, Penllyn was the venue for the annual Glamorgan Hunt Steeplechases. It was an exceptionally pretty location and Bayles[5] records, *"The course is right handed, and the pretty slopes under Penllyn Castle enable the races to be viewed without the assistance of a grandstand. The country is a very good one, and easy to negotiate, over old grassland naturally drained, therefore, the going is never hard or heavy. The fences are of birch and gorse, and most of them form part of a natural country. There is no ridge or furrow on any part, and no fence is jumped twice, which speaks for its extent."*

In 1907, the 'Western Mail' reported, *"Cowbridge is one of the few remaining old fashioned meetings. Unlike Cardiff and Monmouth it has made no pretensions to the dignity of a club, and perhaps, it is the old fashioned flavour it retains that causes it to enjoy such popularity."*

Brian Lee, the racing historian[6], tells how the Great Western and Taff Railways used to lay on special trains throughout the UK to take people to Cowbridge, to attend the Penllyn races. Cowbridge would be decked with bunting to celebrate what was then known as "The Derby Day of South Wales."

He recounts: *"From the primrose-carpeted slopes of the natural grandstand the landed gentry would mix with vagabonds and rogues to witness the racing.*

The First Viscount Lord Tredegar, Godfrey Charles Morgan, whose equestrian statue can be seen in front of Cardiff's City Hall, once won a steeplechase over the course on his famous charger Sir Briggs who he had ridden in the famous, but ill-fated Charge of The Light Brigade at Balaclava.

The famed Anthony and Rees brothers from West Wales enjoyed their early successes at Cowbridge while Sir Harry Llewellyn, of Foxhunter fame, rode his first winner there in 1931 on Theorem, a horse who was destined for point-to-points."

On 8th March 1888, Tim Donovan entered 'Maid of Killarney' in the Farmers' Plate. The course was over two miles and there were four other horses running; 'The Waif', 'Jack', 'Dairy Maid' and 'Needlegun'. 'The Waif' was the clear betting favourite at Evens, while the rest of the field were at 5 to 1. Tim Donovan, who traded as Messrs. Donovan Bros., had bought 'Maid of Killarney' for 25 shillings two years earlier and used her to haul his rag and bone cart through Cardiff, hardly ideal practice for the race meeting! As the race progressed, the horses came to a dry ditch and all bar one, 'Maid of Killarney', stopped, looked and would not attempt the ditch. Eventually, 'The Waif' and 'Needlegun' got over but came in several fields behind 'Maid of Killarney', who took the prize money of 20 guineas. Reportedly, she had raced everything on the way to Penllyn, and yet she still won when she got here!

A sadder story is told in 'Cowbridge & Llanblethian, Past and Present'[7]:
"There are some racing stories which gain rather than lose credence by repetition. The tale of the ill-fated race that took place at Penllyn on 23 May, 1919 is one of them. At this time Dillwyn Morgan of the Bridge Brewery, Cowbridge, owned a fine trotting pony called Daisy, whose coat gleamed like satin and whose speed was a by-word in the borough. She was a dray horse who delivered barrels of ale from the brewery to every corner of the Vale. Mr. Morgan was very proud of Daisy and boasted that his pony could outrace any horse in the locality. He was challenged, however, by a Llysworney farmer who owned a fast hunter. A private race was arranged at Penllyn, wagers were laid, and an enthusiastic crowd of supporters turned up at the racecourse to cheer Daisy on. After a thrilling race she flew past the tapes ahead of her rival. Such a voltage of triumph surged through the jockey's body that he hadn't noticed that Daisy had begun to tremble like an aspen. Within seconds she collapsed on the racecourse and died. The remorse of her owner was so profound that he ordered an inscribed tombstone to be placed over her in the Brewery yard – a lasting testament to her gallant twenty-eight years."

Figure 5 Location of Penllyn Racecourse[8]

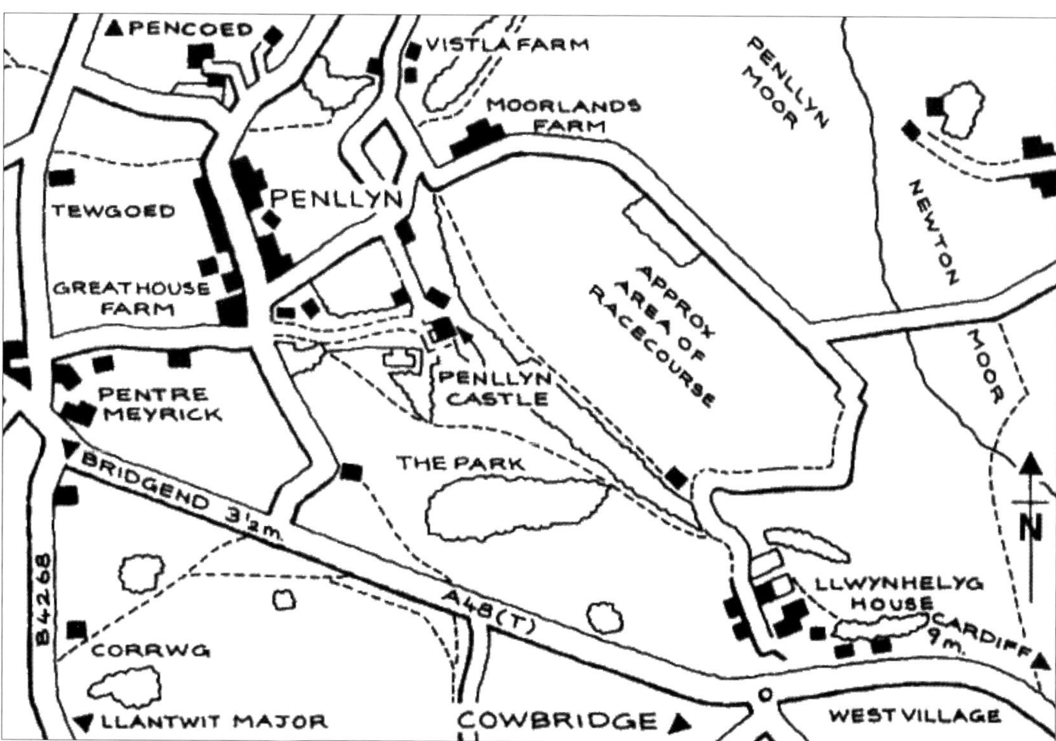

The Hunt and the Races

Colonel Homfray's interest in racing was demonstrated not just by hosting the Hunt Races and attendance at many racecourses, but also by his appreciation of excellence on the track. On 19th March 1937, Evan Williams (son of Fred Williams of the Bear Hotel, Cowbridge) won the Grand National on 'Royal Mail'. On his return to Cowbridge, he was presented with a gold watch at a celebration dinner hosted by the Colonel.

Figure 6. Colonel Homfray and Evan Williams, 27th March 1937

The Last Hunt Race

One special meeting at Penllyn took place on Tuesday 4th May 1939, but with very low attendances:

	Paddock 12s 6d	Cheap 2s 0d	Bookmakers present
1938	275	1813	52
1939	223	1254	49

Figure 7. Cowbridge Races, Penllyn, 4th May 1939

The Mayoress of Cowbridge, Blanche Homfray, is presenting W. Holman with the Sportsman's Hurdle Race Cup, a race he had won riding 'Windy Girl'. W. Holman was probably Walter Holman, the youngest of six sons of William "Bill" Holman, a leading member of the Cheltenham racing set. Walter's brothers included three professional jump jockeys - George, Alfred, and John, and two amateur riders - Walter and Frederick.

The 'Western Mail', on the 5th May 1939, reported the meeting, noting that Harry Llewellyn had nearly ridden three winners, being beaten by a head in one race. However, the paper that day was dominated by international news, with Neville Chamberlain moving the second edition of the Military Training Bill while the leader column reported:

"a meeting today of Herr Von Ribbentrop and Count Ciano, the Foreign Ministers of the Axis Powers" and noted *"Hitler is hardly likely to go all out against Poland unless he is absolutely assured of Italy's active co-operation, and no-one can see what Italy could get out of such a venture commensurate with the appalling risks she would run."*

A few months later, the world would be at war. It may have been the mood of the country, or perhaps the low attendance on the day of the races, which affected confidence, for not one of the winners of the three selling plates received a bid. For Penllyn Hunt racing, it was to prove the last meeting and marked the end of an era.

Point-to-Point

Point-to-point racing is a form of amateur racing for hunting horses, and many jockeys will participate in this code before competing in National Hunt racing. In Glamorgan, all the work of building the jumps and manning the course in point-to-point is done by voluntary hunt members, as the day's racing is one of the principle sources of income for the Hunt. The land is farmed normally, and the bases of the jumps are left in situ, and reconstructed each year.

The first recorded point-to-point in South Wales occurred in April 1887 at St. Mellons, but the second meeting in 1890 was closer to home. The competitors weighed in at Crossways, perhaps the earliest set course, then owned by Ralph Thurstan Bassett, Master of the Foxhounds. The course started between Llandow and Stembridge, crossed the Clemenston brook, took a northerly direction and, turning right and leaving Hilton Farm on the left, followed an almost a straight line over the Pinklands, finishing up at the Corrwg in the south of Penllyn Parish. The Crossways course would be used many more times, though the venue varied over the years.

Figure 8. Point-to-point Race at Crossways, 16th March 1932

This photograph was taken on a delightful spring day in 1932 and features 'Attempt' jumping a fence in the 3:10 Nomination (Open) race over the Crossways course. The horse was a 10:1 outsider and finished an also ran.

Notable riders include Rose Harry who, in 1967 at Penllyn, became the first woman in Wales to ride two point-to-point winners on the same day, riding 'April Witch' to take the Members' race and, later on, 'Zut' to win the Ladies' race.

Another noteworthy rider is John Llewellyn, a legend in hunt-racing circles, born at Moorlands Farm in Penllyn but now farming Newlands at St. Mary Church.

Brian Lee recalls: *"John started riding in point-to-points at 16 but amazingly he didn't ride his first winner until he was 20. He won the Welsh riders' championship on numerous occasions and in 1982 he really put Welsh point-to-pointing on the hunt-racing map when he became the first Welshman to win the national riders' championship outright.*

Under Rules he rode 15 winners at Cheltenham, Newbury, Sandown, Hereford and Chepstow. It was at the last named racecourse, in front of a huge Welsh crowd, that he had one of his most memorable wins on Grenville Richards's Fixed Price in the 1986 Land Rover Gentlemen's Hunter' Chase Championship Final.

When I asked him if the sport has changed a lot since he first started riding he replied, "The standard of riding has vastly improved; the courses are better laid out, the horses are better schooled and there is more emphasis put on the safety of riders and horses." John, who mixed point-to-pointing with competing in local show-jumping competitions, was an expert with novice horses.

He said he kept on riding for more than 30 years because of the thrill of riding winners and every horse he sat on was a new challenge. He certainly knew all about the downside of the sport. During his time in the saddle he suffered broken collar-bones, a broken shoulder blade and hip, a broken wrist and various leg injuries.

John chalked-up his first winner on Highland Myth back in 1966 and towards the end of his riding career he was riding against the sons of the fathers he was competing against in the 1960's."

Figure 9. John Llewellyn, riding 'Timber Tool', Grand Marnier Champion 1990[9]

The Hunt and the Races

In 1952, the Glamorgan and Llangeinor Hunts held their point-to-point on the site of the old racecourse at Penllyn, where the Hunt steeplechases used to take place, a change of venue that met with the instant approval of riders and public alike. John Llewellyn can remember that time well as, at the age of seven, he had a grandstand view of the new course from his bedroom window at Moorlands Farm!

When the Penllyn course finally closed in 1969, the Glamorgan and Pentyrch hunts moved to St. Hilary while the Llangeinor hunt moved to Coychurch. Currently, the Glamorgan point-to-point course is at Ystradowen. With the reversion of the Penllyn course to solely farmland use, Penllyn had ended its 80-year association with horse racing.

The Hunt Today

In 2004, the Government banned certain practices of hunting wild mammals, though there are exemptions. The Glamorgan Hunt carries out trail hunting, drag hunting and hound exercise and meets twice a week through the season. In 2006, the Boxing Day and New Year's Day Meets were attended by over 1,000 people. The Hunt still enjoys hospitality at Penllyn with Meets at the Castle and Penllyn Court.

Figure 10. Boxing Day Meet, High Street, Cowbridge, 2006, Joint-Master Mike Gibson MFH on grey; Huntsman Neil Burton, front

Acknowledgements and References:

We are indebted in this chapter to Brian Lee, the racing historian and author of 'The Races Came Off' and 'Welsh Steeplechase Jockeys', and Chris Pitt, author of 'A Long -Time Gone', for sharing their memories and research on Penllyn's involvement with racing, and to Heather March for her invaluable knowledge of the Hunt.

1 'Cowbridge and Llanblethian: Past and Present', Brian Ll. James/David J. Francis, 1979, pp 181-182; Stewart Williams, Barry and D. Brown & Sons, Cowbridge

2 **www.freewebs.com/glamorganhunt/history.htm**

3 'Cowbridge and District Remembered 1900-1950', Cowbridge Record Society, Jeff Alden (ed)

4 Jeff Alden, Cowbridge Record Society

5 'The Race Course Atlas of Great Britain & Ireland', F.H. Bayles, 1903

6 Brian Lee: 'The Races Came Off', 1986, Welsh Sporting Publications and 'Welsh Steeplechase Jockeys', Cwmnedd Press, 1995

7 'Cowbridge and Llanblethian: Past and Present', B. L. James/D. J. Francis, 1979, D. Brown & Sons

8 Source 'A Long Time Gone', Chris Pitt, Portway Press, 1996

9 Awarded to horse that won the most point-to-point races in a season

Chapter 16

Pubs

While the public house, or alehouse as it used to be known, has been a facet of Welsh life since Roman times, many people would have brewed their own ale, using a mix of herbs (or fruit) for flavouring. This "gruit" often included ground ivy, a herb of the mint family still found in abundance on the Parish Field, that clarified and helped to preserve the ale, known as "gill ale". References to gill ale were not always favourable. George Borrow, in 'Wild Wales', records a drink he spat out in Chester, and quoted the following verse:

"Chester Ale, Chester Ale! I could ne'er get it down,
'Tis made of ground-ivy, of dirt, of bran,
'Tis as thick as a river below a huge town!
'Tis not lap for a dog, far less drink for a man."

PENLLYN

When beer which uses hops, supplanted ale, home brewing still continued locally. On 7th May 1771, the Reverend George Williams, curate of Ystradowen, Penllyn and St. Mary Hill, is recorded as buying 1¾lb hops, at 16d a pound which, with a turnpike fee of 1½d, cost him 2s 5½d.

Brewing was often women's work, hence the term alewife, and at some unrecorded point in time, it is likely that the wife of a local labourer or craftsman would have begun to brew beer for public consumption in a front room of their cottage. The Alehouse Act of 1552 had placed recognizance (bond) and licensing constraints on people wanting to sell beer or ale, and this would have deterred these home-brewing businesses. However, in 1830, the Beer Act substantially reversed licensing policy and it was now possible for any householder assessed for the poor rate to sell beer, ale and cider, without a licence from local justices, by taking out an excise licence from the Excise authorities. This led to a major increase in public house numbers across Britain.

In Penllyn, the position following the 1830 Beer Act, was as follows:

1841 Census	Landlord	Age	1851 Census	Landlord	Age
New Inn	Elias Thomas	30			
Victoria	William David	55			
Barley Mow	John John	45	Barley Mow	Silas Richards	27
Kings Head	Joseph Williams	50	Kings Head	William David	24
Morning Star	Lewis Jones	55	Morning Star	Christopher Harry	66
			Travellers Rest	John Marchant	48
			Fox and Hounds	William David	67

On the evidence of the census reports, and assuming no name changes, as many as seven pubs existed in Penllyn in the mid 19th century, of which just two, the Barley Mow and the Red Fox (previously the Fox and Hounds), survive today. Three pubs, long since gone, were situated at or near the crossroads at Pentre Meyrick. No further information is known about the New Inn and the Victoria, both listed in the 1841 census. Searches of Kelly's and Slater's 19th century directories reveal only references to the Fox and Hounds and the Barley Mow.

Quite often the publican would have more than one trade. William David, at the Fox and Hounds in 1851, lists his other occupations as mason and thatcher; Silas Richards was a carpenter while John Marchant farmed 27 acres.

The Lost Pubs

In 1927, Silurian wrote in the 'Glamorgan Gazette':

"Within a few miles or less, and almost within view of each other, in South Glamorgan are three buildings, whose sturdy walls and roofs for generations sheltered gay, if simple, companies of farmers and farm workmen, whose sound of revelry enlivened the dull countryside, and served at least one good purpose, which was to keep ghosts, goblins and corpse candles at a respectable and safe distance. Goldsmith's "Deserted Village" is melancholy reading, but such, nevertheless, as we would not miss for much, and to me, next to the melancholy of a deserted village, is that of a deserted inn, which for long gave many poor souls their warmest welcome. Your three deserted inns to which reference is made today are The Morning Star, Penllyn; The Crack Inn at the bottom of Crack Hill on the Bridgend-Cowbridge road; and the Bell Inn, St. Mary Hill..........

In days when game was preserved on a much more extensive scale than is the case today, and when poachers were numerous, some of them made the Morning Star, The Crack and The Bell their rendezvous, and their patronage made the extinction of the inns desirable, if not necessary..........

The Crack still provides, or very recently provided, pop and such like delicious drinks, but nothing stronger than water is supplied at The Morning Star. Oh, my countrymen, what a fall was there!"

The Morning Star

The remains of the Morning Star can still be seen as a pile of rubble on the north side of the A48, a few hundred yards east of the Pentre Meyrick cross roads. When the Tithe survey was undertaken in 1840, it was on land owned by Sam Howells and evidently a poor affair, the total tithe for cottage and land amounting to only 1s and 1d. The tenant was Richard Ellis, and his daughter Elizabeth was born at the pub in 1840. One earlier tenant family is recorded. In 1836, Llewellyn Lloyd was born to Mary; wife of David Lloyd listed as an Inn Keeper at the Morning Star.

The Morning Star is shown on the 1847 sketch of the village. William Lewis (Victualler) was the tenant at that time with his wife Catharine. Although Christopher Harry is shown as the publican tenant in 1851, the Morning Star subsequently reverted to use as a cottage and was owned by the newly arrived Homfray family. By the 1861 census, it is shown as being occupied by William David, a tailor, and his wife Mary. Thereafter, tenants of the cottage are recorded as labourers or gardeners.

Silurian recounts one short term resident in 1873, when George Gore visited his elder brother John Gore, who lived in the Morning Star and worked for Mr. Culverwell of Llwynhelig, who farmed Moorlands, Llwynhelig and Great House farms:

"The elder brother had arranged for work for his younger brother, and on Monday morning Mr. Culverwell set the new workman to plough with a pair of oxen. George Gore had never handled oxen, but it was not for an embryo mariner to think or say nay, so he tackled the job. One was a tractable obedient ox, which had previously worked well and long, but the other (Jimmy) was new to the work, and an unmitigated nuisance. He continually tried to bolt, pull sideways, or stood stock still. George knew a few Bible Christian hymns and tunes, and hummed them as well as he could, but the more he hummed, the more intractable the sturdy ox became. Perhaps he was not susceptible to music as most oxen were. The pantomime continued for eight or nine days and then Jimmy became docile and a good worker. The fact was, Gore had subdued the young ox in less than half the time it usually took men to subdue new charges, and the result was that the older ox was taken from him, and substituted by a young and untrained one, to work with Jimmy. Gore saw a repetition of the same pother, resented it and quitted for Corntown............"

The King's Head

Reference to the King's Head can be seen in the 1850 baptismal index, when William David (a publican at the King's Head, Penllyn) and Ann, his wife, attend the baptism of their daughter Catharine. Reference is also seen to the pub in the 1841 and 1851 (but not the 1861) census reports.

While the King's Head is not shown on the 1847 sketch map, we know it existed from the census data. No other facts about this pub are known, but local rumour has it that Crosswinds is the converted pub and the occupants advise that occasionally, there is a strong smell of hops in one of the front rooms.

The Victoria

William David (55) was landlord of The Victoria in 1841, with his wife Catharine (55) and five children Jane (20), Morgan (15), William (14), Ann (12) and William (3). It appears that ten years later, William (24) goes on to run the King's Head while his father became the landlord of the Fox and Hounds. There are no other known records of The Victoria.

New Inn

The only known reference to this pub is the 1841 census record with Elias Thomas (30) as publican, living with his wife Ann (30), children William (6), Edward (3), and Mary (1), and servant Betty John (12).

Pubs

The Travellers' Rest

This was a converted cottage just east of the Pentre Meyrick crossroads. In 1851, it was run as a pub by John Marchant, his wife Sarah and their four children. They had three visitors at the census date - two farm labourers and a blacksmith. In 1858, the tenant was Henry Jones, the pub standing on land owned by William Morgan. This would be where Cross Farm now stands. Though still a pub in 1861, and tenanted by Henry Jones, by 1871 it had reverted to residential use.

Of the above pubs, three, possibly more, were located in or around Pentre Meyrick. Yet in the twenty years prior to 1871, all three remaining Pentre Meyrick pubs had closed.

The principal reason for this decline appears to be a fall in the trade passing through Pentre Meyrick on the turnpike. On 18th June 1850, the first train travelled between Chepstow and Swansea on the new South Wales Railway. It sounded the death knell for the traditional coaching trade. Just 19 days later, on 5th July 1850, the 'Cardiff & Merthyr Guardian' reported, *"The Bristol & Swansea Mail Coaches cease to run from this day. The letter-bags will henceforth be conveyed by the South Wales Railway from Chepstow to Swansea."* Trade in Cowbridge, now bypassed by the railway, was subsequently observed to be "exceedingly dull".

This alone was probably sufficient to make the Pentre Meyrick pubs uneconomic, but the 1869 Wine and Beerhouse Act, which reintroduced stricter controls, would have served as a further deterrent to continuance of marginal businesses.

The Penlline Inn

In 1828, the 'Cambrian' newspaper makes reference to an Edward Morgan being highly commended in the award of premiums[1] to Penllyn residents, and his address is given as the Penlline Inn. This makes the Penlline Inn the earliest recorded pub, but its location remains a mystery. As an Inn it would presumably have provided stabling and accommodation so it may have had a Pentre Meyrick location serving the coaching trade. Alternatively, it may have been the village pub of Penllyn, given its name and the absence of a known pub in the top of the village at that time. Given the listing of an Edward Morgan as joint tenant of a cottage in the 1840 tithe on the current site of the Fox and Hounds, the cottage may well have been the thatched building that was replaced by the Fox and Hounds and to which Silurian refers.

The Surviving Pubs

The Barley Mow

Reference is first seen in the 1841 census when John John and his wife, Ann, ran the pub. This makes the Barley Mow the oldest surviving pub in Penllyn. In common with many pubs at the time, it was and remains a converted cottage, as can be seen from this picture when the Llewellyns were licensees in the early 20th century.

Figure 1. Barley Mow Inn, early 20th century, Landlord William Llewellyn, selling Hancocks beer

The Barley Mow, "the Barley", is a focus of village life in the Graig and continues to be known for its food, beer and as a meeting place for local societies and organisations.

Figure 2 Fox and Hounds Inn, early 20th century, also selling Hancocks beer

The Fox and Hounds

In 1841, there were cottage taverns on the turnpike road at Pentre Meyrick and one at the Graig, but there was no inn suitable for gentry or for the Hunt. When the Homfray family acquired the Penllyn Estate in 1846, this omission was rectified. Since a gentleman could not own a pub, a piece of Homfray land (which the 1940 Tithe had shown as a cottage tenanted by David Thomas and Edward Morgan) was leased to a Cardiff company who undertook to build a suitable inn. The Fox and Hounds appears on the 1847 sketch map and the first landlord was William David.

A succession of landlords, and landladies, followed, probably the best known of which was Margaret Williams, recorded at the pub in both the 1871 and 1881 censuses, the latter at the age of 78.

In 1926, an account by Silurian in the 'Glamorgan Gazette', once again suggests that there was a pub in Penllyn before the current Fox and Hounds, but which also carried that name.

"The old Fox and Hounds, a thatched building, has long been replaced by a substantial, well appointed building, which never knew the straight and genuine old Mrs Margaret Williams, nor her sheep-head one-hand clock, which never indicated the correct time, and which no-one but its owner could ever read, because when it indicated, for instance, a quarter to five, the correct time was 25 minutes past eleven. Some rascal, to whom the old lady refused a drink on trust, once stole one of the clock's weights, out of spite probably. Mrs Williams was sorely tried to find a substitute for the stolen weight. At last she attached tongs to the chain, and behold the old clock went!"

Margaret Williams reportedly died after a fall onto a sharp fender, on the eve of the first Penllyn Races, when she was nearly 90 years old.

After the Second World War, the name of the pub was changed to the Red Fox.

In the mid 1990's the pub was acquired by Peter Karrie, who sang the lead part in 'Phantom of the Opera' in London. In 2000, he decided to try to convert the pub to a private dwelling, which would have required planning permission for change of use. Local residents were extremely concerned at the loss of this historic village institution and, with support from CAMRA, campaigned successfully against its closure. The pub was subsequently sold to the Tomos Watkin Brewery but in March 2002, the assets of Tomos Watkin were sold off and Celtic Inns, acquired its licensed estate. The pub has recently been acquired by new owners.

In Praise of Beer

William Salmon, the centenarian, was in no doubt as to the benefits of beer: *"At Penlline he finds that the bracing air and the abundant outdoor exercise which he takes creates thirst which he is careful to quench with the bright healthy Maidenhead Ale to some of which he treats me. Well brewed ale, the extract of good malt and hops solely, he thought to be as healthy a drink as an Englishman could take. It is the product of good vegetable, purified by fermentation, contained but little alcohol and altogether he considered the moderate use of it much to be commended."* [2]

Acknowledgements and References:

- 1841-1901 Glamorgan census reports
- Slater's and Kelly's directories
- 'Glamorgan Gazette', Silurian's column 1926-1930
- Red Fox:
    - Residents' campaign letter
    - BBC report on closure
- Pers comm. Owner Crosswinds
- Baptismal index
- 'Stage Coaches in Wales', Herbert Williams
- 'Old Cowbridge', Lemuel J. Hopkins-Jones
- London Metropolitan Archives, Licensed Victualler Records
- 'Wild Wales', George Borrow
- Gwent Camra newsletter
- David Jones of Wallington diaries, Cardiff Library

1 Premiums were prizes of money or even pigs, awarded to villagers for the quality of their gardens or crops.

2 David Jones of Wallington diaries, extract courtesy of Cardiff Libraries and Information Services

Chapter 17

Folklore and Legend

This chapter draws on the work of David Jones and of Marie Trevelyan, as well as the recollections of some of the older residents of Penllyn.

PENLLYN

David Jones: We have transcribed below (∢) some of his notes on Penllyn folklore and tales, which he penned in 1882 (extracts courtesy of Cardiff Libraries and Information Services). His handwriting was not always clear and we have indicated (*) if the transcribed word is in doubt. The headings are those of the editor.

Marie Trevelyan was the pen name of Emma Mary Thomas, daughter of a Llantwit Major stonemason. She was born in 1853.

Feast Day Fights ∢

"Bechgin Penlline is a term specially applied to the young men of Penlline and is of very old standing. When the chief local amusements were those to be had at neighbouring fairs and mabsants[1] a fight between the boys ("bechgin") of rival parishes – and every parish had this absurd feeling of rivalry against every other parish near to it – was a common incident in the amusement. I myself can remember when it was part of the gossip of the neighbourhood to enquire after any well known mabsant had been held "and what fighting was there?" surprise being expressed if such an assemblage of the youth … had passed off quietly."

The Child and the Mule ∢

"In the early days of iron manufacture in the hills when of course production was on a small scale, the crude iron was sent down from Llangynwydd (?) to Aberthaw on the backs of mules. The route for this conveyance led through the village of Penlline. More than a hundred years ago (say in 1750) it was part of the traditions of the place that one of these laden animals had killed a child in the village who had chanced to stray across its path, by biting it. The mule in turn was killed by being loaded and loaded until its back broke for it is said that the stubbornness of the mule is shown in the obstinacy with which it will bear excessive weight put upon its back - and that it never bends beneath a load until it breaks down altogether."

As Generous as the Penllyn Cow ∢

"Under the head of parochial charities it has been noticed that a certain bequest of money for the use of the poor was all expended on one particular season of scarcity and was never replaced. There is a rather touching story of this period when in 1820 or thereabout was part of the household lore of the fine people of Penlline. A lady resident in the village (name now forgotten) had for some years provided a cow for the use of the poor to which anyone might go to and milk what they could. The Cow was kept on the "Green" (then a Common open to the use of the villagers for their geese, donkeys etc) and in this period of scarcity, when the distress in the village was very great, it mattered not at what time of the day or the night the starving people went to the Cow - she always gifted them enough milk for their most pressing wants. It was spoken of years afterwards by those who had passed through that season of stern privation as a thing which bordered if it did not quite touch the miraculous. This I had from one who well*

knew Penlline and its traditions from 1812 to 1820. The circumstances had occurred some years before that time, but there were many still living then who recollected it. One or two elderly persons connected with the village to whom I related the tradition – Mr Salmon being one – had not heard of it before."

Marie Trevelyan: *"When a supply of any kind appears to be inexhaustible, the people say, "It's like the Penlline Cow." A lady living at Penlline kept one of her cows especially and only for the sake of the poor. The cow was daily milked by those for whose benefit she was set apart. This animal grew venerable, and was regarded as almost sacred. The yield of milk was enormous, and at whatever time of the day or night she was milked, the supply never failed. In fact, the Penlline cow was regarded as a miraculous animal."*

The Corpse Candle ∢

"Whether Penlline has its haunted house or its haunted lane or cross roads I cannot say. If it has not it will be rather remarkable among Glamorganshire villages. I have not met with any story of the kind or I would put it upon record. The present is not the "golden age" of ghost stories and one has no great success in enquiring for them at present. Tales of the supernatural: the Canwyll Corph[2], the Caehyraeth[3], Death Warnings and so forth are more common.

Here is one of about the year 1740 of the "Canwyll Corph". It used to be told by my grandfather and the appearance was witnessed by himself. He was returning from Penlline one night and was threading his way down the narrow lane now done away with[4] and through into the park when he thought there was something or somebody following him. He looked around and saw a light as if a candle carried in the hand by somebody walking. Wondering who could be going along in that way at so strange an hour he got as quietly as he could in some place of concealment, behind a bush or something of that kind and waited until the person should pass him. That person came steadily along holding a naked light of some kind in his hand and he recognised the bearer as a young fellow of about his own age, a native of Penlline whom he knew well. The bearer of the light passed on silently at a steady walking pace in the direction of Llanfrynach[5], the light going up and down with the motion of the body. On the following Sunday my grandfather was again at Penlline and saw this young man in the afternoon at or near the chapel where he was engaged in keeping the score of a party of ball players who were I think having their game against the Chapelwall. The time of year must have been in the early part of November for the foddering of cattle had just begun; the young man met with an accident on the Monday while taking some hay out to fodder from the effects of which he died in a day or two, and was in his grave before another Sunday came round."

The Spectre Funeral

"Llanfrynach, from its loneliness, inclines those who have a belief in the supernatural to associate the weird and the awe-inspiring with it. Burials however take place there but rarely; and so notwithstanding its weirdness there is little danger seen even by the person who has the gift of seeing the supernatural should he or she spend the midnight hour in its approaches of seeing that which will harrow★ up the soul. Still it is possible it seems to have an adventure of an unexpected kind in Llanfrynach lane. A Penlline man (about 1836 I think) was making his way on a dark night across the Carrwks[6] and on reaching a narrow part of this lane found the way blocked up with horses and a large vehicle beside which he tried to pass. The whole affair was standing still; and as he pressed his way between the standing objects and the hedge he found that an accident had happened and that the body of the vehicle lay over and close upon the side of the hedge completely stopping his further progress. Wondering much what this could mean he put his shoulder to the displaced vehicle and lifted it up into its proper position. After which he went home as fast as he could. He had been assisting a spectre funeral out of a mishap! And as preshadowed had to assist the real one also out of like case. Shortly after this nocturnal adventure a funeral from a distance came to Llanfrynach; the lane was exceedingly rough and narrow and the hearse either broke one of its springs or fell over on its side, at the very spot where the man had to force his way by. More strange still the man happened on the day of the funeral to be working in a field near to the scene of the accident and was appealed to for help: he came, and had to lift up the body of the real hearse just as, some four nights before, he had put his shoulder to the phantom one."

The Banshee

"The Caehyraeth, of which a description may be read in 'The Vale of Glamorgan' was not of such frequent appearance as the Canwyll Corph. A hundred years or more ago a person was crossing the fields by the pathway which leads from the end of the "new road" towards Llanfrynach when the Caehyraeth passed by him with a sudden rush, uttering an unearthly shriek, and knocking him down flat on his face. It was all done in a moment. Nothing whatever was seen."

The Elm Tree and Big-Bellied Men

"One of the greatest natural curiosities in the parish is the gigantic elm tree in the farmyard at Trevychan[7]. It has been hollow far beyond the memory of man: but has a head of fine branches. A wager was made as far back as the year 1790 (or thereabout) that a large number of the stoutest men in Cowbridge should fit inside it and drink a stated number of gallons of beer also large. Cowbridge had then a goodly number of big-bellied men and great drinkers. The feat fitted admirably with the taste and humour of the time; the big men went up to Trevychan, squeezed themselves inside the tree and drank their fill of liquor to the admiration of many beholders. Tun-bellied Kayes was one of the party; Rowland Williams of the White Hart[8] also a big man, another; a Cooper (name forgotten) whose outside helping★ was immense, a third. The rest of the party I have often years ago heard traditionally named, but the rest of their names I

have forgotten. My impression is that the number was about twelve. In printed accounts of this elm and the capaciousness of its hollow I have seen it stated that 18 men once stood inside it; while Nicholson in the 'Cambrian Travellers Guide' places the number as high as 36. His exact words are these "On the farm of Captain Howell is an elm tree; it measures in circumference 28 feet. It is hollow and capable of containing 36 full grown persons. The entrance is similar to an ancient gothic doorway."
The tree was a really fine object as late as 1870 but when I passed in August 1881 it was a dreadful wreck. Its noble head had all disappeared and nothing remained but about ten feet of the shorn and hollow trunk. There was a little sign of life and that was all."

Winged Serpents ≺

"In ancient legends winged serpents are by no means uncommon. A curious pamphlet of about 1640 gives an account of one then existing (or the writer said) at a particular spot in Sussex. But what will be said of some such being natural as a snake with wings having been killed in Penlline woods as late as about the year 1836? It was one of the stories current in the neighbourhood in my childhood. What is more the daughter of the man who killed the reptile (a man named Bowen shepherd to Mr Ballard) was in my father's service and used to horrify me as a child with the "true and authentic" tale of its slaughter. In later years when I wished to discover what really had been killed I could learn nothing more than it was some reptile of uncommon form and size – which one person (who had heard of it) thought might be an overgrown lizard. It was killed upon a tree, and was said to be able to fly from one tree to another in the wood."*

Marie Trevelyan: *"The woods around Penllyne Castle, Glamorgan, had the reputation of being frequented by winged serpents, and these were the terror of old and young alike. An aged inhabitant of Penllyne, who died a few years ago, said that in his boyhood the winged serpents were described as very beautiful. They were coiled when in repose, and "looked as though they were covered with jewels of all sorts. Some of them had crests sparkling with all the colours of the rainbow." When disturbed, they glided swiftly, "sparkling all over," to their hiding places. When angry, they "flew over people's heads, with outspread wings bright and sometimes with eyes, too, like the feathers in a peacock's tail." He said it was "no old story," invented to "frighten children," but a real fact. His father and uncles had killed some of them, for they were "as bad as foxes for poultry." This old man attributed the extinction of winged serpents to the fact that they were "terrors in the farmyards and coverts."*

Figure 1. Penllyn Winged Serpent as interpreted by DRAGONS website[9]

Mari Lwyd (Grey Mare/Grey Mary)

Figure 2. Mari Lwyd (artist Nick Hawksworth)

Recollections

(A.P.) Yes we used to go carol singing and Mari Lwyd. **(H.G.)** I was scared stiff of the Horse's head. **(K.H.)** Do you know what that is Steve? **(S.W.)** No I don't know what that is. **(K.H.)** Please can we have an explanation of the Mari Lwyd for Steve. **(E.P.)** Well I know that they would dress up with a Horse's head and they would put a cloth, a white linen cloth over it. And they would decorate it with little bells and such. (Herbie starts singing the Mari Lwyd song). **(E.P.)** Now my wife's uncle until four years ago continued this tradition up in Llangynwyd, which is where my wife is from. And if you go to the pub, which is there now, there is a signpost outside, with my wife's uncle and the Mari Lwyd. It was an old grey horse and they would take it about and they would knock on the doors wherever they would go and sing outside, in rhyme, and ask for entry and for food and drink and whatever. And those inside the house must respond, and this is impromptu as they go along. And they rhyme and they sing and the tune would stay the same but the words can alter. And you have to best the guy inside until he runs out of words or verse and then you can get in and have your drink and whatever. And it is a very old tradition and it is still going on to this day up in Llangynwyd. **(K.H.)** And it happened here in Penllyn? **(N.J.)** Yes, they used to come around here. **(K.H.)** Was it a special day for Mari Lwyd? **(E.P.)** Yes at Christmas.

The horse's skull would be covered by a white sheet, with empty bottle ends for eyes, and decorated with ribbons and bells. A pole was attached to the head so that it could be lifted and moved and another stick attached to the lower jaw so that its mouth could move and bite. The person operating the Mari stood under the sheet and Trefor Owen[10] recounts: *"It was then carried about and the first intimation often received was the sight of this prowling monster peeping around into the room, or sometimes shewing its head by pushing it through an upstairs window. One case was recorded, by my mother, of a sudden death through fright of this. It almost always created a collapse of some and the scamper of others"*. After the rhyming competition and once admittance was gained, the Mari would pay particular attention to the women of the house, nudging, neighing, blowing and biting them. If admittance wasn't gained, it would bring bad luck to the household members and their crops.

Whatever the pagan origins of the Mari Lwyd, and its possible links to other wassailing and fertility customs, its heyday was in the 1860's[11] and the practice died out in Penllyn many years ago, possibly due to its association with drunkenness. To see the Mari Lwyd today, visit the Old House pub in Upper Llangynwyd at about 2pm on New Year's Day.

The White Lady

"Morgan Jenkins used to relate that, during the Civil War, there was a sortie from the Castle to try to get to St. Fagans and they had treasure with them. They got as far as the farm at Llwnhelig and were caught there. The wife of one of them, a white lady, is supposed to haunt the castle and if you see her you die. Apparently a footman did." (from Jean Dale's notes on Penllyn history)

Recollections

J.B. "Do you remember? Perhaps you wouldn't ... Eddie Collier, the American, he lived in the Graig, he was American mind, and he came in the pub one night and he said "Ye God", he said, "I was walking up" he said, "and I saw a lady, all dressed in white" and I looked at Eddie ... and he said "I actually stopped and asked how she was, and she just vanished."

Woodlands' Crying Child

"Morgan Jenkins said that, when living in Woodlands, they often heard a child crying and on asking round they were told a couple had lived there with a mentally handicapped child. They had to lock it in to go to work and it could be heard crying." (from Jean Dale's notes on Penllyn history)

1 Mabsant was a local saint's day celebration. The feast day for St. Brynach is 7th April.

2 Canwyll Corph was a Corpse candle, a light seen in connection with death, say where a fatal accident had occurred or was about to occur, or marking the route of a funeral.

3 Caehyraeth also Cyhiraeth or Cyhyraeth, which used to be a Celtic Goddess of streams but then became synonymous with a banshee, or unearthly cry, often associated with death or multiple deaths.

4 He is probably referring to the original route from the castle to the A48 highway, traces of which can still be seen, which was closed after the Homfray family acquired the castle.

5 This path was used to bear coffins from Penllyn for burial at Llanfrynach, the coffin stiles can still be seen.

6 Now shown as Corrwg on the Ordnance Survey map, an area south of the A48

7 Part of Llwnhelig Farm, per David Francis 'The Border Vale', now known as Dre-fechan

8 Landlord from 1788-1799, 'Old Inns and Alehouses of Cardiff', Cardiff Record Society

9 **www.colba.net/~tempest**

10 'Welsh Folk Customs', Trefor Owen, 1974

11 Per Emma Lyle, National Museum and Galleries Wales

Chapter 18

Leisure and Celebration

Leisure activities in Penllyn have never been the sole preserve of the gentry, even if not all could boast the spectacular setting enjoyed by the lawn tennis players in the photograph (Fig. 1). The Penllyn Lawn Tennis Club was set up in 1977 and two hard surface courts were laid out on the Winchfield. These facilities are still enjoyed today by the villagers and members from further afield. While the tennis club has thrived, other village organisations have formed and then disappeared as interests and enthusiasms have waxed and waned.

PENLLYN

Figure 1. Tennis on the castle lawns, 1934

Recollections

(A.P.) Well yes, there used to be a football team and they played in the field on Moorland Road, from the Village Hall. Remember, they used to have black and white squares – do you remember that Albert, the football team colours? **(A.N.)** No, I don't. **(A.P.)** You know Wendy Wright and Robbie Llewellyn, well that field there – that was the football field **(H.G.)** Behind where I lived. **(A.P.)** Yes, and they had black and white colours, because I remember running the line there and they used to have hockey on a Saturday and on Sunday at Pentre Meyrick.

(E.P.) So where did you play then? **(J.B.)** Well that was the drawback. We didn't have a good ground, so what we did, we used to play a lot of the games away in Cardiff and all round the place. But before the war Mr. Dunn, his sister Margaret was a hockey international and she had a hockey ground there in the field, next to the house, and it was halved off. I think Mr. Thomas or Davies who was in the farm before used to graze half. **(B.T.)** It would be Glyn, yes, Bill's father. **(J.B.)** And when the hockey was finished they would obviously have the field mowed and Mr. Dunn would make a lovely wicket square......... J. C. Clay played on there. I'm not sure if a Maurice Turnbull but I am sure J. C. Clay, because Mr. Thomas, Jack, he was a very good cricketer, Jack. **(B.T.)** You were all good cricketers.................**(J.B.)** And we had a game against Cowbridge and what they would do is send up a mixture of first and second teams.............. and we would be on the verge of beating Cowbridge and they would send down for some more players!

Figure 2. Research notes recalling Penllyn Football Club 1973-88, with other notes not football related!

Cricket, football and hockey teams have come and gone, but are sometimes reformed for events such as the Village Fete. Past cricket matches between Penllyn and the Graig, often very convivial events, were given extra spice by the need to avoid cowpats on the outfield. No such problem for football on the Winchfield, although the rivalry between the two halves of the village was such that trips to hospital for the injured players was sometimes the result. Even the village ladies formed a football team for the celebration of the Silver Wedding Jubilee of Queen Elizabeth II in 1977.

Figure 3. Ladies' Football Team, Silver Wedding Jubilee Fete, 1977

More recently, Boules matches have been played between teams from the Barley and the Fox, with far fewer injuries.

Figure 4. Boules, 2003, Barley Mow Car Park

In addition to Penllyn Lawn Tennis Club, many other organisations have played their part in village life.

Penllyn & District Women's Institute

On 20th October 1964, a group of fifty-one women met at the Village Hall, Penllyn to discuss the formation of a local W.I. It was decided that the Institute would be known as Penllyn & District in order to reflect the wide area represented, as evident in the addresses of the first members. They included Penllyn, Craig Penllyn, Pentre Meyrick and Cowbridge, and also Llangan, Llansannor, St. Mary Hill, Pencoed, Coychurch and Coity. Membership was open to women and girls of 15 years and above.

The first meeting of the new Institute took place on Tuesday 17th November 1964 at 7.30pm at what was then the Village Hall. Forty-eight members were enrolled, each paying a subscription of 5 shillings. It was agreed to hold monthly meetings, to take place on the third Tuesday of each month. This was, however, changed in 1967 to the first Tuesday of the month, which would conveniently coincide with the arrival of the County Letter, the monthly communication from the Glamorgan Federation of Women's Institutes to all the Institutes in the county, then numbering in excess of one hundred.

At the inaugural meeting a committee of 15 was chosen by secret ballot. Mrs. Joanna Cory of Penllyn Castle was elected President, Mrs. Joan Francis of Brynawel Farm, St. Mary Hill became Secretary and Mrs. Joan MacDonald of the Old School House, Penllyn was elected Treasurer. In the early days the meetings began with 'Jerusalem' and ended with 'The Queen' being sung, or occasionally, the Welsh National Anthem. It is not clear when these traditions died out. The programme for the first year of the Institute began with a demonstration of Christmas decorations for the December meeting and included the first fund-raising event, a Whist Drive, in February 1965.

The first outing for members of the Penllyn & District W.I. took place in July 1965 and was a mystery tour via Bridgend, the Bwlch and Rhigos mountains to Caerphilly, where a meal was taken at the Bluebell Hotel. It was suggested that the members should pay £1 for the tour and the supper, with any money left over to go to the Institute's fund. The sum of £3 10 shillings remained after all expenses were paid. In August 1965, Penllyn ladies entered the Co-operative class in the W.I. section of the Vale of Glamorgan Show and won first prize. They have entered that competition on thirty-two subsequent occasions and have won first prize seventeen times. Mrs. Cory donated this prize, now known as the Penllyn Cup, in 1969.

From March 1983, while the old Village Hall was being demolished and rebuilt, meetings were held at the Castle, at Church House, Penllyn, in the upper room of the Old Chapel, Craig Penllyn or the Village Hall in Treoes. The meetings resumed in the present Village Hall in February 1984. Meetings have been cancelled on just three occasions, all because of bad weather. In January 1979, cold weather caused burst pipes when the water pipes at the Village Hall froze. The snow that winter was above head height in the Graig. Snow also caused closure in February 1966 and January 1985. In the past, the Penllyn and District W.I. used to hold carol services in various local churches, most often in Penllyn. The service had to be cancelled December 1975 during the power crisis, when heating was not allowed in public places.

It has been said that those who tread the corridors of power at Westminster and in Whitehall tremble when the massed forces of the National Federation of Women's Institutes take up a cause, and over the years the Institute at Penllyn has played its part. Each May, the members discuss various resolutions and send a delegate to represent their views at the annual National General Meeting on such topics as toxic waste disposal, genetically modified food, child care services, domestic violence, housing on brown field sites and human rights issues.

Penllyn and District W.I. members have also over the last three and a half decades taken an active interest in several local issues, most often on safety and environmental concerns. They have drawn the attention of the appropriate authorities to what used to be a dangerous turning from the A48 to Penllyn, to the speed of traffic on the road past Llangan School and have pressed for better and safer transport for school children. They have also been actively involved in local environmental matters. They have encouraged the County Council to clean up the corner near the Barley Mow public house, prevented the development of housing on the Parish field, demanded the removal of abandoned cars from Ruthin Common and supported the preservation of the red telephone kiosk outside the Old Post Office in Penllyn.

Other activities during the lifetime of the Penllyn and District W.I. include various fund-raising occasions in addition to the popular Whist Drives. Pancake Races, Christmas Fayres, a St. David's Day Supper and Line Dancing have all added to their own funds. Members have also individually and collectively supported various charities financially and by personal effort. They have supported the W.R.V.S. work at Hensol Hospital, a Children's Renal Unit at Cardiff Royal Infirmary and the Macmillan Nurses organisation, amongst others. Members have also been involved in house-to-house collections for various charities.

Over the years, members have taken part in debates, quizzes, choirs, various entertainment programs, darts and table tennis matches, skittles, tenpin bowling and many other competitions.

In November 1999, Penllyn and District W.I. celebrated its 35th Anniversary with a party to which founder members; other past members and representatives from the Glamorgan Federation and from other Institutes in the West Vale Group were invited.

Penllyn Table Tennis Club

It was Jane Griggs, a resident of Craig Penllyn, who suggested forming a table tennis club in 1974. During a chance meeting with Wendy Wright, Jane asked if she thought people would be interested in playing table tennis in the small Village Hall. They duly went around the village knocking on every single door to see how many people would be interested. The second house they called at belonged to Mr. & Mrs. Howlett who were then in their 80's. This certainly raised a laugh (even though 3 of the current members of the club are ladies well into their 80's) but this didn't deter them and they carried on raising enough interest to start a Table Tennis Club. Jane was the only person who knew the rules and regulations and how to play table tennis, but through her encouragement, an active club developed. In time, other residents used to come along for the social evening to play games and cards, and it was through this that life seemed to generate in the hall once more.

It was not all plain sailing. Having eventually purchased a table, the funds were pretty low so some members used to pick up all the papers that had been left out for the dustmen and collect them for recycling. They were stored in the garage of one of the members until someone came to collect them and the small amount of money raised helped the Table Tennis Club and also the Hall Fund.

Jane Griggs recalls the first tournament held in the club when both she and Pat Smith played together. As it was supposed to be a mixed doubles tournament the other members insisted that Jane wore a false moustache for the game. Cups and trophies were presented to the winners, although not the elaborate ones available today. With funds stretched to the limit, the cups were cheap eggcups covered with tinfoil. In fact, one of the members still has a wooden vase inscribed with Dymo-tape 'P.T.T.C Ladies Singles 1975'.

Playing in the old village hall was a little hazardous for the more active members who often ended up running into the walls, which were so thin, that members could have gone flying through the wooden walls of the hall.

The standard of play improved to such an extent that members felt confident enough to enter a League. To meet the requirements of the League a new table and strip lighting were needed. A kind donation by Konrad Meier ensured that Penllyn T.T.C entered the Cardiff and District Table Tennis League for the season 1980-1981 and in the first season finished a commendable 7th place in Division 5, where they obtained 101 points.

Figure 5. Official Table Tennis League Handbook, 1981-82

One away match held in Cardiff was abandoned half way through, when a security watchman came in to tell the teams that it was snowing very heavily and that several roads were closed. The roads through Cardiff itself were quite clear, but when travelling up Tumble Hill on the way out of Cardiff, the car driven by Geoff Payne, one of the team members, veered across the road. Luckily, instead of going through the hedge he ended up sliding back down the hill. Never has there been so much silence in a car following a match. A second attempt was made but it wasn't until the members reached Penllyn and tried to get out of the car that they realised how much it had been snowing. It came half way up their legs!

Although several club members played league games for Penllyn T.T.C, the main stalwarts of the team were Geoff Payne, David Wright, Alun Evans and Chris Smith.

The female members of the Penllyn T.T.C also felt the standard of table tennis had reached a level that enabled them to take part in the Women's Institute Table Tennis Tournaments. They have travelled to Sophia Gardens in Cardiff, to Carmarthen and even to Aberystwyth, returning with trophies and certificates for winning both the singles and the doubles tournaments.

Membership has fluctuated over the years. Older members have moved from the village but thankfully new members have joined this thriving club. The Penllyn T.T.C is the oldest surviving club in the village and as the proud owners of two table tennis tables it could certainly cater for even more members, all due to that chance meeting all those years ago.

Badminton

Not all organisations survive. The minutes of the inaugural meeting of the (now defunct) Badminton Club stated that it would commence activities on 9th February 1984, this being a Thursday night and one of only two nights during the week when the Village hall was available. The committee was Blanche Smith (Treasurer), Monica Munson (Chair) and Pat Smith (Secretary).

Graig and Penllyn Residents Association

The Association was formed in 1986 in response to what many villagers considered unacceptable planning proposals. Over the years it has maintained a watching brief over the buildings and natural environment of the parish, raising funds for maintenance and improvements via a wide range of social activities. The committee are elected annually and meet quarterly.

Figure 6. Flower Festival entries in Village Hall, 2004

Figure 7. Spirited rendition of Mustang Sally by villager Steve Madeley at a fund raising social event

Figure 8. Residents Spring Clean, 2005

Figure 9. One of the more challenging tasks of recent years was the refurbishment and enhancement of the children's play area in the Winchfield, finally completed in October 2003

Village Hall Committee

The Village Hall is an integral part of village life and the current hall is the second to occupy the site, its predecessor dating back to at least 1912. At that time there was no Church Hall for social events as a counter attraction to the village pub in an age when temperance was a major social issue. Nor was there a place for the Parish Council to meet when the new School Board in Bridgend objected to the traditional use of the Village Schoolroom. The new hall, or village reading room, was a gift of the Homfray family and it was the custom for the daily papers delivered to the Castle to be taken the following day to the reading room. Many local clubs took advantage of the new facility, a Sunday School was arranged and the Parish Council had their regular meetings there.

The minutes of the Penllyn Men's Club for 1928 and 1929 show that members were charged 1/- per month and they used the reading room on Monday, Thursday and Friday nights. The Red Cross Society met every Tuesday and the Women's Club every Wednesday. The Men's Club provided fire and light and charged the Women's Club and Red Cross Society 6d a night towards the cost of fuel, while dance organisers had to pay 1/-. Another source of income was takings from the air rifle box. Residents can still remember Johnny Thomas, a crack shot from Pentre Meyrick, lying on his back on a trestle table shooting targets with the air rifle. Expenditure at the hall was mainly on coal, mantles, cleaning and petrol but on 18th October 1929 a Whist Drive and Dance was held *"in view of the fact that the amusements of the room were very few"*. The proceeds were to be used to purchase a Table Skittle game. The dance was evidently successful for, on 1st November 1929, B. S. Bird & Co. of Cowbridge supplied the Club with a bagatelle board for £6 10/- and Table Skittles for £1 15/-. The hall also had a piano, used by Billy Taylor and his trio at dances. These were popular affairs and, despite the temperance movement, the hall was not strictly alcohol free, for flagons would be readily available outside the back of the hall.

Maintenance of the structure appears to have been by the Castle estate but by the 1960's the fabric had deteriorated. In 1974, the Homfray family offered to replace the hall and this was erected in 1983 using steel and timber. Responsibility for running the hall passed to the village through an elected committee responsible to nominated trustees, and this continues today. The hall is now used regularly for Table Tennis and Whist and remains popular for meetings and social functions.

Figure 10. Village Hall, 2004

Major Celebrations

From time to time major local, national, or even global events were recognised by the community and, for a short while, village life would be put on hold while everyone joined in the celebrations. The following selection of photographs records some of these events:

Figure 11. Penllyn Carnival to celebrate the Silver Jubilee of King George V, 1934

Recollections

(J.B.) We were talking about Ernie and Ernie was the drummer in the village band, the Top and Bottom. **(E.P)** Right, so there was a village band. They played in the hall did they? **(J.B.)** No, no, no. This was for the King George VI father's Jubilee. And the top had a band and the bottom had a band. And the bottom had a goat. But our band was the best musically, you know. Anyway, in the park, I think it was perhaps the Colonel, but he said the bottom band was the better of the two. And old Fred Dunn said, "Hey, hold on", he said "It may have a goat, but ours is the best musically" So how they settled it, they had to sing a song. Somebody had to sing and my mother, she crawled under the wagon because my father said "I'll sing". He'd had a drink as well, and he got up and sang 'Oh for the Wings of a Dove'. He had a nice voice, you know. So, there was a compromise and I think it was a draw.

Figure 12. The Graig (or bottom) band celebrating the Coronation of King George VI, 1937

Figure 13. Carnival to celebrate the Coronation of King George VI, 1937

Figure 14. Golden Wedding celebrations 1939, L-R, Colonel Homfray, Blanche Homfray, Lord Dunraven

Figure 15. Children dancing round the maypole on the Winchfield, Silver Jubilee Queen Elizabeth II, 1977

STOUTS

Figure 16. Procession through Cowbridge to mark the end of World War II

Recollections, re end of war celebrations

(A.P.) Well we did. We had a carnival didn't we? There were several carnivals that we had and of course there were the Jubilee and the Coronation ones. I have got some photographs. I can hear Nancy and Betty talking about the time when we all met with Arthur Llewellyn of Great House and what we did was we had these tractors and trailers and people rode on them and we went all the way to Cowbridge and we stopped at the Station entrance and we all had photographs taken and then we went around to Aberthin and back up through the Village.

Chapter 19

The Parish Field and Coed y Graig

The Parish Field and Coed y Graig are situated at the northern end of the carboniferous limestone ridge that underlies Penllyn and Craig Penllyn. Whilst the field slopes gently southwest to the stile, and moderately west to Cae Rhedyn, Coed y Graig has steep, mainly north facing slopes. The field and Coed y Graig form a candidate SINC (Site of Importance for Nature Conservation) and are part of the Thaw Valley Special Landscape Area.

Figure 1. Parish Field, July 2003, with display of Common Knapweed (Centaurea nigra)

The field's average ph is around 6, weakly acid despite the underlying carboniferous limestone. The west slope appears more oligotrophic (nutrient poor). Nutrient rich areas are seen along the east hedge, the lower hollow right of the path, the sacrificial compost areas and by the south hedge east of the stile.

Banks, Hollows and Borrow Pits

The field exhibits a number of apparently man-made features. There are ditches and hollows adjoining the east and southeast boundaries, which are apparently associated with the hedge banks and boundary walls. The east hedge bank appears to have been constructed of earth and then "clothed" with a stone layer. The southeast boundary, associated with the site of a ruined cottage, was made of stone with lime mortar, apparently using the field stone immediately adjacent, leaving a depression of some four feet in places. The west boundary exhibits a small quarry, possibly a borrow pit associated with the construction of a house on Cae Rhedyn. East of the public footpath in the field are two depressions which do not appear to bear an obvious relationship with the boundaries. A suggestion that these were Home Guard look out posts has been rebutted by local knowledge. Another theory, still current, is that these were test pits for lead or spar, both having been mined locally.

The Parish Field and Coed y Graig

History and Land Use

Local clearance of woodland for pasture has been occurring for over several thousand years, and we cannot say when the Parish Field was first cleared, though the composition of plant communities suggests it has been pasture for many years. Our first certain knowledge about the Parish Field occurs in 1839, when the tithe map shows it as part of field 28, which had a total area of 37 acres, 1 rood and 17 perches, was part of the Commons and used as pasture. This map, though inaccurately drawn in parts, clearly shows that Coed y Graig was also part of the same field 28, implying that the wood was not present at the time.

It is here that plant evidence and map evidence appear to differ. Coed y Graig has several plants in abundance that are recognised as ancient woodland indicator species[1] including dog's mercury, bluebell, pignut, ramsons, wood anemone and yellow archangel. Coed y Graig also exhibits some signs of ancient coppicing, particularly one sweet chestnut tree that appears several hundred years old. It is possible that Coed y Graig, marginal land at best with its steep north facing slope, was one of the last areas to be cleared, or was only partially cleared, and was one of the first areas to be replanted with trees or allowed to regenerate naturally as woodland. The east hedgerow of the Parish Field has dog's mercury and another ancient woodland indicator, the curious moschatel plant, or town hall clock, so called because its flowers face in four directions like a public clock face.

In 1860, the 20 acre area now occupied by Coed y Graig was split into 13 strips and allocated to cottars at the Graig, but at some point thereafter, the Homfray family acquired the strips of land and woodland use was re-established. In the 1960's, aerial photographs show a mature wood being felled with only small areas of trees remaining. The wood nowadays comprises mostly trees planted after that felling, though the diverse understorey of woodland plants has survived well.

After the enclosures, the Parish Field, numbered field 14c, totalled just four acres. With nearly all 178 acres of the remaining Commons enclosed, provision had to be made for the exercise and enjoyment of the poor of the parish. The Parish Field was allocated for this use and administered by the Churchwardens and Overseer for the poor.

There was also provision for allotment gardens for the poor and an area of just under one acre was allocated. Shortly after the end of the Second World War, with the approval of the Charity Commissioners, the allotment gardens were sold to Herbert R. Thomas. The extent of these allotments can be seen today by hedge banks and tree lines. All other evidence is that the remaining 3.095

acres of the field remained as pasture. It is worth noting the 1930 condition of the "allotments" sold to Herbert R. Thomas. This land is now entirely wooded through natural succession. The grassland plant community has been replaced with a woodland understorey, though not of the diversity seen in Coed y Graig.

Figure 2. Parish Field, 1930, with Coed y Graig in background and the rectangular outlines of the allotments to the left

Before the Second World War, the field was let to Albert Edwards, who used to graze his cows there. They were milked in a small shed in the quarry/ borrow pit, evidence for which can be seen by a ring affixed to the wall of the quarry and the remains of parts of a concrete floor. Mr. Edwards used to get the local village boys to watch the cows as they grazed on the common land[2] of the Rhiw up towards Cymle, and reward them with whistles cut from plant stems.

One resident recalls: *"It has been rented out to various farmers or smallholders. The first person that I can remember renting it was Albert Edwards. He used to rent it for £3.00 a year. I remember several people renting the field, David Thomas – The Vistla, Alan Williams, he had it for a time and Suzanne Morris, the lady who rides the big white horse."*

In 1974, the charitable nature of the field was formalised in a deed *"In the matter of the Charity for Allotments for the Labouring Poor, in the Ancient Parish of Penlline, in the County of Glamorgan, comprised in an enclosure award of the 1st March 1860"*. Trustees to the Charity were the Parish Council of Penllyn (now Penllyn Community Council). The deed noted that the field was let to Mrs. Serena Homfray for the sum of £10 pa and she used the field for horse grazing.

Subsequently, the field/allotments were the subject of a planning application for residential development, which was turned down. A further proposal, to apply fertiliser to the field to improve the grazing, was also rejected. If any of these proposals had been successful, the biodiversity of the field would have been damaged irreparably.

The Parish Field and Coed y Graig

Grazing by horses ceased in approximately 1990, at which point the land was let on several short-term leases to the Residents Association who arranged for the flatter areas of the field to be cut. However, even in 1990 the scrub had encroached on the grassland and, despite some scrub cutting, the area occupied by scrub and succession woodland continued to increase.

By 2002, the lease to the Residents had expired and neither the field nor the hedges had been cut since 1999. One Vale naturalist noted in 2001 that the *"field (is) full of flowers but needs management/mowing"*. Refusal by a gas supplier to deliver Liquid Petroleum Gas to the Rhiw in August 2002, as a result of the condition of the hedges, brought the unsatisfactory state of the field to the attention of both the Residents Association and Penllyn Community Council.

A new lease was granted to the Residents Association by Penllyn Community Council and, in September 2002, a programme of restoration work commenced with the following objective *"to preserve the Parish Field as a species rich (primarily grassland) habitat for community and local educational use."*

Management

Management of the Field was divided into remedial and maintenance:

Remedial management, which commenced in Autumn 2002 and is now complete, included:

- Removal of scrub and immature trees to encourage natural regeneration of grassland
- Removal or mitigation of field hazards:
  - Removal of barbed wire, glass, litter, metal and asbestos sheets
  - Felling of diseased trees if considered dangerous
  - Erection of quarry fencing
  - Repair of boundaries
- During this period biodiversity was enhanced by new micro habitats:
  - Dry stone wall on south boundary
  - Deadwood from cut trees and scrub cutting (stacked to minimize grassland lost)

Maintenance management, which includes:

- Encouragement of biodiversity by retention of scrub in thickets, boundaries and windbreaks
- Annual cut of grass to prevent further scrub encroachment and dominance by aggressive species. The timing of the cut, in early autumn, recognises the late flowering Knapweed and Devil's Bit Scabious, and allows them to set seed.

- Removal of leavings to prevent litter build up and nutrient enhancement. The leavings are then composted in sacrificial compost areas.
- Annual cut of roadside hedge
- Control by topping, of bracken, creeping thistle and rosebay willowherb

In winter 2003, the bulk of the remedial management was completed, leaving the field with an increased proportion of grassland but with a mosaic of scrub retained on the west slope. The intent was to allow natural grassland colonisation of the areas cleared of scrub, assisted by the presence of the seed bank in the adjacent established grassland.

The remedial management of the field was a partnership between villagers, other individual volunteers and bodies such as Pencoed College, Glamorgan Heritage Coast Project and Penarth Explorer Scouts. Financial support was provided by Environment Wales, an initiative of Wales Assembly Government.

Figure 3 Residents in characteristically happy mood, 2004, dedicating a new green oak bench in the field to Norman Whitehouse, who lived at White Cottage. The inscription on the bench reads: *"When the oak is felled the forest echoes with its fall, but a hundred acorns are sown silently by an unnoticed breeze"*

Biodiversity

The Parish Field comprises largely species-rich unimproved grassland. Since the Second World War, some 98% of the UK's lowland species-rich grassland has been lost as a result of development, "improvement" by fertilising or reseeding with Italian Ryegrass, conversion to arable land or, when none of the above are suitable, by being abandoned. Such grassland is a semi-natural habitat, as lowland grassland does not normally occur without intervention by cutting or grazing. These interventions stop the grassland reverting to scrub and then on to climax woodland.

Figure 4. Comma butterfly nectaring on Hemp Agrimony

The dry mesotrophic (of intermediate fertility) grassland of the Parish Field is mainly MG5 (Centaurea nigra-Cynosurus cristatus) with sub communities of MG5a (Lathyrus pratensis), MG5b (Galium verum)[3] and MG5c (Danthonia decumbens). It also has a small amount of MG1 (Arrhenatherum elatius) grassland as well as scrub and bracken. As the MG5 grassland community is mainly confined to the British Isles, the UK has special responsibility for its conservation.

Figure 5. Adder's Tongue Fern

Countryside Council for Wales Survey

The Countryside Council for Wales surveyed the field in 1993 as part of its lowland grassland survey. It reported: *"Graig Penllyn supports a small total area of good quality MG5, an uncommon grassland community, which shows little sign of agricultural improvement. Three sub communities are represented (MG5 a, b and c) with some interesting transitions and zonations between them. This is an unusual combination and MG5b is particularly restricted in Wales. The site also has some species interest and is considered to be of moderate to high conservation value for its grassland vegetation overall."*

In the past few years, several uncommon species have been recorded here, including the carder bumblebees, *Bombus humilis* and *Bombus muscorum*. The unusual Adder's

Tongue fern can be seen in April, while a month later the field has thousands of cowslips. The field supports plentiful invertebrate and small mammal populations in the summer that provide food for predators such as slow worms, grass snakes, owls, foxes and badgers.

Heritage

The Parish Field and Coed y Graig are part of Penllyn's heritage and a living link with past agricultural practices. They are as significant as Penllyn's built heritage and should be recognised accordingly. In this context it was much appreciated by the residents when the restoration project won a series of awards namely; Best Kept Village, Village Feature; The Campaign for the Preservation of Rural Wales Award and Vale of Glamorgan Biodiversity Award (overall winner 2005).

More importantly, the field and woodland include irreplaceable local genetic material and a wealth of flora and fauna. They provide a heady mix of floral displays and of vistas across the Vale, including a distant view of the sea through the valley of the Ogmore River and a panoramic view of the Thaw Valley from the footpath[4] on Coed y Graig.

---

1 Certain plant species, usually those that spread relatively slowly by vegetative means, are known to be either entirely restricted to, or only rarely found outside, ancient woodlands. These are known as ancient woodland indicator species. Where a number of these species are found together, there is a high likelihood that the wood in which they occur is of ancient origin (source, Heritage Woodlands).

2 The Rhiw's common land, previously pasture, has now reverted to woodland. It is now the sole remaining common land in the parish.

3 MG5b grassland is uncommon in Wales. This field accounts for circa 1½ % of the Wales total.

4 Footpath 16. The wood and field are featured in two Valeways walks: Castle, Court and Wells; and Craig Penllyn and Penllyn, which can be found on the website **www.valeways.org.uk**

Chapter 20

Images

Penllyn (the top of the village)

This southern end of the village (villagers consider Penllyn and the Graig to be part of the same village, not two separate villages) has its origins in the establishment of the castle, though most buildings are of far more recent construction.

PENLLYN

1. Penllyn Village Street.
Early 20th century postcard of the pre-tarmac village street. Houses are **Pear Tree Cottage** (left), **Forrest Cottage** (centre) and **The Meads** (right).

2. Avenue of trees.

These trees, 106 in total, lined the new road from Penllyn to the A48 and presumably, were the ones planted by John Homfray c1846. In April 1963, the Minister of Housing and Local Government revoked a Glamorgan County Council tree preservation order. The trees were considered to be dangerous and all were felled.

3. Crossroads.
1920, looking east with "Penllyne Farm" (now **Great House**) to immediate left, castle drive ahead, flanked by **St. John the Evangelist Church** and **The Lodge**, village road to left and new road to right.

4. War memorial.
1921, erected in memory of the fallen in the Great War.

5. First Floor Hall House.
These are the remains of a T-shaped 14th century First Floor Hall House, surviving only as a full height cross wall with fireplace, foundations and first floor doorway. The ground floor would probably have been the kitchen area with the living space on the first floor. This was the kind of house occupied by the gentry between the 12th and 16th century. A large collection of pottery and building ceramics was found in the adjacent garden, which on examination indicated occupation between the 14th and 16th century, confirmed by the find of a long-cross penny of 1307-9.

6. The Lodge.

Pre 1846 a priest's house and glebe garden were on this site. The priest's house was demolished and the stone used for the boundary walls. The lodge was then built, but on a different alignment, by the Homfrays. Note the carving of the otter above the door.

7. Keeper's Lodge.

This lodge house would have been built c1860 and also bears the carving of the otter, though the fletching on the shaft is no longer clear.

8. Otter. Appearing on both **The Lodge** and **Keeper's Lodge**, the otter was the crest to the Homfray coat of arms, with the motto "Vulneratur non vincintur" or " Wounded but not vanquished."

9. Chapel House.

This property probably predates Miss Gwinnett, but has been extensively altered with addition of stables to the rear, contemporary with the castle rebuild around 1800. It was previously the estate coachman's house.

10. Great House.

Early 20th century. This is a 17th century house which once had extensive farm buildings and orchards around. Documentary evidence is sparse but from 1800 it appears to be owned by Nicholl of Cowbridge but it was always rented or leased, usually to the incumbent of the church (Llanfrynach and the chapel of ease, now St. John the Evangelist). There was never a parsonage and the living was always split between three families in turn. The third storey of the house appears a later addition, the previous roofline visible when last re-rendered. Note the number of occupants of Great House and also the iron railings, now outside Great House Farm.

11. Great House Farm.

This house is the renovated barn (photo pre-renovation) of the original farmhouse (**Great House**) next door to the right. In living memory it saw use as a bakery and the loft space used as accommodation by itinerant workers at harvest. To the front of the house is a pond, actually a large paved water trough.

12. Milking Shed for Great House Farm. Prior to residential conversion, now renamed **The Old Mill**.

13. Post Office/Stores.
Early 20th century. Now **Forrest Cottage**, which, before expansion, still found room to host both the village stores and the post office.

14. Old Post Office:
14.1. Exterior. House expanded in 2005, this was the last Post Office and stores in Penllyn.

14.2. Interior.
Many houses in the parish retain original features such as large fireplaces, bread ovens and stone staircases.

15. Barns and milking shed.
Prior to the residential development of 9 houses at **The Meadows**.

16. Village Farm.
The whitewashed gable wall of Village Farm retains its 16/17th century form and structure. Its stonework and main timbers are original and it retains its cistern.

17. Court Farm with **The Old Byre** to rear and **The Old Machine Shop** to the left. Court Farm was probably the home farm of Penllyne Court. It is now situated on the west of the Village Street but once spread either side, and the highway passed through the farmyard with a stream from the wells alongside. Now the road realigned, the stream culverted, and the old barns reused for boundary walling, it has become a road for commuting car traffic but the evidence remains for the discerning eye.

Rosevine and the missing houses

To the east of Court Farm is the dense woodland (Coed-y-Parc), which hides the ruins of at least two cottages, a farm (Blaydon Lodge) and a bridleway. To west and east are two main parish roads, Groesel road and Heol Langdon, which once formed a main cross roads. They show what all parish roads were like 200 years ago in the Vale. Between 1900 and 1960 the parish appears to have lost many original dwellings, which is why it now appears as two ends with countryside in between. The last cottage, 'Rosevine', was rescued and now appears as a modern house. Opposite is the old farm Vistla (Pen-fistla) one of whose barns was converted into residential accommodation in 2005. Originally the bridle path went through Vistla and continued down the slope into the Thaw Valley to Llansannor and Llanharry by Stanby road. This is probably part of the packhorse trail mentioned by David Jones of Wallington, which took iron and lead ores to the coast at Colhugh or the Leys.

18. Heol Langdon, 2005. One of the old parish roads, now a bridleway.

19. Rosevine Cottage 1969, pre renovation:

19.1. Exterior. The roof level of Rosevine was raised during renovation, and an extension was added to the western end of the house. All the first floor level and extension was carried out in brick creating a patchwork wall of stone and brick, then smooth-rendered. This has been replaced recently by roughcast render more in keeping with local construction.

19.2. Interior.

Unfortunately, the majority of the original features were removed during the refurbishment but the original stone built Tŷ Bach (Little House or outdoor toilet) pigsty and corrugated Andersen Shelter still remain in the garden.

Images

The Graig (the bottom of the village)

As late as 1937, Craig Penllyn, "the Graig", did not have tarmac surfaced roads. Much of the land north of Court Farm was originally Common land, which, together with the moors, was enclosed in 1860. Of the 70 or so households comprising Penllyn at this date, 28 were crofts worth less than £15 and most of these were in the Graig. Some of these crofts would have originated as tiny cottages erected overnight on common land and so received tenure under the 'tŷ-unnos' tradition[1]. Many of the tenants relied on charitable distribution of food and coal from the Salmon family and later the Clarendon and Homfray families right up to the inter-war years. The restriction of the 1947 Town and Country Planning Act on new building in the countryside gradually created a market for these poor dwellings, which with permission for modernisation or development could often yield a good profit. Together with infill development of large gardens, it created the area of housing which is the Graig today.

20. Winchfield, 1930.

This flat grazing land appears to have been excluded from the Common Land and was retained for grazing rental until the Homfray family purchased it from Lord Dunraven and leased it to the Parish. In 2005 the Homfray family trusts gifted the land to The Winchfield Recreational Charity, a new charity set up by Penllyn Community Council to receive the land and use it for the benefit of the residents of the Parish. The Winchfield is named after the winch, part of the mechanism of the deep well dug near the southern boundary, which was sealed off by Sam Dobbs when piped water reached the Graig.

---

1 Tŷ Unnos literally means a 'One Night House'. People believed that if you built a house overnight on common land, and if smoke rose from its roof at dawn, you could claim the house and surrounding land to the distance of a stone's throw. These structures were flimsy in their construction, being made of turf and soil, but if the house was allowed to remain, a more permanent building would be erected later on the same site, and a piece of untamed land would become a smallholding. (source BBC Wales history)

21. Outbuildings at Winchfield Farm (now Winchfield House) and the David family c1915.

Robert Edward David (who built Winchfield House in 1906) is at the wheel of the car and his wife, Mary Ann, is far left. Their daughter, Gwyneth May, is the young girl at the back. Mary's brother is sat next to Robert David, his wife stands behind the car and their son is sat in the back. Robert and his wife were featured in the 'Observer, Leader & Free Press' in 1952, each then being 87. In his later years he moved to 111 Cowbridge Road, Bridgend, but while at Penllyn he was "at one and the same time the clerk and attendance officer to the Penllyne School Board, an assessor and collector of Land Tax, an assistant overseer, a deacon, treasurer and organist at the Presbyterian Chapel".

22. Cymle.

Behind **High Lanterns** is the stone dwelling Kimred (1799), Cimle (1831), Cymtha (1847), Kymdu (1881), Cymle (1919), a sub-Medieval Glamorgan Cottage probably from 1550/1600. Its status in this part of the village suggests it could have been built by the Lord of the Manor to house the village reeve. Much of the original form of the building remains. To judge from the Tithe map, in its original form it would be set in the centre of a large yard with pens for geese and plots of vegetables around.

23. Merida (top left in above photo) circa 1930.
Now a private residence, it was previously used as the chapel vestry and as a place of rest. **Quedgeley** (middle). A tiny cottage, originally with no name, which underwent many changes including use as a lodging for itinerant preachers with outhouse used as a chapel mortuary. This was before renovation and extension to form the modern dwelling. **Tŷ Fry pond** (foreground). The young boy is Anthony Powell, whose father Jack Powell can be seen outside **Tŷ Canol** in the chapter on mining. **Tŷ Fry** was a 16th century cruck-framed longhouse opposite the **Barley Mow** and is just visible in the aerial photo on the inner cover. **Tŷ Fry** burned down in the 1970's, the remains were demolished, the pond was filled in and it now forms the car park for the **Barley Mow**.

24. Rhyd Cottage, 1930, (in foreground).
One of the few remaining survivors of village redevelopment and infilling. **Rose Cottage** (in background). This cottage was demolished circa 1971 and two new properties, **Ashfield** and **Hilltop**, erected in 1973. On the boundary of **Hilltop** and **Tanglewood**, remains of an old rubbish dump yielded some crockery, rifle shell casings, candleholders and a chamber pot! The **Parish Field** (with **Coed y Graig** behind) can be seen upper left.

25. Copse Edge, 1962, middle top in photo.
This property was used as the Graig's Post Office and the steps opposite (now the "Dolly Steps", previously "the Alley") gave access from the village road adjacent to Winchfield. **Rhyd Cottage** can again be seen to the left, while **Timberscombe** is middle right, and the council houses (**Half Way Tree** and **No. 1**) are far right.

26. Archway Cottage, 1963**,** now renamed **Argoed.**

27. Craig House, 1961 photo prior to construction of **Craigie Lea** and **Woodview. White Cottage** (pre renovation) is just visible to rear.

28. Salmon's Wood, example of cruck frame construction. Where the modern housing known as Salmon's Wood now exists, there used to be a cruck framed old cottage named **Celynen-chwith** (1877) previously Cymtha Wyth (1847). We think Manoah David may have lived here in the 19th century but cannot be sure. The last resident, Moses Bassett was known as 'the poorest man in the parish' who, in the 1914/18 war was given permission by the Parish Council to cultivate the roadside verges with potatoes.

29. Ham Farm:

29.1. Ham Farmhouse (left) and outbuildings 1968. The outbuildings were later converted into separate residential accommodation. **Ham Farm** is located on the river terraces of the Thaw and is overlooked by the north slopes of Coed y Graig

29.2. Ham Farm Barn (now Is Coed), pre renovation. Is Coed has retained, as features, the openings seen on the main structure. These would have been used to allow wagons access to the barn's interior.

30. Residential Housing, previously Fferm Goch Farm Settlement.

Fferm Goch (Red Farm) and Fferm Goch Farm Settlement ("the Settlement")

While Fferm Goch is within Penllyn, the Settlement is across the road in Llangan. It was part of a Utopian scheme by the Welsh Land Settlement Society to give unemployed miners a new start in life, by providing them with residential accommodation linked to work on the farm. Settlers were paid the standard wage for farm workers and the land was worked co-operatively as one large farm. The Settlement consisted of 24 semi-detached houses designed by T. Alwyn Lloyd.

Text of a letter from the Secretary of the Society:

The Welsh Land Settlement Society Limited
Principality Buildings,
Queen Street,
Cardiff

25th November 1939

Dear Sir,

I have pleasure in informing you that your application for employment on the above-named Society's Farm Settlement, Fferm Goch, Llangan, Nr. Bridgend, has been successful. Your employment is subject to the relevant terms and conditions set out in the pamphlet which you acknowledge in your form of application to have seen and understood.

It is desired that you should note carefully the following instructions in connection with your transfer to Fferm Goch Farm Settlement:
1. You will report to the Manager of Fferm Goch Farm Settlement on the day of your arrival at the Settlement.
2. You and your family will occupy one of the newly erected houses known as No. 9, Fferm Goch Farm Settlement, for which you will pay a rental of 4/- a week to be deducted from your wage.
3. Before entering into occupation of the house you will be asked to sign a Tenancy agreement.
4. It is to be clearly understood that the wage payable to you will be in accordance with the Agricultural Rate for the County fixed from time to time. The present rate of wage for the County of Glamorgan is 36/-.
5. You should take with you your Unemployment and Health Insurance Contribution Cards and Medical Card. The latter is required in connection with your transfer to a Panel Doctor in the new area.
6. Your appointment will be for a probationary period of twelve calendar months. If at the end of that period your services, in the opinion of the Welsh Land Settlement Society, are considered satisfactory you will be eligible to become a member of the Co-operators Society when formed. It is anticipated that a Co-operators Society will be registered not later than 1st February, 1941. It should be understood that in the event of a transferee's services being unsatisfactory they may be terminated by the Society at any time during the Probationary Period, by one week's notice in writing.
7. All necessary information with regard to the removal of your furniture and family will be communicated to you by the Employment Exchange.
8. All facilities with regard to the Society meeting the cost of removals <u>from</u> the Settlements of the Society have been withdrawn.
9. You will, of course, be expected to observe the regulations of the Society, and I am sure you will co-operate in using your best endeavours to make a success of the scheme.
10. Please acknowledge the receipt of this letter on the attached form, which should be addressed to the Secretary at the above address.

Images

Pentre Meyrick

This crossing point is at the centre of a Bronze Age landscape. A hundred metres south on the Llysworney road is a robbed out barrow, which contained a funerary urn. Just to the north are further barrows and locations of flint scatters. Some 500m to the south-west are the lumps and mounds of Mynydd Bychan, known locally as "Humpty Dumpty". They mark the site of the fortified Iron Age settlement excavated in 1950 by H. N. Savory, which was occupied from 50BC to 100AD, and at a later period was a medieval settlement.

Recollections

(J.B.) My dad dug up a Roman coin just across the road from there. And I showed it to Dr. Savory from the Welsh Museum when they were excavating in the Humpty Dumpty and "Oh", he said, "It's a first issue of Roman coinage" So there was a Roman presence here. He said that the coin must have been a month's wages for that legionnaire or whatever. He must have been very annoyed when he lost that!

There are two current versions as to how Pentre Meyrick (Meyrick's/Meurig's Village/Homestead) came to be so named. The first is that it was named after Meurig ap Tewdrig (born circa 596 – died circa 665). He was the son of St. Tewdrig, King of Gwent and Glywysing, and Meurig succeeded his father in the early 7th century. Interestingly, Meurig is credited by some as being King Arthur's father, but we make no such claim.

The second version is rather more recent. Thomas Meyrick (born 1768) was working as a labourer for Edward Thomas of Treoes. Edward's sister, Florence, (born 1744) was sickly, and had been advised by the village ladies that a husband would improve her health. This resulted in Thomas marrying Florence on 5th March 1791 and, with her dowry, Thomas was able to acquire land, settle at Pentre Meyrick and the settlement took its name from him and his dynasty. As always, there are stings in the tail. Florence was 47 when she was married, compared to Thomas at 23. We can find no record of her bearing a child but Thomas is named as the father of Mary, born 28th October 1792, only 19 months after the marriage. The mother's name is not given. Mary died early, at the age of 31. Florence's health seems to have improved, however, for she finally died in 1821, aged 77. Thomas meanwhile, only survived her by 5 years, dying in 1826 aged 58. And Thomas' mother, Ann, outlived them all – she was aged 99 when she died in 1834. Thomas is sometimes credited with residing at Pentremeyrick House, but the Ordnance Survey of 1877 shows fields where the property now stands.

31. Nash View.
It has been suggested that T. Alwyn Lloyd, who designed the housing at Fferm Goch, may also have designed the houses at Nash View, but this has not been confirmed.

Images

The Moors

Penllyn and Newton Moors, formed by glacial sediment, would have been marshland and shallow lakes before drainage activity created today's dry landscape. The water table remains high, ready to bog down the incautious driver straying off the narrow roads.

32. Stanby cottage. Pre redevelopment, now **Chatwood House.**

33. Moorlands Farm.

Early 1960's, painting by Nancy Richards a Veterinary Surgeon from Llansannor. Moorlands was farmed by Noel Llewellyn and his wife Cissy (Cecilia), who can just be seen looking over the hedge. Their son, John, was a famous point–to–point rider who now farms Newlands at St Mary Church.

34. "Duck pond" being cleaned in 1933.
Note the paved lining, which would stop cattle slipping, and help prevent damage to the puddled clay, itself needed to stop the water draining into the underlying limestone. There used to be 11 ponds in Penllyn, used mainly for watering the livestock, but these have all been filled in with the exception of the pond outside Great House Farm. Another essential use for the water was for fighting the fires that all too frequently broke out in homes and outbuildings.

35. Hay Barn burning, 1925.
This must have been a terrible blow after the tremendous labour of the hay harvest. The body language of the exhausted workers tells its own story.

Cowbridge

36. Llwynhelig, 1901.

It is sometimes not appreciated that the Penllyn parish boundary reaches this far into Cowbridge. Llwynhelig was shown as Willow Bush on the 1799 Yates map. The older parts of Llwynhelig appear to date to the 17th century (and possibly earlier). It is now much extended and gentrified, perhaps by James Ballard who farmed 307 acres and employed nine labourers in 1851. The mid 19th century redevelopment was done so as to give an external appearance only of that date, although the window spacing does give a clue to the two builds. It is shown in the present outline on the tithe map of 1839. The house has not been altered externally since the mid 19th century except for the addition of a porch circa 2000, which re-established a previously recorded feature of similar design. At the time of this 1901 photograph, the census revealed that Evan Thomas, a farmer aged 74, lived there as head of the household, with his wife Elizabeth (62) and their son George (24 and single) and daughter Eliza Cath (27, also single). Servants were William Harken, (single, 24, horseman teamster on farm), Louisa Jenkins (single, 25, general domestic) and Charles A Newman, (single, 17, cowman).

Images

Vale of Glamorgan

37. Vale of Glamorgan Agricultural Society Show. Based at Penllyn from 1953, the show is fondly remembered by villagers. It was the annual occasion when the whole Vale descended on Penllyn, with the Cowbridge A.T.C. (then, as now), valiantly directing the mass of traffic attempting to enter and exit the parking areas. The last show at Penllyn was on 20th August 1997, with John Homfray, President; Edward Rees, Chairman; Anthony Thomas, Vice Chairman and David Llewellyn, Vice President. In 1998, the Show moved to its current location at Fonmon Castle. These final images of Penllyn were taken at the 1997 Show, attended (and enjoyed) by some 16,000 people.

37.1. (L-R) Robert Llewellyn, Mary Llewellyn and David Llewellyn, presenting the Peter Llewellyn Memorial Trophy to Tim Prichard, of Castellau Fawr farm, for his Charollais sheep.

37.2. (L-R) John Homfray, awarding The Pinkstone Perpetual Challenge Cup to Mr. David Davies, of Lower Monkton Farm, for his Hampshire Down ram, supreme champion of the sheep classes. Mr. Davies can remember competing at the Vale Show when it was held at the Bear Field in Cowbridge, prior to its move to Penllyn.

37.3. Aerial photograph of show field looking north. In the hazy mist, the images of the village houses can just be distinguished. After a few days all the tents and stands would be taken down for the last time. Events such the Vale Show and Penllyn Steeplechases evoke bittersweet memories; the sadness of their departure from Penllyn offset by all the fun at the time of those great occasions.

The history of Penllyn was, until very recently, of people making a living in a farming parish. It seems appropriate to close with one last recollection from John Bagg, recounting his memory of Arthur Llewellyn (Robert and David Llewellyn's grandfather) at the prelude to his own two year stay, at the Adelina Patti hospital (Craig Y Nos) and at Llandrindnod, while suffering from tuberculosis and pleurisy:

Recollections

(J.B.) We are lucky to have always had nice people. I always remember Mr. Llewellyn, Arthur. A lot of people would shudder with Mr. Llewellyn because he was a bit crusty you know. No harm in him. I used to pinch his swedes. Well, not pinch them. If I wanted one, I would take one, especially during the war. And then a couple of weeks after, he would say, "Moving the sheep, Johnny." And you would go. And you wouldn't take three or four swedes, you would just take one. You wouldn't trouble if he saw you, you know. Now when I went to the sanatorium, very few people had a car in those days, he knocked on the door. And he knocked on the door and he said, "You're off to hospital." He said to my father "I'll be picking you up" he said "tomorrow." And we had a nice picnic. I'll always remember that picnic. Because I knew then that I'd be there and not coming back. It was like the last supper to me.

Appendix 1

The Methodist Chapel, Craig Penllyn, Inscriptions and Location of Headstones

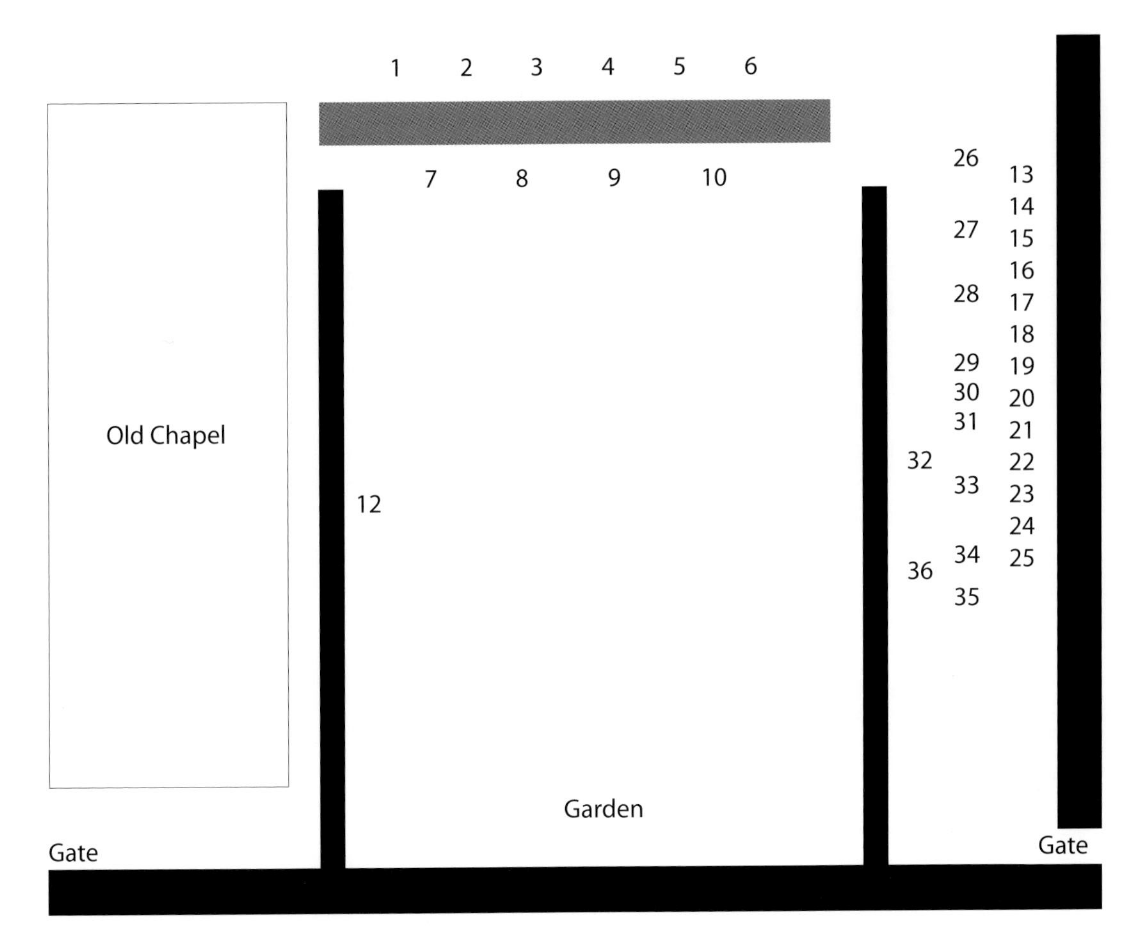

Figure 1 Plan of headstone locations

1. In Loving memory of REES, beloved husband of CATHERINE ROBERTS of Village Farm, Penllyne. Who died Oct 13th 1933 aged 63 years. Also CATHERINE beloved wife of the above who died Dec. 27th 1967 aged 92 years.

2. In loving memory of WILLIAM beloved husband of ANNIE THOMAS of Vistla. Who died Sept 16th 1931 Aged 54 years. Resting. Also the above ANNIE THOMAS who died Jan 11th 1961 aged 81 years. Re-united.

3. In loving memory of THOMAS RADCLIFFE of Great House. Born July 3rd 1830, Died Sept 19th 1908. Mi a Ymdrechais Ymdrech Deg, Mi a Orphenais Fy Ngyrfa, Mi a Gedwais Y Fydd[1]. Also JANE wife of the above named, who died Feb 1st 1915 Aged 82 years

4. In loving memory of ASHLEY Son of WILLIAM and the late ELIZABETH RADCLIFFE Penmark Place Who died Oct 24th 1921 aged 20 years

5. Also the aforesaid ELIZABETH RADCLIFFE Who died at Penmark Place Jan 24th 1920 aged 62 years also the aforesaid WILLIAM RADCLIFFE who died March 20th 1932 aged 74 years

6. In remembrance of SUSANNA JOHN, the beloved wife of DAVID JOHN of Argoed-Uchaf Born July 25th 1854, Died Sept. 27th 1915 Be thou faithful unto death, and I will give thee a crown of life Also the said DAVID JOHN Died Sept 2nd 1929 Aged 78 years. In hope of eternal life, which God, that cannot lie, promised before the world began

7. Er Cof Am RICHARD Annwyl Briod REBECCA DAVID Bu Farw medi 28 – 1883 Yn 77 Oed. Hefyd REBECCA ei Briod Bu Farw Hefydd 8 – 1895 Yn 90 Oed Hefyd Rachel Eu March, bu Farw Meh 1 – 1866 yn 25 Oed.
   Coffad Wrissth y dyfiawyn bydd sydd fendigewdig[2]

8. In loving memory of Catherine wife of RICHARD WILLIAMS of Penllyne. Who died Dec 2 1908 aged 79 years. "life's work well done, God's rest well won". Also the above RICHARD WILLIAMS who died Dec 21 1914 aged 83 years

9. In loving memory of MARY, beloved wife of JOHN R THOMAS who died Feb 26 1943 Aged 74 years Rest in Peace. Also JOHN R THOMAS Husband of the above died Jan 17th 1948 Aged 78 years. Reunited.

10. In loving memory of MARY, beloved wife of EDWARD HOPKIN WILLIAMS of Graig Farm who died March 1st 1927 aged 68 years. Also EDWARD HOPKIN WILLIAMS who died July 14th 1954 aged 90 years

11. In loving memory of MARGARET JANE THOMAS wife of DAVID W THOMAS daughter of THOMAS & JANE RAD-CLIFFE of Great House, in this Parish died Oct 26th 1901 aged 28 years "Precious in the sight of the Lord is the death of his Saint"

12. In loving memory of CATHERINE beloved wife of THOMAS GRIFFITHS who died July 6th 1935 aged 66 years. Thy will be done. Also of the above THOMAS GRIFFITHS who died April 26th 1958 aged 87 years. Also DILLWYN their dear son, died April 22 1970 aged 59 years

13. In memory of THOMAS the son of DAVID and MARY REYNOLDS Jun. Of this Parish who died the 23rd Day of April 1848 aged 1 year. Also ALICE Daughter of the above named who died the 8th day of Oct 1852 aged 4 mths. Also JOHN, son of the above named who died the 2nd day of May 1865 aged 26 years, Also the above named MARY REYNOLDS who died Sept 29th 1895 aged 87 years. Also the above named David Reynolds who died June 19th 1903 aged 96 years. We are gone to rest.

14. In loving memory of Rachel the beloved wife of WILLIAM JOHN late of Coity who died Nov 28th 1896 aged 40 years. Also of ANNE daughter of the above who died Dec 10th 1909 aged 15 years. "Thy will be done"

15. In loving memory of WILLIAM the beloved son of DAVID & JENNETT THOMAS of this Parish who died May 2nd 1895 aged 29 years. "Watch therefore for ye know not what hour your lord doth come" Also the above named DAVID THOMAS who died May 19th 1905 aged 69 years. "Blessed are the dead which die in the Lord" Also the above named JENNETT THOMAS who died Aug 24th 1916 aged 72 years "Ni Frysis Yr Hwn a Credo" [3]

16. In memory of REBECCA the wife of JOHN JENKINS of this Parish who died August 3rd 1858 aged 44 years. Also the above named JOHN JENKINS who died Sept. 26th 1870 aged 58 years

17. In Loving memory of WILLIAM JOHN SAMUEL Son of JOHN & MIRIAM SAMUEL of this Parish died July 28th 1878 aged 15 years. Also the above named JOHN SAMUEL who died June 5th 1908 aged 77 years. Also the above named MIRIAM SAMUEL died January 13th 1913 aged 76 years

18. In loving memory of REBECCA WOOD wife of George WOOD of this Parish who died April 18th 1910 aged 57 years. "We loved her, God loved her and called her home to peace and rest" Also the said GEORGE ELWORTHY WOOD who died Sept 20th 1922 aged 72 years. "Sweetest thoughts shall ever linger around the place where he is laid"

19. In affectionate remembrance of Hannah daughter of MANOAH & MARY DAVID who died December 10th 1880 aged 6 years. Also the above named MANOAH DAVID who died May 27th 1913 aged 83 years. Also the above MARY DAVID who died July 1st 1919 aged 85 years

20. In memory of CATHERINE wife of EDWARD WILLIAMS of the Parish who died Oct 18th 1871 aged 74 years. Also the above EDWARD WILLIAMS who died May 30th 1885 aged 85 years

21. In memory of THOMAS JOHN of this Parish who died Oct 14th 1856 aged 59 years. Also THOMAS JOHN son of the above who died Jan 29th 1868 aged 44. Also MARY JOHN who died Dec 2nd 1913 aged 84. Thy will be done.

22. In loving memory of ELIZABETH the beloved wife of WILLIAM BURKE of this Parish who died Feb 8th 1880 aged 47 years. "And so shall we ever be with the Lord" Also CATHERINE second daughter of the above named who died Dec 8th 1894 aged 30 years also ELIZABETH their daughter who died Sept 26th 1900 aged 30. Also WILLIAM BURKE who died Dec 16th 1907 aged 77. Thy will be done. also ELIZABETH ANN BURKE daughter-in-law of the above WILLIAM BURKE born 1873 died FEB 27th 1900

23. Sacred to the memory of MARY NICHOLAS daughter of THOMAS & CATHERINE NICHOLAS of this Parish who died April 16th 1834 aged 3 years. Also of the said CATHERINE NICHOLAS who died Oct 9th 1841 aged 38. Also their son THOMAS NICHOLAS who died 20th Oct 1841 aged 5 years. Also MARY their Mother who died 27th of May 1901 aged 83

24. In memory of DAVID son of MORGAN and MARY PRICE of this Parish who died March 9th 1855 aged 23 years, Also the aforesaid MORGAN PRICE who died April 6th 1884 aged 78 years. Also of MARY PRICE who died June 27th 1894 aged 87 years.

25. In memory of MARY JENKINS died Oct 13th 1886 aged 74.

26. In memory of JOHN BASSETT of this Parish who died 20th Oct 1881 aged 87

27. In loving memory of DEWI beloved child of RICHARD & MARTHA WILLIAMS who died Dec 25th 1911 aged 3 years. "Suffer little children to come unto me". Also RICHARD WILLIAMS who died March 31st 1943 aged 76 years and Martha his loving wife who died July 1961

28. In loving memory of ANN D. the wife of MORGAN JOHN of Argoed Uchaf who died Oct 30th 1898 aged 42 years. Also the above named MORGAN JOHN who died Sept 16th 1900 aged 52.

29. In Memory of John son of JOHN REES by ANN his wife who died July 7th 1839 aged 16 years. Also JOHN REES who died on Sept 2nd 1862. Also ANN REES who died March 1st 1862.

30. In Memory of ANNE wife of WILLIAM FREDERICK who died September 24th 1894 aged 68. Also the said WILLIAM FREDERICK who died Dec 18th 1898 aged 75. Also in memory of RACHEL daughter of WILLIAM and ANNE FREDERICK who died on Dec 12th 1850 aged 14 months. Also THOMAS their son who died on Jan 29th 1864 aged 5 weeks

31. In loving memory of JOAN beloved wife of CLIFFORD JAMES HAYBALL of this Parish who died on Nov 19th 1891 aged 49 also the above CLIFFORD JAMES HAYBALL who died on Dec 27th 1915 aged 75 years, Thy will be done, also DAVID HAYBALL son of the above who died Dec 3rd 1962 aged 78. Rest in Peace

32. In loving memory of ANN GWRAIG JOHN ROWLANDS O'R PLWYF HWN[4]. A fu Farw Ebril 24 1872 aged 65. HEFYD JOHN ROWLANDS A fu Farw Mawrth 15 1877 aged 64

33. In loving memory of EVAN WILLIAMS of this Parish who died on July 16 1853 aged 66. Also Catherine wife of the above named who died on Nov 10th 1868 aged 72, also THOMAS WILLIAMS son of the above who died on Oct 11th 1879 aged 51. For whom the Lord loveth he chasteneth

34. In memory of ELIZABETH wife of DAVID JENKINS of this PARISH who died on Oct 1st 1881 aged 74 years Also the above named DAVID JENKINS

35. In loving memory of WILLIAM beloved son of WILLIAM & CATHERINE LEWIS late of HAFOD who died Nov 22 1900 at 57 Eirw Road Britania aged 42 years. Also Willie their grandson who died on March 26th 1898 aged 15 years. Though sad we mark the closing eye, If those we loved in days gone by, Yet sweet in death their latest song, we'll meet again, will not be long Also the above named CATHERINE LEWIS who died on Nov 13 1903 aged 81. Mi a ymdrechais, ymdrech deg, Mi a orphenais fy ngyrfa, Mi a gedwais y ffydd[5]

36. In loving memory of WILLIAM dearly loved Husband of Gwen Roberts, dear father of REES and BARBARA who died 3rd May 1954 aged 43 years. Also the above Gwen beloved wife and Mother. Died 26th April 1995 aged 82

Please note that while care has been taken to accurately record the monumental inscriptions, it is not possible to be certain that all inscriptions have been correctly transcribed. A personal visit is recommended if confirmation of any inscription is required.

1 I have fought the good fight, I have finished the race, I have kept the faith (Timothy 4:7)

2 The memory of the just is blessed (Proverbs 10.7) (translation by Welsh Language Board / Bwrdd Yr Iaith Gymraeg)

3 He that believeth shall not make haste (Isaiah 28.16) (translation by Welsh Language Board / Bwrdd Yr Iaith Gymraeg)

4 ANN WIFE OF JOHN ROWLANDS OF THIS PARISH

5 I have fought the good fight, I have finished the race, I have kept the faith (Timothy 4:7)

Appendix 2

The Village Wells: Post Excavation analyses and notes

1. Report by S. H. Sell of Glamorgan Gwent Archaeological Trust (G.G.A.T.) on Ceramics and Glass recovered from Ffynnonau y Pentre, Penllyn

A very large assemblage including (93.6 Kg.) of post medieval and modern ceramics and (6.6 Kg) of glass, nearly all of it from bottles, and a small group of clay tobacco pipes, was recovered from unstratified surface deposits adjacent to a group of three springs/wells known as Ffynnonau y Pentre (or Salmon's Wells) at Penllyn.

Almost 90% of the assemblage of over 6000 sherds was 'local' coarse earthenwares. It was not possible to undertake a detailed analysis of this group, such was its size, but substantial proportions of some vessels were noted. Most of the common types, e.g. heavy pans, bowls and dishes, chamber pots, jugs and drinking vessels were noted. Nearly all vessels were glazed, with glazes varying from buff through to blackish; most were clear (brown). A number of the jugs and other hollow wares had been partially dipped in slip and others showed trailed slip decoration, which was also noted on some of the flatwares. Rim forms tended to be plain, everted or flanged among the hollow wares, and clubbed or ledged in the flat wares, with some of the heavier vessels bearing a decorative thumbed strip to strengthen the rim.

The dating of these ubiquitous coarse wares is imprecise and the researcher is best guided by the chronology of other associated artifact types; in this case we are dealing with an assemblage which may have been accumulating over some considerable period of time, making close associations difficult. Much, if not most, of this group is likely to have its origins at Ewenny, where pottery production flourished during the 18th and 19th centuries; the slip-decorated designs are certainly typical, but only two sherds have decoration in sgraffito in the style identifying them with the later period of production at Ewenny.

The only other groups of any size consist of stonewares (1.5% of the group) and industrial white earthenwares, chinas and other modern ceramic types (3.4%). Most are probably of 19th century or more recent date.

Also among the assemblage were very small numbers of Staffordshire/Bristol buffwares (16 sherds), tin-glazed earthenwares (10 sherds), including the base of a drug jar and Staffordshire salt-glazed stonewares (4 sherds). A date from the first half of the 18th century onwards may be appropriate for these types. North Devon gravel-tempered wares were almost entirely absent (0.12% of the total) but this has probably more to do with the general date of the group, covering the later post-medieval period when North Devon imports had largely died out, than to the inland location of the site.

Appendix 2

Two sherds from jugs of medieval date, and part of the crest of a glazed ridge tile of possibly early post-medieval date, were also noted.

The glass consisted in the main of bottles of 19th century or later date, with only a small proportion (4%) of window glass. The group included some modern pieces, whose inclusion may be attributed to bottles continuing to be discarded as rubbish in comparatively recent times rather than representing the date of the group as a whole. The date range here is consequently the widest with the neck of an onion bottle of late 17th century date being the earliest piece among this group.

The clay pipes (a total of 23 stems and 3 bowls) fit broadly within the date range, with 19th century styles predominating, but there are two early heels with maker's stamps, both of which may belong to the late 17th century and are of Bristol style. A waste flint flake was also noted amongst the assemblage.

1.1. Dating

Apart from a very little early material, the group appears to belong broadly to the 18th and 19th centuries. The local coarsewares are difficult to date, but it is assumed that their place begins to be taken towards the end of the eighteenth century by the mass produced industrial wares, at least in many of the areas of domestic use. The relative absence of North Devon products and pre-industrial finewares may indicate that the bulk of the coarsewares could be contemporary with the white earthenwares, rather than belong to an earlier period. Alternatively the assemblage may be seen as a representation of the changes in vernacular pottery throughout the 18th and 19th centuries. Where secure dating can be attributed, it belongs in the main to the 19th century. There is not enough earlier material for its significance to be assessed. Technically, however, an accumulation of rubbish, relating both to the use of the well and the discarding of household items from the 13th/14th century to the present day could be postulated, with the 19th century being the period when almost all of the deposition took place.

2. R. H. Caple, post excavation notes

Completion of work to the repair of the revetting wall to the overflow stream revealed that the whole embankment was ground raised above the shale outcrop level. It appears to be mainly loose stone from demolished buildings mixed with broken pottery. There were a number of pieces of worked sandstone 80mm thick and around 200mm x 180mm, possibly furnace liner and various pieces of slag and some lead ore.

The revetting also showed straight joints with a suggestion of steps behind, but all built up later.

After examination and classification by G.G.A.T., over 100 kg of pottery fragments recovered from site clearance were reburied on site in woodland to N.E. of stream. In excavating this pit, it was noted that under the 80mm of demolished building stone was encountered a smooth bed of yellow lime mortar. For the small area of the pit this mortar was explored to show a thickness of 20mm above some 80mm of layered ash from coal related industrial use above clean sub-soil.

It is suggested that there is probably evidence of some local small industrial use adjacent to the spring area though no known maps, i.e. post 1840, show any buildings here. They would be approached over the stream and later through the gap in the revetting, until passing out of use and being buried in their own rubbish and clearance from the stream and use of the wells.

The site was finalised by cleaning out Wellhead No. 1 which had been fouled with rubbish. This produced a total of 21 copper/alloy coins (value 6 shillings, three pence and one farthing) from the period 1940 to 1990 plus one 1898 penny. It rather confirmed the evidence of Parish records, which showed regular cleaning of the wells up to 1937. The well was seen to be a shallow cut basin into the sandy-shale of the water bearing strata with masonry built up in stages above it. Depth from bottom of shale to the overflow hole in the large stone slab of the well entry is 90mm. The water cleared within a few hours of cleaning.

Appendix 2

3. Schedule of Finds

3.1. Pottery and Glass

Description Pottery 18th to 20th century.	Sherds	Weights Kg.	Pots
Local coarsewares including slip-decorated wares	6075	84.568	270
Local coarsewares, with sgraffito decoration	2	.018	
North Devon G.T. Wares	11	.100	
West country slipwares (possibly local)	2	.010	
Buffwares, yellow glazed	11	.048	4
Buffwares, brown glazed	5	.018	
Tin glazed earthenwares	10	.130	
Staffordshire salt glazed stonewares	4	.005	
Red/Black stonewares	7	.042	
Modern stonewares, all types	100	3.940	3
White earthenwares, all types including creamwares	220	1.160	43
Other earthenwares (modern)	45	.566	5
Misc. non-earthenwares (post medieval/modern)	17	.038	1
Pottery Early post-medieval			
Crested ridge-tile fragment	1	.026	
Pottery Medieval			
Glazed jug fragments	2	.012	
Other materials Post-medieval to modern			
Clay pipes, including 3 mouthpieces and 2 stamps	26	.016	3
Clay Marble	1	.006	
Glass bottle / vessel, clear / greenish	182	3.375	11
Glass bottle / vessel, dark green	153	2.830	
Glass bottle / vessel, brown	25	.358	
Glass window	15	.034	
Prehistoric			
waste flint flake	1	.002	

3.2. Other Material Found

Description Coins	Date
Bronze halfpenny George II	Illegible (1746/54)
Bronze halfpenny George III	1799
Bronze halfpenny Bun head Victoria	1860 / 94
Bronze halfpenny Bun head Victoria	1875
Shilling	1920
Shilling	1947
Halfpenny	1950
Various post decimal coins	1971 and later
Collection of coins from clearance Wellhead No. 1	All post 1940
Other material	
Copper alloy locket	Mid 19th C
Two Copper alloy buckles	Mid 19th C
Various Bone, China and stamped metal buttons	All 18th to 20th C
Unglazed and unpainted pipe clay figurine of 'political cartoon' type approx. 160mm height (see 3.3 below)	Late 19th C
A decorated pewter spoon 180mm long and cast with initials IM. This is a dog nose spoon of Queen Anne's coronation and dated to c.1700. Information per M. Redknapp of N.M.G.W. This spoon is now donated to the N.M.G.W. collection.	Circa 1700

Appendix 2

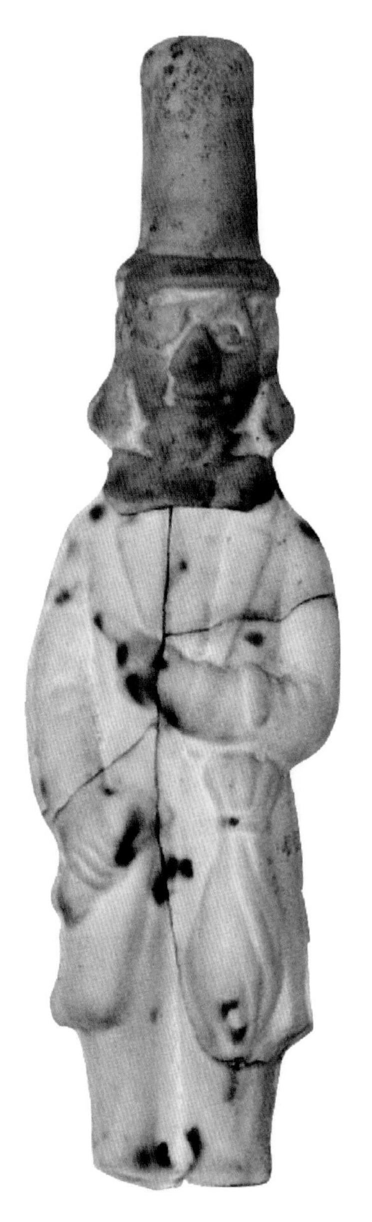

Figure 1 Pipe clay figurine found during Village Wells excavation

3.3. R. H. Caple, notes on pipe clay figurine

3.3.1. Introduction

The fragmentary figurine was excavated from a well deposit in Penllyn. The head of the figurine was recovered first, followed by the remaining extant pieces, which together depict a man wearing a frock coat, top hat and bow tie. There is a scroll in the right hand and an umbrella is suspended from the left arm, which is crossed over the chest. The character possesses collar length hair and a patch over the right eye, with the remaining eye appearing sunken and the nose, bulbous.

The artifact was recovered in five large joining pieces, which comprised the head, two torso fragments, two lower body fragments and a flake that fitted between the last four. All had clean break edges. Differential staining of a dark greyish-purple colour - in this case marks that are discontinuous between the fragments - might suggest that the artifact was broken in the ground, and underwent taphonomic changes that resulted in the visual anomalies. The stains might pertain to solubilised inclusions in the ceramic body or the ingress of chemical species during burial. Concretions on the head piece seem to be evidence for the accumulation of insoluble salts on this portion of the figure.

3.3.2. Conservation

Conservation work was undertaken in the summer of 1999, in order to prepare the figurine for display. The break edges of the fragments were degreased with neat IMS (Industrial Methylated Spirits) on cotton wool swabs, then, using a soft brush, the edges were sealed with 30% Paraloid B-72 (an acrylic co-polymer) in 50:50 IMS:acetone. Having established the assembly order of the pieces, proprietary Paraloid B-72 was brushed along the joining break edges of Pieces 1 and 2. These fragments were aligned, brought together, pulled apart for two seconds to create a better key and then rejoined. The joins were held together with masking tape placed at right angles to the breaks. Piece 3 was added to 1 and 2 applying the method described above, and then taped. Finally, Pieces 5, 4 and 6 were adhered to the existing section. When the joins had been taped, the figurine was placed horizontally in a tray of bird seed, to achieve a full cure. Excess adhesive was shaved away with a sharp scalpel blade.

3.3.3. Investigation

During and after the conservation process, research was carried out in order to attempt to establish the identity of the character depicted by the figurine. Shortly after excavation the figurine had been identified provisionally as an artifact manufactured by one of the Staffordshire potteries in the nineteenth century. Letters, photographs and illustrations were then sent to the various extant Staffordshire potteries and potteries museums in the area. David Barker, Keeper of Archaeology at "The Potteries Museum and Art Gallery", Hanley, disclosed that little seemed to have been written about "pipe clay" figurines (pers. comm.). This was perhaps a result of the apparent paucity of evidence for such artifacts in the archaeological record.

According to Barker (pers. comm.), the figurine might be nineteenth century in date, but the absence of a stamp or maker's mark is a loss of vital information for the date and origin of manufacture. Barker conceded that the figure could indeed originate from pottery-producing centres such as Stoke [-on-Trent] although he had never encountered the like in excavations there. Perhaps a clue to the provenance of the figurine might be derived from the negative evidence returned from the Staffordshire potteries and British ceramics societies. The Wedgwood Museum, The Spode Museum, The Royal Crown Derby Porcelain Company, Royal Doulton and The British Ceramics Federation did not recognise the artifact as one manufactured by their companies or region. This outcome shifted the line of enquiry from Staffordshire.

To gain more information, ceramic specialists at the Victoria and Albert Museum, London, were approached. Terry Bloxham (pers. comm.) of the Ceramics Department deduced, from a photograph, description and illustrations of the figurine, a date of around 1880. It was possible to assign such a specific date to the artifact, because the manufacture of the piece from slip cast, hard paste porcelain, along with the stylistic design, were indicative of ceramics from the German Thuringer factories. Many similar figurines were produced in the period of 1860 - 1890.

The manufacture of such figurines, often referred to as 'fairings', was undertaken on a modest scale by the Staffordshire potteries. "Fairings" were gifts won or bought at a village fair. It has been speculated that fairing is a condensed version of "fair earning" (Vogel & Vogel: 1997). Despite the Staffordshire contribution to the fabrication of fairings in the Victorian era, it is known that the German factories exported vast numbers of figurines to the Welsh and English markets (Bloxham: pers. comm.) Many of the fairings bear the impressed hallmark of a shield depicting a bent arm bearing a sword. This is the mark of Springer and Oppenheimer of Elbogen, in East Germany (but now Loket in Czechoslovakia). However, it was subsequently discovered that works assigned to the aforementioned company were actually produced by another organisation with the same hallmark - Conta and Boehme of Pössneck, Saxony (Bloxham: pers. comm.; Vogel & Begley). It is possible, therefore, that the figurine was manufactured by the latter organisation. Further evidence to support this assertion is the fact that such figurines were sometimes exported unpainted, where they might later be decorated by Victorian ladies, as a pastime (Bloxham: pers. comm.).

One reason the German companies were employed to produce fairings was their development of cheap techniques for mass production, which were aided by proximity to high quality kaolin (Henderson), against which the British manufacturers could not compete (Vogel & Begley). What is more, the companies would accept commissions for the manufacture of figurines depicting local celebrities, be they heroes or villains. In this way, short and unique production runs of specific characters could be ordered (Bloxham: pers. comm.).

3.3.4. Identity

The hallmark for a fairing would usually appear on its underside. In the case of Conta and Boehme figurines, the impressed hallmark would often be accompanied by a four-digit number. The numbers of the first series ranged from 2850 – 2899, and the second series from 3301 - 3380s. Yet other figurines known to be manufactured by the company might bear numbers outside this range, or no numbers at all (Vogel & Begley). In the case of the Penllyn figurine, it is not possible to say which combination of features, if any, would have been present, since the diagnostic base is missing. However, even if the origin of manufacture is uncertain, there are some clues that might help to reveal the identity of the figure. The character is portrayed holding a scroll in his right hand - a detail that is included in the portrayal of many figurines of politicians. In the Victorian era, politicians were said to be admired, (Harding: 1998; 12) making them suitable subjects for such pieces. Over the right eye is an eye patch, signifying blindness. This evidence should improve the chances of determining the identity of the character depicted. An alternative method of portraying blindness in one eye was to model the figure with a closed eye. An example of a figurine depicted with one eye closed is that of "Christmas Evans," the Baptist Minister of Anglesey between 1792 and 1826. Evans lost his eye in a religious brawl in 1778 (Harding: 1998). Although the identity of the Penllyn figurine is still elusive, the features it retains might well be sufficient for a future identification.

Appendix 2

3.3.5. Bibliography

Caple, R., 1999, *The fresh water supply of a village in the Vale of Glamorgan*
Harding, A. N., 1998, *Victorian Staffordshire Figures: 1835 - 1875 Book 1*; Schiffer Publishing Ltd., Atglen, USA
Harding, A. N., 1998, *Victorian Staffordshire Figures: 1835 - 1875 Book 2*; Schiffer Publishing Ltd, Atglen, USA
Henderson, J. D., *Bohemian Export Porcelain - A Legacy of the Habsburg Empire*- **www.execpc.com/jamesk**
Vogel, J. & Vogel, R., *Porcelain Trinket Boxes* - **aarf.com/fetrin97.htm**
Vogel, J., Vogel, R. & Begley, *Victorian China Fairings* - **www.uscrsglobalnet.co.ukIfairing**

3.3.6. Personal Communications

Allen, C., British Ceramic Confederation, Stoke-on-Trent
Baddeley. S., Royal Doulton, Fine China Division, Stoke-on-Trent
Barker, D., Keeper of Archaeology, The Potteries Museum & Art Gallery, Hanley, Stoke-on-Trent
Blake Roberts, G., The Wedgwood Museum, Stoke-on-Trent
Bloxham, T., Ceramics Department, Victoria and Albert Museum, London
Jones, J., Royal Doulton, Stoke-on-Trent
Sargeant, M., The Royal Crown Derby Museum, Stoke-on-Trent
Woolliscroft, P., The Spode Museum, Stoke-on-Trent

penlline

.org.uk